TAX RETURN WORKBOOK

James Carlisle

BOXTREE

First published 2002 by Boxtree
an imprint of Pan Macmillan Ltd
Pan Macmillan, 20 New Wharf Road, London N1 9RR
Basingstoke and Oxford
Associated companies throughout the world
www.panmacmillan.com

ISBN 0 7522 6500 8

1 3 5 7 9 8 6 4 2

A CIP catalogue record for this book is available from the British Library.

Designed and typeset by seagulls
Printed by Bath Press

Contents

Preface

Who are these Fools?

The Motley Fool name harks back to the Fool of the Middle Ages, that character so beloved of Shakespeare, who was the only person who could tell the king the truth without getting his head chopped off. The Fool kept his head because he used humour to convey a sometimes unpalatable reality.

So what's the Foolish truth when it comes to finance?

Partly, it's that the financial world preys on ignorance and fear. Throughout your life you'll have found financial professionals doing their best to sell you their own version of financial 'Wisdom', often designed to benefit them rather than you. Meanwhile, the basics of personal finance and investing are not taught in any effective or consistent fashion in our schools. As if this wasn't enough, successive governments have seemed to delight in producing a system of taxation and benefits that makes the head spin. All this serves to leave a bewildered Joe Public at the mercy of a financial services industry that has been more than happy to take advantage.

Stockbrokers, banks and financial advisers strive to present an image of financial success, experience and utter responsibility. At the same time, the reality of their actions – often selling to their customers high-charging, under-performing investments – is entirely at odds with this image. It is this behaviour that Fools know as conventional Wisdom. The Wise have made enormous amounts of money from fools (note the small 'f') in the past, but times are changing. The peasants are revolting.

Most of us have been fools at one time or another. We've handed over a chunk of our financial future to people we trusted to give us good advice. Many of us have bought endowments or been sold an overcharging pension. We've signed up and handed over our money. Only after the event did we realize that these investments had little chance of keeping pace with more efficient, cheaper alternatives. Typically, we discovered this at around the same time we realized that a slice of our hard-earned money had gone to pay commission to those people we trusted. Oh, we were so foolish!

Somehow, lessons in the importance of reading small print always seem to cost so much more than other forms of learning. So, the Motley Fool set out to try to teach people some of these lessons before it was too late. We've made a song about those nasty endowments and we've made a dance about those overcharging pensions. Above all, we've tried to cut through the blather that pervades the financial world. In our efforts, we've been helped by thousands of Fools who've turned up on our website with their own experience and knowledge. The power of that community is what makes the spirit of Foolishness so much greater than the sum of its parts.

So what is this spirit of Foolishness? Well you'd probably get a different answer from every Fool you asked, but there is very definitely an ethos that ties it all together.

First and foremost, the Fool is about enjoying life. Relax, be cool, have a jam sandwich. The moment financial matters take over your life is the moment the cart is put before the horse. Having said that, the Fool is keenly aware that a lack of money can cause a lot of strife. Providing for yourself and your family, now and in the future, is an important business and it's important to stay on top of your personal finances. As we'll see later in this book, this starts with getting out of debt – and staying out. It then involves putting together a balance of savings and investing that suits your own ambitions and tolerance for risk. No one can do this for you, because nobody understands you better than you do. Not only that, but you're the one who has your own interests closest to heart.

There is also quite definitely a Foolish way of thinking. You could call it common sense, but there's more to it than that. It's a question of looking at the available evidence and reaching a rational conclusion – of thinking laterally, without being driven by preconceived ideas. Most importantly, a Fool will say 'show me why', rather than take the 'conventional Wisdom', as read.

The final element of the Fool comes down to the individual and the community. The basic premise is that if you want something done right, you'd better do it yourself. The more you rely on others, the more you risk your affairs being conducted without your best interests at heart. But despite this individual responsibility, the Motley Fool is passionate about the power of the community to help others learn and come to their decisions. We all have our own particular range of knowledge and ability and by putting it all together, we can learn and understand things that none of us could fathom on our own.

So there you go. That's the Fool. Sound OK? Nothing too dodgy? ... Yes? ... Sure? ... Onward!

Introduction

What this book is about

For most people, dealing with their financial affairs is like heading to the dentist for some root canal work, only less appealing. This is entirely understandable but, just like that toothache, it won't go away if you ignore it. Sooner or later it needs sorting out and, if it's later, things will probably have just got a whole lot worse.

The good news is that your finances don't require constant monitoring. There's no need for a daily grind of checking bank balances and shuffling money around. For all but adrenalin-fuelled stock market junkies, a once-a-year check on your finances is all that's neccessary, and is all that's really desirable. It's not so much a question of 'is it a good time to move more money into shares?'; more, 'is the balance between my short-term and long-term savings right, given my age and overall circumstances?' Your age only changes once a year and your overall circumstances don't often change much quicker.

It also so happens that tax returns, if you have to fill them in, happen on a yearly basis. We at the Motley Fool can't help thinking that this is a useful coincidence. The thought of getting out all our bank statements, credit card details, investment statements and what-have-you more than once a year is too awful to contemplate. So you can save yourself a lot of trouble by killing two birds with one pile of noxious paperwork.

Of course, you can get an accountant, or other tax adviser, to do your tax return for you. If you've got truly complex tax affairs, then this might make sense, since they'll probably be giving you advice on other matters as well. All that advice can end up costing a lot, though, and as good Fools know, the best way to make sure you have lots of money is to waste very little of it. It will also set you back several hundred pounds to get a relatively simple tax return done professionally. That extra money on your savings and investments each year can make a lot of difference to your long-term future.

In any case – and give me the benefit of the doubt here – filling out your tax return and sorting out your finances can be quite a rewarding exercise. No, honestly! Out there, beyond the customary fog of pain, guilt and anxiety about all things financial sits a promised land, a serene plateau where everything is in order and every day is the weekend. In this financial utopia, your bills are paid on time, you have savings for a rainy day and your retirement is secure. Here, too, your tax return gets done with a minimum of fuss.

As images go, a plateau represents things quite well, because although it can be a small struggle to get there, when you arrive there are no more hills to climb and it really only takes a minimum of effort to keep things moving smoothly. Once you've got everything more or less in order, the changes from year to year are also only likely to be slight. That goes both for your finances and, presuming you don't radically change the way you earn money, your tax return too, where cribbing heavily from last year is positively encouraged.

The long and the short of it, then, is that we've tried to provide a guide to help you negotiate the twin headaches of your tax return and your personal finances, all in one mad swirl of excitement. Well, excitement is probably too strong a word for it, but we hope we've made things useful, understandable and, dare we say it, occasionally amusing. We certainly can't answer every question that everyone might have, so we haven't tried; but where there may be deeper problems to sort out, we've tried to give pointers to where you might next go to look. Sometimes this might involve seeing a pro. Far be it for the Motley Fool to suggest seeking professional advice, but sometimes it really is the only option.

How the book is organized

In the light of these twin aims – helping you do your tax return and helping you conduct your financial health check – the book (once you've got past this rambling introduction) is organized into two sections. The first half, which we've decided to call **Part One – Doing the Tax Return**, is all about filling in your tax return, while the second half, or **Part Two – The Health Check**, is where you give your finances the once-over. We reckon it's a pretty easy structure to follow.

First, though, you need to plough through the rest of this introduction, because it contains quite a bit of important stuff. For one thing, it closes by working out which bits of the tax return you actually have to fill in. Depending on how complicated your life is, there should be quite a few bits that you can ignore. Of course, if you can ignore a particular section of the tax return, you can also ignore the corresponding chapter in this book.

At last, you make it to Part One – filling in the tax return. This follows the way the Inland Revenue numbers the boxes on the return. The Employment section, which is the first one that most people come to, has boxes numbered 1.xx and

1.yy and so forth. So we've made the Employment section the first chapter of this book.

The tax return takes us up to Chapter 11 but, by the time we get there, the numbering thing has broken down a bit. Chapter 10, for instance, deals with the 'main body' of the tax return, which starts off with boxes numbered 10.xx, but which then goes on to 11.xx, 12.xx and so on up to 24.xx.

Part One finishes with a warped mathematical process designed to calculate how much tax you owe. As we'll see, you can opt to let the Inland Revenue do this for you, but they're happy for you to do it yourself if you want. Mostly it's a question of filling in boxes, but it does require some patience!

Part Two of the book is where you send the auditors into your personal finances. The process is similar to checking on the financial health of a company. It starts, in Chapter 12, 'Mr Micawber's Happiness/Misery Test', by looking at your personal cash flow statement. We establish, hopefully, that there's more coming in than going out. Chapter 13 is then an audit of your personal balance sheet or, to cut out the blather, 'What Have You Got?'

The next few chapters look at the different segments of what you've got. This starts in Chapter 14 with the nasty business of debts. Chapter 15 looks at what we've called chattels. These are basically the personal items, like your car or your TV, that you use to make life comfortable. The process here is rather like what's known as 'working capital control' in a company. You need to have enough to keep things ticking along smoothly, but too much is an inefficient use of your money.

Chapter 16 is where we look at your short-term savings, what you need and what to do with them. Chapter 17 is about your long-term investments. Again this involves what you need and what to do with them, but we also look at the tax-protective wrappers, such as pensions and ISAs, that you can use to keep the tax man away from them.

Chapter 18 is all about your home and your mortgage, assuming you have such things; and then Chapter 19 looks at the subject of insurance, which you'll need to cover the things that your savings and investments can't handle. Finally, we get to Chapter 20, where we wrap things up and attempt to leave you with the warm satisfaction of a job well done.

The tax return – do you need to fill one out?

Let's hope so! At least, if you've already bought this book, let's hope so.

If you pay higher rate tax, or if your financial affairs are the slightest bit quirky, then you need to fill out a tax return. It's called self-assessment and it's the law. You can sulk all you like, but if you don't comply, they'll keep fining you until you do. There is an explanation of who needs to complete a tax return in the 'Self-Assessment Frequently Asked Questions' section of the Inland Revenue's website at **www.inlandrevenue.gov.uk/sa/faqs/general.htm**. It starts off by saying that self-assessment applies to:

- Self-employed people including business partners
- Company directors
- Other people with more complicated tax affairs including people who pay higher rate tax
- Pensioners with more complex tax affairs
- People who received rent or other income from land and property in the UK
- Trustees and personal representatives
- Trustees of approved self-administered pension schemes
- Non-resident company landlords

You're then pointed to more detailed notes for the different categories. These can be found at **www.inlandrevenue.gov.uk/sa/index.htm**. The largest category is 'other people with more complicated tax affairs including people who pay higher rate tax'. Since self-employed people and business partners are included in a different category, the other people being referred to here are employees, give or take a few rich kids that don't work at all.

If you get sent a tax return and you don't fit one of the categories listed, or you don't think your affairs are very 'complex', then you should call up your local tax office and have it out with them. Otherwise, self-assessment it is, and this book is designed to help you through it.

How to do the tax return

Basically, you have a choice: you can either do your tax return with a pen on the hard copy tax return that you were sent in the post, or you can do it online. Which process you opt for is up to you, but there are some advantages to doing it online. For starters, the software you use (you can get it from the Inland

Revenue and other places) will calculate how much tax you owe automatically. As we'll see, doing it yourself is hard work. The process is also partially automated at the Inland Revenue's end, so things should happen more quickly and efficiently. So long as it's just the Employment or Self-Employment pages that you need to fill in, you can use the Inland Revenue's software package, but if you need other supplementary pages (we'll explain what these are in a moment), then you'll need to pay for someone else's software (check that your pages are supported!) or complete the return on paper.

To do the return online, you'll need to get yourself registered with the Government Gateway at **www.gateway.gov.uk**. You'll need your Tax Reference number from the front of your tax return, as well as your postcode or National Insurance number or both. Within seven days you'll be sent your User ID, which enables you to log onto the service. You need to do this within fourteen days to activate your account. With all this behind you, you're in a position to do your online tax return. There's more information about the online process at **www.ir-portal.gov.uk/index.jsp**.

If you do your tax return the old-fashioned way, then you must use blue or black ink, write clearly, and only in the spaces provided. In this book, we've assumed that you're doing it this way, although it should make little difference to what is said.

However you do it, there are several things to bear in mind. The tax return essentially asks a series of questions, to which you answer 'yes' or 'no'. If it's 'yes', then you need to fill in the various pages and boxes that apply to you. Where a box doesn't apply, it can be left blank. Numbers should be used for all amounts and, where indicated, losses should be entered in brackets. Remember that if you add a bracketed (that is, negative number) to a positive number, then it is like deducting it. So 60 + (40) = 20.

Figures for your income and gains should be rounded *down* to the nearest pound, while tax credits and deductions should be rounded *up* to the nearest pound. All the boxes should be rounded down or up, not just the totals boxes. In some cases, this might mean that the boxes don't tally exactly, but that doesn't matter (an example might be boxes 10.12, 10.13 and 10.14, where you're asked to detail income from UK savings after tax has been deducted, the actual tax that has been deducted, and the amount before the tax was deducted, because boxes 10.12 and 10.14 will be rounded down while 10.13 will be rounded up).

When to do the tax return

The tax year ends on 5 April every year, and this sets the ball rolling. On **6 April**, the Inland Revenue sends out the tax returns and they should land on your doormat soon afterwards.

The next key date is **30 September**, when the Inland Revenue likes to have your completed tax return back. If you make this date, the Revenue will calculate how much tax you have to pay them. It also means that they'll tell you what you owe before it's due on 31 January (which we'll come to), and that means you'll be able to make that date and avoid paying interest. What's more, if you get your return in by 30 September, you might also be able to organize having your tax collected through next year's PAYE code. If you miss 30 September, things get a lot more complicated (and I can vouch for that), so don't!

31 January is the final deadline for getting your tax return in for the year that ended on the previous 5 April. Miss this, and you'll be hit with a £100 fixed penalty (assuming you owe some tax). This is also the deadline for paying your tax and, if you miss it, the Inland Revenue will start charging you interest on what you owe. (On top of that, there'll be an automatic surcharge on any tax you owed on 31 January if the Inland Revenue doesn't get it by **28 February**.) Depending on your tax calculation, you may also have to make a 'first payment on account' for the next tax year. There's more about this in Chapter 11.

If you're still dragging your feet come **31 July**, things start to get really nasty. There's a second £100 penalty for tax returns that were due in on 31 January and a second 5 per cent surcharge for tax that was due on that date. If you're one of the people who have to make 'payments on account' (see preceding paragraph), then this will also be the date to make your second such payment.

So, as you can see, it doesn't get any easier as time goes on. In fact, it gets a fair bit harder and, if you're really sloppy, it'll get more expensive too. It's not something that's going to go away… so get on with it! Make 30 September and have a relaxing Christmas and New Year (and Bonfire night and all the rest of it, come to think of it), without having to worry about getting around to doing the tax return sometime.

Getting the bits together

What you get from the taxman
As we've seen already, the people who need to fill in tax returns are, for the most part, higher-rate taxpayers, the self-employed, people in business partnerships,

company directors, trustees and personal representatives (you should know what these are if you are one). If the Inland Revenue thinks you fall into any of these categories, it will send you various bits and pieces in the post. These are:

● The tax return
● Any supplementary pages they think you need
● A guide to filling out the return; and
● A guide to calculating your tax.

It's your responsibility, though, to decide for yourself if you need to do a return. Just because you don't get a form doesn't necessarily get you off the hook. If you're at all uncertain about whether to fill in a return, then you should start by contacting the Inland Revenue's general tax advice helpline on 0845 9000 444.

If you think you do need to fill in a return, but haven't been sent the bumph, then you'll need to get hold of it. You can do this by calling the document orderline on 0845 9000 404, by emailing **saorderline.ir@gtnet.gov.uk**, or by going to the Inland Revenue website at **www.inlandrevenue.gov.uk/sa**. Read the rest of this section of the book before doing it, though, because you're about to work out which bits you'll need. You'll also need to get hold of the *Inland Revenue's Tax Return Guide*.

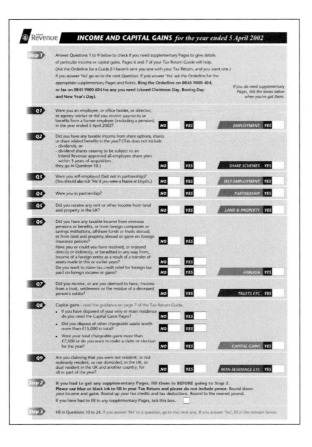

The supplementary pages

The tax return is made up of a main bit that everyone fills in, and various extra bits, called supplementary pages, that you fill in if they're relevant. You should have been sent the supplementary pages that the Inland Revenue thinks you need but, again, it's up to you to make sure you have the right ones. To decide this, look at page 2 of your tax return. You just have to scoot down the page answering the various 'yes' or 'no' questions in blue or black ink. We've reproduced it here.

The first step with anything is typically the hardest, so it's good of them to make this bit relatively straightforward. Why not try it now? In just a few short moments, you'll have reached the end of the first phase and feel you're getting somewhere. I can vouch for that, since this is where I started writing this book and has left me with a satisfying glow of achievement. Only another couple of hundred pages to go. Onward!

Whenever you answer 'yes' to a question on page 2, you need to check that you have the relevant supplementary pages. So, if you've ticked the 'yes' box for 'were you an employee… in the year ended 5 April 2002?', then see if you have the supplementary pages marked 'Employment' at the top.

If you have the extra pages, the Inland Revenue likes you to put a tick in the box on the far right of the question, just to show that you're awake. If you don't have the necessary extra pages, then you need to make a note, because you'll have to get hold of them. You can do this by phoning the hotline on 0845 9000 404, or you can download them from the Inland Revenue website at **www.inlandrevenue.gov.uk/sa.** Of course, if you've opted to fill the form in online, then the bits you need should be there.

The second question, 'Did you have any taxable income from share options, shares or related benefits during the year…?' is rather more scary. So much so that I'm not going to go into it here. On the whole, you should know if you definitely have any share options or whatever, but if you think you might have some, then it can be hard to work out if this applies. If you're not sure, start by asking your employer or the trustees of the share option scheme.

Each of the next nine chapters of this book deals with an individual set of supplementary pages, so if you're having trouble answering any of the questions on page 2, you can skip ahead for a bit more information. The chapters are as follows:

1   Employment (SA101)

9 to 5 down at the shoe factory? You should know if you're in this category.

2   Share Schemes (SA102)

These can be rewarding. Unfortunately they're a bit tricky on the tax front.

3   Self-Employment (SA103)

Take life by the scruff of the neck and be your own boss. Very Foolish!

4 Partnership (SA104)

That feeling of togetherness!

5 Land & Property (SA105)

Whether it's bricks and mortar or just a muddy field, if you're getting an income from it then these pages are for you.

6 Foreign (SA106)

Perhaps you rent out a villa in the south of France – or just have a savings account in Ecuador...

7 Trusts etc. (SA107)

You might be a fully-fledged 'it-girl' or it might be more mundane, but if you have the benefit of a trust, then this is for you.

8 Capital Gains (SA108)

Capital gains are great, but they can make a mess of your tax return.

9 Non-Residence etc. (SA109)

Even living overseas may not remove you from the grasp of the UK taxman. If you have income and gains in the UK, he'll want a slice.

There are also help notes on pages 6 and 7 of the *Inland Revenue's Tax Return Guide*. If you're still not sure how to answer any of the questions, there are also the detailed guidance notes for each set of supplementary pages, which you can get from the orderline (0845 9000 404) or from the Internet at **www.inland revenue.gov.uk/sa.**

What else?

On top of the Inland Revenue Forms, you'll also be needing the various financial records that you've been keeping safe throughout the year. Haven't you? If you take nothing else from this book, take this piece of advice: it will be about a thousand times easier to do your tax return if you keep a small file or drawer somewhere labelled *Tax Return*. Filling in your tax return is mostly a question of copying in numbers from elsewhere, but that ain't easy if you haven't got the 'elsewhere' to hand. So, when you get nasty-looking things like a 'P60' or a 'dividend voucher' or a 'statement of interest received', pop it in your drawer ready for future reference, instead of slipping it down behind the sofa.

The documents that you'll need for your tax return are, broadly speaking, ones which either set out how much income you've got from somewhere, ones which set out how much you have by way of expenses, and ones which show how much tax you've already paid. Sometimes, as with a P60 from your employer, it might tell you something about all three. If you're self-employed or rent out property, then you'll need quite detailed information about your sources of income and expenditure during the year, so a whole filing cabinet and, more than likely, a whole set of accounts might be required. For the full low-down on record keeping, you can get hold of the Inland Revenue leaflet 'Self Assessment – A general guide to keeping records' from the document orderline on 0845 9000 404 or the internet at **www.inlandrevenue.gov.uk/pdfs/sa-bk4.htm**.

If you didn't keep good records in the last tax year, it's a bit late to do anything about it now. Instead, as you come across the chapters that affect you, see what you need and whether you've got it. Where you can't find a particular document, you should be able to get hold of a replacement. Otherwise it'll be a case of making your best estimate and explaining, in the relevant additional information section, why you don't have the exact details. Just remember to be more organized next year!

Part 1
Doing the Tax Return

Employment

Hopefully, filling out page 2 of the tax return didn't cause you too much trouble. Unfortunately, though, if that was relatively straightforward, the same can't be said of the Employment supplementary pages. The good news is that for most people, it will be their only supplementary section, so at least when you've got to the end of it you'll be well and truly on your way.

What you'll need

The first things you need, of course, are the Employment supplementary pages themselves. In fact, you need one complete set for each different job you had during the tax year. On top of this, you should have a form P60 from the employer you were with at the end of the tax year (they're required to give it to you by 31 May following the end of the tax year). For any other jobs that you left during the tax year, you'll need the P45 form that you should have collected on leaving, instead of the P60.

If you had any employment benefits other than pay during the year, you should also get something called a P11D. This summarizes all the benefits-in-kind (such as a company car) that you received during the year. You should get one P11D from each employer that you had during the year, and they're required to give it to you before 6 July following the end of the tax year.

If you're someone who gets involved with a lot of employment expenses, then it's also worth asking your employer about any dispensations that they have with the Inland Revenue. We'll look at these in more detail in a moment (under benefits and expenses), but it's as well to be ahead of the game.

You should also have the Employment guidance notes, which you can get from the Inland Revenue orderline on 0845 9000 404 or from the Internet at **www.inlandrevenue.gov.uk/sa**. If you happen to be a Minister of Religion or a Member of Parliament, then you'll need an entirely different version of the form.

Boxes 1.1 to 1.7 – Details of employer

Start by putting your employer's details into boxes **1.1** to **1.7** (remember that a separate set of supplementary pages is required for each different employer). The information for question **1.1** comes from your P60 or P45. Other than that, the only slightly tricky ones here are **1.6** (were you a director of the company?) and **1.7** (if so, was it a close company?).

Question **1.6** is only relevant if you're a full-on director in the legal sense. It makes no difference what your job title is. It probably won't make much odds, but they need to know. Question **1.7** is rather more complicated. First of all, you only need to bother with it if you were a director (and ticked box **1.6**). 'Close companies' are, broadly speaking, companies that are owned by five or fewer people or by any number of people if they're also directors. If you think you might be a director of a close company, you should check with your local Tax Office.

Details of employer

Employer's PAYE reference - may be shown under 'Inland Revenue office number and reference' on your P60 or 'PAYE reference' on your P45

1.1 [   ]

Employer's name

1.2 [   ]

Date employment started
(only if between 6 April 2001 and 5 April 2002)

1.3 [/   /   ]

Date employment finished
(only if between 6 April 2001 and 5 April 2002)

1.4 [/   /   ]

Employer's address

1.5 [   ]

Postcode

Tick box 1.6 if you were a director of the company

1.6 [   ]

and, if so, tick box 1.7 if it was a close company

1.7 [   ]

Boxes 1.8 to 1.11 – Money

This is where you put all the money earnings you received from your employer. This will include things like salary, bonuses, commissions and overtime. Other more esoteric inducements such as tips or 'golden hellos' should also be included, along with things like sick pay paid by your employer. The section looks like this

Income from employment		
■ **Money** - see Notes, page EN3		Before tax
● Payments from P60 (or P45)		**1.8** £
● Payments not on P60 etc. - tips		**1.9** £
- other payments (excluding expenses entered below and lump sums and compensation payments or benefits entered overleaf)		**1.10** £
	Tax deducted	
● UK tax deducted from payments in boxes 1.8 to 1.10	**1.11** £	

Things to leave out of this section include the benefits and expenses that go in boxes **1.12** to **1.23**, lump sums paid in relation to leaving your job (these go in boxes **1.27** to **1.29**), sick pay and other benefits paid by the Department of Social Security (these go in the main body of the tax return) and anything to do with share schemes (which go in the Share Schemes supplementary pages). Also, don't include contributions to your employer's pension scheme or any charitable donations made through your payroll (such as Give as You Earn).

The good news is that all this ought to be summed up nicely on your P60 (or P45 if the employment has ended). In any case, the first box to fill in, **1.8**, will come directly from there and is probably called something like 'net pay after superannuation'. In certain circumstances, if you provide services to a 'client' via a company, but where you are to all intents and purposes an employee of the 'client', you may be treated as receiving 'deemed Schedule E payments'. This basically means that the money needs to be treated as employment income and, as such, should be included here. There is more about this in the Inland Revenue leaflet *IR175: Supplying services through a limited company or partnership* and *IR2003: Supplying services. How to calculate the deemed payment*.

The next box, **1.9**, is for tips. They don't generally come to you via your employer, so they won't be reflected on your P60 (or P45); but they still form part of your income. Box **1.10** is for any other employment-related payments that didn't get included in the other two boxes. If you're not sure how to classify a particular payment, start by asking your payroll people at work. Otherwise, try the Employment guidance notes or the Inland Revenue's general tax advice helpline on 0845 9000 444.

Finally, box **1.11** is for the tax that's already been taken off your employment earnings, via your employer's payroll. You should be able to lift this figure directly from a box on your P60 (or P45).

Boxes 1.12 to 1.23 – Benefits and expenses

You need to fill in this subsection if you've received any 'benefits in kind' from your employer. This means anything of value, other than cold hard cash. To confuse things, you have to enter the 'cash equivalent amount' of any benefits. For example, if your employer kindly gave you an old office computer to take home for your own personal use, you need to insert the computer's second-hand value, *even if you don't go ahead and sell it*.

Note that you only have to fill in this subsection if your earnings were 'at a rate of £8,500 or more per year', or if you were a director of your employer company.

Most of the information needed here should be included in the form P11D that you get from your employer. So it should be a relatively simple matter of copying the numbers from the P11D to the tax form. It's worth checking the numbers as you go though, since it's not unknown for employers to get the figures wrong. If there is a mistake, just put the correct figure in the tax return. If you're not sure about any of the boxes, the first step would be to talk to your employer about it. After that, there's the Inland Revenue *Booklet 480: Expenses and benefits – a tax guide* and each of the boxes has its own helpsheet (these are available from the document orderline – 0845 9000 404 – or the Internet at **www.inlandrevenue.gov.uk/sa**). Where appropriate, the helpsheets include worksheets for calculating the 'cash equivalents' of the various benefits.

The example of the second-hand computer would be an asset transferred to you by your employer and would go in box **1.12**. You should also include in box **1.12** anything that you could give up at short notice for a higher cash wage, like board and lodging, or any payments made by your employer to someone else on your behalf, like rent paid directly to your landlord.

Box **1.13** is for vouchers, credit cards and tokens. Vouchers are basically anything that you can exchange for money, goods or services: things like gift vouchers, luncheon vouchers and season tickets. Credit cards and tokens are things that enable you to get money, goods and services on credit, or with

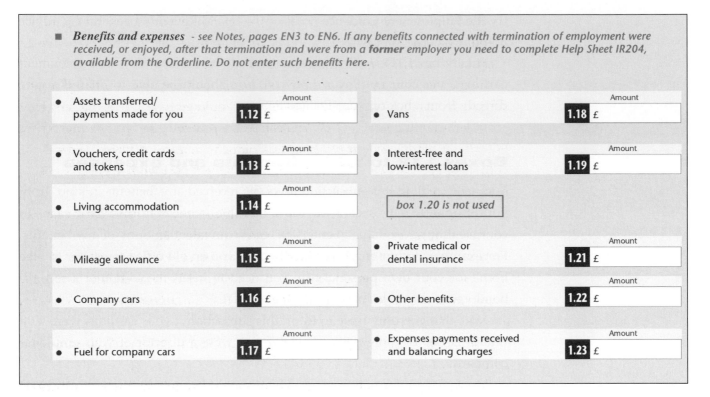

someone else settling the account: the obvious example is the infamous company credit card. So, you should put in box **1.13** the total amount of vouchers you've received in the year, and the total amount that you've spent on company credit cards (or tokens, whatever they might involve).

There are, however, a few fairly obscure types of voucher and credit card payments that the taxman will let you get away with, and these should not be included in box **1.13**. There's a list of these in the Inland Revenue helpsheet *IR 201: Vouchers, credit cards and tokens* (which you can get from the document orderline on 0845 9000 404) – but it's probably easiest to start by asking at work.

Any living accommodation you or your family get from your employer should be included in box **1.14** (the difference between this and 'board and lodging' in box **1.12** is that the latter could be given up at short notice for a higher cash wage). Your employer should give you a figure for this, but if you want to look into the detail, get hold of helpsheet *IR 202: Living accommodation* from the document orderline on 0845 9000 404.

If you get an allowance from your employer for using your own car or other vehicle for business journeys, and it's more than what's allowable for tax purposes, then the difference should go in box **1.15**. If you don't get an allowance, or it's less than what's allowable, then you can claim the expenses in box **1.32** (there's a bit more about this when we deal with that box in a moment). If you can't work out whether or not you have an excess, have a look at help-sheet *IR125: Using your own car or motorbike for work.*

If you have a company car for private use, your employer should give you a figure for its cash equivalent. This figure should go in box **1.16**, and any fuel provided should go in box **1.17**. You can read up on the nitty-gritty in helpsheet *IR 203: Car benefits and car fuel benefits.* Company vans for private use are dealt with separately in box **1.18** (and even they have their own helpsheet – *IR136: Income tax and company vans*).

Note that these boxes are for *company* vehicles for *private* use. Where you use your *own* car for *business* use, refer to boxes **1.15** and **1.32**.

Your employer should give you a figure for the cash equivalent of any interest-free or low-interest loans and this should be entered into box **1.19**. If you want to check on your employer's sums, the details are in *IR145: Low-interest loans provided by employers.*

Box **1.20** is no longer in use, which is nice. Shame there can't be more like that. (It used to be for mobile phones.)

If your employer pays for, or contributes to, any private medical or health insurance, they should give you a figure for it and it should go in box **1.21**.

Box **1.22** is a catch-all for any benefits that didn't fit into the earlier boxes. These might include relocation expenses or the costs of a crèche paid for by your employer, but in some cases they won't be taxable. If you think you might have something to put in here, start by talking to your employer.

Box **1.23** relates to what your employer has paid to you for expenses that you incurred in the line of duty. In other words, the total of all your monthly expense claims. Your employer should provide you with the details. The idea is that the expenses that you claim (and receive) get added to your employment income, but later on (in boxes **1.32** to **1.36**), we deduct them again. The difference should reflect the amount by which your income has been bolstered by the net expense payments you've received (if you've overclaimed) or reduced by the net expense payments that you've made (if you've underclaimed). If you're in the first category here, you'd better hope your employer doesn't mind. If you're in the second category, you should be asking yourself (or even better, your employer) some serious questions. Although you might pay a little less tax, it's only because you're effectively being underpaid!

Clearly the process of putting every last employment expense into the tax return, just to be netted off against a claim for those expenses, can be a bit cumbersome for those who like their business lunches (and the cab home afterwards). To simplify things a little, the Inland Revenue might come to an arrangement with your employer so that certain expenses need not be mentioned on either side of the equation. These are called 'dispensations' or PAYE settlement agreements. Your employer should let you know if there are any of these things in place.

The final nuance with box **1.23** is something called 'balancing charges'. It only matters if you have claimed on your expenses, some time in the past, for buying something that you use for work (like, perhaps, a laptop). This would be included in box **1.35** and is called a capital allowance. If you then go ahead and sell the laptop, or just stop using it for work, the Inland Revenue will want you to account for the value of it at that point. That's called the balancing charge and you have to include it in **1.23**. Otherwise, we could all go out and get tax relief for our laptops, use them for work for a day, and then shift them to our own personal use. It's fair enough really. If you have a balancing charge that needs accounting for, you should get hold of the helpsheet *IR206: Capital allowances for employees and office holders* (from the orderline or Internet).

Boxes 1.24 to 1.30 – Lump sums and compensation payments

This is where things get really tricky, but you shouldn't have to fill in this bit unless you've received a lump sum payment as a result of a change in the terms of your job, or on being made redundant or dismissed. It's unfortunate that the Inland Revenue throws this at you just when you could do without the complications, but then I guess the tax man isn't known for his sensitivity. Anyhow, commiserations come from us Fools and we hope you can turn it into something positive. Before then, though, we'll need to get this bit of the tax return out of the way.

If all you got was a redundancy payment, against which your employer allowed a tax exemption for up to £30,000, then things are comparatively simple. You enter the amount of the payment (after deducting the exemption) in box **1.29**; and enter the amount of the exemption in box **1.24**. Only enter positive numbers or zero, though. So, if you received a £7,500 redundancy payment, all of it covered by the exemption, then you'd leave **1.29** blank, but enter £7,500 in box **1.24**. If, however, you received £40,000, of which £30,000 is exempted, then you should enter £10,000 in box **1.29** (that is, £40,000 minus £30,000) and

■ **Lump sums and compensation payments or benefits including such payments and benefits from a former employer**
Note that 'lump sums' here includes any contributions which your employer made to an unapproved retirement benefits scheme

*You must read page EN6 of the Notes **before** filling in boxes 1.24 to 1.30*

Reliefs

● £30,000 exemption   **1.24** £

● Foreign service and disability   **1.25** £

● Retirement and death lump sums   **1.26** £

Taxable lump sums

● From box B of *Help Sheet IR204*   **1.27** £

● From box K of *Help Sheet IR204*   **1.28** £

● From box L of *Help Sheet IR204*   **1.29** £

● Tax deducted from payments in boxes 1.27 to 1.29 - *leave blank if this tax is included in the box 1.11 figure.*   Tax deducted   **1.30** £

the £30,000 exemption in box **1.24**. You also need to put the amount of any tax already paid in respect of the redundancy payment into box **1.30**.

If your situation is more complicated than this, we're afraid you either need to stick your finger in the air and guess, or plough through the worksheets contained in the Inland Revenue helpsheet *IR204: Lump sums and compensation payments*. Needless to say, the Inland Revenue doesn't take too kindly to guesswork. The worksheets seem designed to confuse and they do a very good job of it. So, don't be scared of making full use the general tax advice helpline (0845 9000 444).

Box 1.31 – Foreign earnings not taxable in the UK

This subsection, as the title suggests, relates to income earned while you weren't resident in the UK. If you're sure you *didn't* receive any income during the year that related to employment when you weren't UK resident, breathe a huge sigh of relief, ignore the nasty-looking box **1.31** and move on to the next section – 'Expenses you incurred in doing your job'. Off you go and count yourself lucky.

■ **Foreign earnings not taxable in the UK in the year ended 5 April 2002** - *see Notes, page EN6*   **1.31** £

For those of you who are still here, we're afraid things are about to take a turn for the worse. You'll need to fill in the Inland Revenue helpsheet *IR211: Employment – residence and domicile issues*. You can't really do that, though, until you've worked out who you are and where you come from, which means filling in the 'Non-Residence etc.' supplementary pages. These are covered in Chapter 9. So off you go, too, and we'll see you back here when you're done with Chapter 9 and have come up with a number to go in the evil box **1.31**.

Boxes 1.32 to 1.36 – Expenses you incurred doing your job

This bit, relatively speaking at least, is a doddle. You simply have to insert all the expenses you paid out during the year that were 'wholly, exclusively and necessary for your employment'. This includes any expenses that you actually claimed back from your employer because, if you remember, we included those payments to you as part of your gross income back in the benefits and expenses section (boxes **1.12** to **1.23**), so now we have to set off what you actually paid out.

Remember that, as we saw when looking at box **1.23**, your employer might have a dispensation with the Inland Revenue whereby for certain things, neither the benefit nor the associated expense should be entered in the tax return. On top of expenses that you've reclaimed from your employer, though, it's perfectly fair for you to include expenses even though you didn't (for whatever reason) get reimbursed for them. However, if your employer wasn't prepared to pay for them, the Inland Revenue will take some persuading that they were 'wholly, exclusively and necessary' for your employment.

You might have thought that travelling to your place of work was 'wholly, exclusively and necessary for your employment', but apparently not. The theory is that commuting merely puts you in a position to do the work, it doesn't help

■ *Expenses you incurred in doing your job* - see Notes, pages EN6 to EN8		
● Travel and subsistence costs	**1.32**	£
● Fixed deductions for expenses	**1.33**	£
● Professional fees and subscriptions	**1.34**	£
● Other expenses and capital allowances	**1.35**	£
● Tick box 1.36 if the figure in box 1.32 includes travel between your home and a permanent workplace	**1.36**	

you do it. Or something like that. It seems pretty tenuous, but you're not allowed a deduction for the costs of 'ordinary commuting' to and from your permanent place of work, except in unusual circumstances. You are, though, allowed a deduction for travel to a temporary place of work, unless the trip is 'for practical purposes substantially ordinary commuting' (in other words, broadly in the same direction and broadly the same length). If you are allowed a deduction for a particular trip, then you're also allowed a deduction for the meal and accommodation costs that go with it. You should add up any allowable travel, meal and accommodation expenses and put the figure in box **1.32**. If you're unsure about how your various trips fit into all this, start by asking the people at work. If you're still not sure, try the Inland Revenue general helpline on 0845 9000 444.

Box **1.32** should also be used to enter the costs of running your own car or other vehicle for the purposes of your employment. If you receive an allowance from your employer for these costs, then you can only include these expenses to the extent that what's allowable for tax purposes exceeds the allowance (see the comments about box **1.15** on page 22). There are two ways of calculating the amount of tax relief, called the 'exact basis' and the 'simple basis'.

With the exact basis, you claim for your travel costs for each and every mile travelled during the year for business purposes. The travel costs include cost of fuel, but also the proportion of repair and maintenance costs that relate to business use. To work out the exact proportions, you have to keep records of all your travel expenses, as well as mileage for both business and private use. There's more detail about how to work things out on the exact basis in helpsheet *IR125: Using your own car or motorbike for work*.

The simple basis, not surprisingly, takes a rather more broad-brush approach. For motorbikes, you get a straight 24p per mile of business use, for bicycles it's 12p. With cars, it depends on the size of the engine and whether you do more or less than 4,000 miles for business purposes. The detail is in the table below.

TRAVEL EXPENSES - SIMPLE BASIS	Engine Size	Up to 4,000 Business Miles (pence per mile)	Over 4,000 Business Miles (pence per mile)
	Up to 1,500cc	40	25
	1,501 – 2,000cc	45	25
	Over 2,000cc	63	36

Box **1.33** is for 'fixed deductions' negotiated with the Inland Revenue by a trade union or similar. The idea is that they come to an agreement for how much certain types of workers should be able to claim – for example, for tools. You enter this figure here. However, if you think it will come out higher, you can work it out for yourself and make a claim under box **1.35**, 'Other Expenses'. The Inland Revenue will want a pretty good reason, though, why you're different from everybody else.

If you have to pay fees and/or annual subscriptions to approved professional bodies to carry on your profession, then these should be entered in box **1.34**. You should be able to find out how much to enter from the relevant professional body.

Box **1.35** is the general catch-all for other expenses, but remember that the expenses must be 'wholly, exclusively and necessary for your employment'. This is a pretty severe test. It wouldn't include the purchase of a business suit, but it might well include the purchase of specialist clothing. You'd hope, for instance, that David Beckham manages a claim for those white boots of his – but it might be different if he kept using them for a kick-around in the back garden with Brooklyn. And to be allowable, the expense must also be incurred in actually carrying out your job, rather than just putting yourself in a position to do it. So Goldenballs might struggle to charge for his Deep Heat. Actually though, I doubt he'd have to pay for his boots or his Deep Heat… in fact, maybe we'd best leave Beckham's tax return out of it. I dread to think how it would look. But no doubt someone gets paid plenty of money to fill it in.

Box **1.36** is just to be ticked if you included, in box **1.32**, any expenses for travel to and from your permanent place of work. This might surprise you since we said it couldn't be included, but we did add *except in unusual circumstances*. If you've spoken to the people at work or the Revenue and you think you're in an unusual circumstance, then good luck to you, but don't forget to tick box **1.36** to alert the taxman! You could also add a brief explanation in box **1.40** ('additional information').

Box 1.37 –
Foreign earnings deduction for seafarers

Box **1.37** is pretty straightforward, unless you happen to be a seafarer. A seafarer is defined as 'someone that performs their employment duties on a ship'. If this isn't you, then skip the box and move on. If you think you might qualify, then you'll need to start by getting hold of helpsheet *IR 205: Foreign Earnings Deduction: Seafarers*.

■ *Foreign Earnings Deduction* (seafarers only)	**1.37** £
■ *Foreign tax for which tax credit relief not claimed*	**1.38** £
■ *Student Loans repaid by deduction by employer* - *see Notes, page EN8*	**1.39** £

Box 1.38 – Foreign tax for which tax credit relief is not claimed

Despite the nasty looking title, this one's simple enough as well. If you didn't pay any foreign tax on your employment income during the tax year, then skip box **1.38** entirely. If you did pay foreign tax on your employment income, you can potentially claim a relief, or tax credit. If so, leave box **1.38** blank and fill in the Foreign supplementary pages (see Chapter 6). If, for some reason, you don't want to claim the credit, enter the amount of foreign tax you've paid in box **1.38**.

Box 1.39 – Student loans

From April 2000, student loans (proper student loans, that is, not the inevitable overdraft) now work so that the money you've borrowed is recouped by the Inland Revenue when you pay tax. It's almost like an extra tax on people who got government money to go through higher education, except that how quickly you pay it back will depend on how much you're earning. Anyway, box **1.39** is where you enter your student loan repayment for the year. It should have been deducted by your employer and should therefore be found on your P60. If you've changed employments during the year, look at the payslips from your previous employer(s) to find the amount to enter on each separate set of Employment pages.

Box 1.40 – Additional information

You can probably guess what this is for, but it's hard to actually pin down what might go in it. The broad answer is anything else you feel would help the Inland Revenue to check on your tax. So, if you included something as an 'expense' that might not normally be allowable, then you'd want to explain why you're different. Remember they have millions of these things to go through, so they won't thank you for a long essay, but if you've got something to add, add it here.

Share schemes

Share schemes can be a wonderful incentive to get you out of bed and into work in the morning, but they're a nightmare as far as tax is concerned. Successive Chancellors, each keen to be seen to be doing something, have added so many

---

Inland Revenue

Income for the year ended 5 April 2002

SHARE SCHEMES

Name

Tax reference

Fill in these boxes first

If you want help, look up the box numbers in the Notes.

Share options

Read the Notes on pages SN1 to SN8 **before** filling in the boxes

■ Approved savings-related share options

		Name of company and share scheme	Tick if shares un-listed	Taxable amount
● Exercise	2.1		2.2	2.3 £
● Cancellation or release	2.4		2.5	2.6 £

■ Approved discretionary share options

		Name of company and share scheme		
● Exercise	2.7		2.8	2.9 £
● Cancellation or release	2.10		2.11	2.12 £

■ Enterprise Management Incentive options

		Name of company and unique option reference		
● Exercise	2.13		2.14	2.15 £
● Cancellation or release	2.16		2.17	2.18 £

■ Unapproved share options

		Name of company and share scheme		
● Grant	2.19		2.20	2.21 £
● Exercise	2.22		2.23	2.24 £
● Cancellation or release	2.25		2.26	2.27 £

Approved Share Incentive Plans

Read the Notes on page SN2 **before** filling in the boxes

		Name of company and share plan		
● Shares ceasing to be subject to the plan	2.28		2.29	2.30 £

Shares acquired

Read the Notes on page SN8 **before** filling in the boxes

		Name of company and share scheme		
● Shares acquired from your employment	2.31		2.32	2.33 £
● Shares as benefits	2.34		2.35	2.36 £
● Post-acquisition charges or lifting of risk of forfeiture	2.37		2.38	2.39 £

■ Totals

● Total of the taxable amounts boxes (total boxes in the right-hand column, starting with box 2.3) total column above 2.40 £

● Any taxable amounts included in boxes 2.6 to 2.39 which are included in the Pay figure on your P60 or P45(Part 1A) 2.41 £

Total taxable amount box 2.40 minus box 2.41 2.42 £

SA102

BS 12/2001net TAX RETURN ■ SHARE SCHEMES: PAGE S1 Please turn over ➤

You must complete a separate copy of Pages S2 or S3 for each taxable event (explained on page SN1 of the Notes) in the year ended 5 April 2002 that relates to your share options or shares acquired. If you had more than one taxable event in the year, ask the Orderline for more copies, or photocopy these Pages. (If you use a photocopy, please put your name and tax reference at the top.)

Share options

Read the Notes on pages SN2 to SN8 **before** filling in the boxes

Name of company and share scheme 2.43

Class of share (for example, 10p Ordinary) 2.44

		Options granted	Options exercised	Options cancelled/released
2.45	Date option was granted	/ /	/ /	/ /
2.46	Date option was exercised		/ /	
2.47	Number of shares			
2.48	Exercise price: option price per share	£ .	£ .	
2.49	Amount, if any, paid for grant of option	£ .	£ .	£ .
2.50	Market value per share at date the option was granted	£ .		
2.51	Market value per share at date the option was exercised		£ .	
2.52	Amount received in money or money's worth			£ .

Enterprise Management Incentive options

Read the Notes on pages SN3 to SN6 **before** filling in the boxes

Name of company and unique option reference 2.53

Class of share (for example, 10p Ordinary) 2.54

		Options exercised	Options cancelled/released
2.55	Date option was granted	/ /	/ /
2.56	Date of disqualifying event	/ /	
2.57	Number of shares		
2.58	Exercise price: option price per share	£ .	
2.59	Amount, if any, paid for grant of option	£ .	£ .
2.60	Market value per share at date the option was granted	£ .	
2.61	Market value per share at date of the disqualifying event	£ .	
2.62	Market value per share at date the option was exercised	£ .	
2.63	Amount received in money or money's worth		£ .

BS 12/2001net TAX RETURN ■ SHARE SCHEMES: PAGE S2

different types of plan, with so many different rules, that you could probably devote an entire book to the subject. No doubt such books exist, but we wouldn't recommend trying to read one except as a cure for insomnia. So, we're going to keep things very brief, and stick to giving you an idea of where to start with this section.

Let's start by noting that this section is not designed for any capital gains you made on shares, or any dividend income you received from them during the year, even if they were shares in your employing company. Shares are investments and the income (that is, dividends) and gains you make from them should be entered elsewhere in the tax return (capital gains have their own supplementary pages, while dividends go in question 10 of the main body of the tax return).

What we're concerned with here is where you get shares, in the company you work for, as a benefit of your employment. Note the last bit – *as a benefit of your employment*. If you had to pay the full market price for the shares, then they

wouldn't be a 'benefit' and the taxman wouldn't care about them (at least as far as this section is concerned). So for the shares to be a benefit, they need to be given to you free or cut-price. As well as shares, you need to worry about any options to buy shares in your company ('share options'). Since they too have a value, being granted share options can also be a benefit of employment.

To confuse matters further, the shares and share options can be given to you in a variety of ways and, depending on which way is chosen, the tax you have to pay on the benefit can be reduced or removed entirely.

So, the first question you have to ask yourself is 'did I receive any shares, or rights over shares (such as options), in my employing company during the tax year?' If you say 'no', then you can forget this chapter and move forward. If your answer is 'yes,' or even, 'er, yes, maybe, well I'm not entirely sure,' then you need to ask yourself 'how was I given them?'

Better than asking yourself, though, is to ask your employers. With a bit of luck, they might even be able to tell you how to enter the information in your tax return. If they can't tell you where it goes, then you'll need to fall back on the Inland Revenue's *Guidance notes on the share schemes supplementary pages* and the particular helpsheet that relates to your breed of share scheme. There's a list of them below and your employer should at least be able to tell you which of the helpsheets applies to you. They can be ordered from the Inland Revenue's order-line on 0845 9000 404. On the Internet, there's a special section of the Inland Revenue's website devoted to share schemes from which the various documents can be downloaded: **www.inlandrevenue.gov.uk/shareschemes**.

Document No.	Document Name
SN1	Notes on Share Schemes supplementary pages
IR16	Share acquisition by directors and employees
IR95	Approved profit sharing schemes
IR97	Approved Save as You Earn share option schemes
IR101	Approved Company Share Option Plans
IR2002	Share Incentive Plans
IR2006	Enterprise Management Incentives
IR216	Shares as benefits
IR217	Shares acquired: post-acquisition charges
IR218	Employee shares: Operation of Pay As You Earn (PAYE) and National Insurance contributions (NICs)
IR219	Shares acquired from your employment
IR287	Employee share schemes and Capital Gains Tax

IR HELPSHEETS ON SHARE SCHEMES

Self-Employment

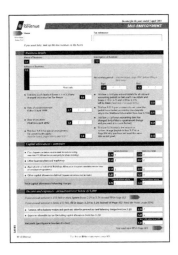

If you did any work during the year, in the UK or abroad, as a self-employed person, these pages are for you. Self-employed means that you are trading as an individual, rather than through a company or in a partnership with others. If you work through a company, then you'll be an employee of that company and you need to fill in the Employment pages (Chapter 1). If you work in a partnership with others, then you'll need the Partnership pages (Chapter 4).

Having said that, there can be a fine distinction between a contract of employment with a company and a contract to do work for a company as a self-employed individual. Which camp you fall into basically comes down to whether you're your own boss. In deciding that, there are a number of pointers that the Inland Revenue will consider. For instance, a self-employed trader is

● likely to be able to decide where, when and how the work is to be done
● likely to be paid on a fee basis, rather than on an hourly or daily rate
● likely to be capable of making a loss, or extra profit, depending on how well the job is done
● unlikely to have a contractual right to paid holidays or sick leave.

All these factors tend to make someone their own boss and, therefore, self-employed. If you're not sure where you fit in, you should phone the Inland Revenue general advice line on 0845 9000 444. It's also possible to be both employed and self-employed where, for instance, you have a day job, but undertake additional freelance work. In that case, you have to fill in both the Employment pages and the Self-Employment pages. If you run more than one business, you need to fill in one set of Self-Employment pages for each business.

What you'll need

As we've said, you need one set of Self-Employment supplementary pages for each business that you operate. You should also make sure you have the Inland Revenue's *Notes to filling in the Self-Employment pages*, and there are a number of helpsheets for specific areas, which we'll refer to as we go along. As ever, you can get the Inland Revenue's various documents from the orderline on 0845 9000 404 or the website at **www.inlandrevenue.gov.uk/sa**.

In addition to the Inland Revenue documents, you'll need your business accounts. If you don't have accounts, then you need your business records. You're required to keep records of all your business transactions, so you should have these!

Finally, if you're a farmer, doctor, Lloyds underwriter, writer, artist or subcontractor in the construction industry then you're a special case (books about tax returns are the only place you'll see these occupations grouped together). Lloyds underwriters have their own special pages to fill in, while some of the other categories have their own helpsheets. These are:

- *IR 224: Farmers and market gardeners*
- *IR 232: Farm stock valuation*
- *IR 231: Doctors' expenses*
- *IR 234: Averaging for creators of literary or artistic works*

Those operating professional businesses have some extra issues and should get hold of *IR 233: The 'true and fair' view for professions and the 'adjustment' on withdrawal of cash basis*. Doesn't sound too hot, does it? But it's there to help you.

What's your accounting period?

You need to account for your business profits (and losses) in 12-month chunks, but you can choose when the 12-month periods end. This might be the anniversary of when you started the business, it might be the 31 December or, if you really want, it can be your birthday. Of course, you can save yourself a lot of trouble by using 5 April, so you match the tax year exactly. One of the main factors that you might want to consider is the seasonality of your business. If you operate an ice-cream van, for instance, you wouldn't want to have a year-end of, say, 31 May, since the summer months are better used making money than fiddling around with your accounts. It will also be easier to work out your profit or loss if you pick a quiet time of year when things like stocks and work-in-progress are low.

The accounting period that you use for the purposes of your tax return, called the *basis period*, is the one that ends in the relevant tax year. So, if your accounting period runs to 31 December, then for your 2001/2 tax return, you'd use the 12-month period ending 31 December 2001. However, this is confused if you've just started or ceased to be in business, or if you decide to change your accounting period. It makes life a lot easier if you don't do this very often.

Starting out

In your first tax year of being self-employed, you simply work out your profits from when you started to 5 April. In the second year, you're into the normal phase and you use the accounting period that ends in the tax year. So, if you start a business on 1 January 2001, then the basis period for your 2000/1 tax return will be the three-month period from 1 January 2001 to 5 April 2001. For your 2001/2 tax return, you're into the normal swing of things and you use the accounting period that finished in that tax year, which will be the one that ended on 31 December 2001.

Now it doesn't take a genius to spot that you've actually been taxed twice on your profits from 1 January to 5 April 2001. That might seem like a swindle, but it isn't really. After all, for the 2001/2 tax return you've avoided paying tax on the profits for the three months from 1 January to 5 April 2002. Assuming that your profits have increased (or your losses have decreased) in your first 15 months of operation, it will actually benefit you.

The Inland Revenue is just trying to keep things simple (and not making too bad a job of it). The idea is that in each tax year, you get taxed for a whole 12 months of trading and, as near as possible, the idea is that you get taxed, at some point, once for each and every month you've traded. The three months don't get forgotten, though. Instead, they get tucked away in the memory bank tagged 'overlap', along with the taxable profits made in them. When we get to the bit about 'closing up shop', you'll see that it all sorts itself out.

Changing the accounting date

If you change your accounting date and, as we've said, we don't recommend you do it very often, then things will be messed up for a year or two. Keeping to the same example, let's say that some time during 2002, you decide to shift your year-end back a month to 31 January. That means that for the 2002/3 tax year, your basis period will be the *thirteen*-month period ending 31 January 2003. A bit of a pain, but not the end of the world. What does happen, though, is that you get to use a month of your overlap; that is, you deduct your taxable profit for your first month's trading, and your stored-up overlap correspondingly reduces to two months.

If, instead of moving to 31 January, you decide to shorten your accounting period so that it ends on 31 October 2002, then your 2002/3 basis period will be the ten-month period from 1 January to 31 October 2002. And, you've guessed it, your overlap increases by two months to five months. Overlap just reflects the months in a tax year that you've traded for, but not paid tax on.

Closing up shop

When the time finally comes to pull down the shutters for the last time, you get taxed for the period up to when you actually stop trading. Let's go back to the earlier example, assuming that we didn't change the accounting date (so we still account for periods ending 31 December and have three months overlap); and say that we stopped trading on 31 June 2005. For the 2004/5 tax year, our basis period will be the 12 months ended 31 December 2004 as usual. In the 2005/6 tax year, we'd be taxed on the period from 1 January to 31 June 2005.

So, including what went on when we started up back at the beginning of the millennium, we can see that we've been taxed on every month that we've traded for, *but...*we've been taxed on the first three months' trading twice. We didn't mind before, but now it seems to have caught up with us. So, what happens is that the taxable profit that we made in our overlap period of three months now gets deducted from our final lot of taxable profits. Rather elegantly, it's only fair to say, everything's come out in the wash.

OK, so hopefully we've now got our bits together and we know which period we're getting taxed on. If none of the stuff about accounting periods made sense, then you'd better take a look at the *Notes on Self-Employment* and/or the helpsheet *IR222: How to work out your taxable profits*. Better still, give the Inland Revenue helpline a call on 0845 9000 444.

Value Added Tax

The first thing to say about VAT is that it's not part of your taxable profits or the tax you pay on them. It's different. In most cases, you'll have to register for VAT if your business's annual turnover hits the VAT threshold (£54,000 from 1 April 2001). Below this, you can decide whether or not to register. If you do register, then *generally speaking* (it does get fiddly), you charge your customers VAT on what you provide to them, deduct the VAT that you've been charged on things that others have provided to your business, and pay the difference to Her Majesty's Customs and Excise. The idea is that this net amount reflects a tax on the value that your business adds to things as they pass through it, which is why it's called Value Added Tax.

Anyway, since the VAT doesn't form part of your business profits, it needs to be stripped out for the purposes of your income tax. So, if you write VAT-inclusive figures in your tax return, you need to include the net amount of VAT paid as 'other expenses' in box **3.63**, or as other income in box **3.50** (we'll get to these boxes as we go through the form). Any additional explanation (perhaps if the VAT relates to equipment you've bought) should go in the additional information section.

If you're not registered for VAT, you don't charge your customers VAT. Any VAT you pay on things you buy for the business simply counts as part of the cost of those things, and should be included in the figures that you enter.

Right, with all that out of the way, we can move on to the tax return.

Boxes 3.1 to 3.13 – Business details

Boxes **3.1** to **3.3**, business name, description and address, are straightforward. The business may simply have your own name, or you might have a trading name. Whatever it is, stick it in. If the details have changed since your last tax return, then you also need to tick box **3.6**. Boxes **3.4** and **3.5** are for the accounting period covered in the tax return, as per the earlier discussion.

If your business commenced trading after 5 April 1999, you need to put the start date in box **3.7,** and if you stopped trading or sold your business between 6 April 2001 and 5 April 2002, then you need to put the end date in box **3.8**. If you do complete either of these boxes, then the rules about accounting dates will be slightly different and you should look at page 3 of the helpsheet *IR222: How to calculate your taxable profits*.

Box **3.9** requires a tick if you are claiming that you're a special case. Details of the particular special cases are given on pages 10 and 11 of the Inland Revenue's *Notes on Self-Employment*. If you're included, you may also need to get hold of the relevant helpsheet.

Business details

Name of business

3.1

Description of business

3.2

Address of business

3.3

Postcode

Accounting period - *read the Notes, page SEN2 before filling in these boxes*

Start

3.4 / /

End

3.5 / /

- Tick box 3.6 if details in boxes 3.1 or 3.3 have changed since your last Tax Return

3.6

- Date of commencement if after 5 April 1999

3.7 / /

- Date of cessation if before 6 April 2002

3.8 / /

- Tick box 3.9 if the special arrangements for certain trades apply - *read the Notes, pages SEN10 and SEN11*

3.9

- Tick box 3.10 if you entered details for all relevant accounting periods on last year's Tax Return and boxes 3.14 to 3.73 and 3.99 to 3.115 will be blank *(read Step 3 on page SEN2)*

3.10

- Tick box 3.11 if your accounts do not cover the period from the last accounting date (explain why in the 'Additional information' box, box 3.116)

3.11

- Tick box 3.12 if your accounting date has changed (only if this is a permanent change and you want it to count for tax)

3.12

- Tick box 3.13 if this is the second or further change (explain in box 3.116 on Page SE4 why you have not used the same date as last year)

3.13

Things begin to get a little murky at box **3.10**, with the instruction to tick the box 'if you entered details for all relevant accounting periods on last year's tax return'. You'd be forgiven for thinking that the Inland Revenue had reverted to its much-favoured gobbledygook. I'll try to explain things, but it will mean going round the houses a bit.

When we looked at accounting periods, we saw that it's possible to have a basis period that isn't the same as your accounting period (particularly if you have a start date after 5 April 1998). If that's the case, then you have to take the relevant portion of each accounting period. So, if your basis period includes three months of accounting period 1, and nine months of accounting period 2, then you'll need a quarter of the figures for accounting period 1 plus three-quarters of the figures for accounting period 2. Now it's possible that you included information for some of the accounting periods in last year's tax return. If so, you don't have to repeat the information. If you included details of **all** the accounting periods that make up this year's basis period in your last tax return, then you should tick box **3.10**. If you do this, you'll be able to get away without repeating the accounting information in boxes **3.14** to **3.73**, and **3.99** to **3.115**. You will, however, always have to fill in boxes **3.74** to **3.98** to make various adjustments and arrive at your taxable profit.

Box **3.11** needs a tick if there's a gap between the end of your last accounting period and the beginning of the one that forms your basis period for the current tax return. If this is the case, you'll also need to explain yourself in the additional information section (box **3.116**). And make it good.

If you've changed your accounting period since the last tax return, you need to tick box **3.12**. If this is the second time, or more, that you've changed the accounting date since 5 April 1994 (or since 5 April 1999 if the business commenced before 6 April 1994), then you also need to tick box **3.13**. Again, you'll have to provide an explanation in the additional information section at **3.116**.

Boxes 3.14 to 3.23 – Capital allowances – summary

Capital allowances are the taxman's equivalent of depreciation. Depreciation is the process by which the cost of an asset is spread over its useful life. So, if I buy a car for £10,000 and reckon it will last five years before conking out and being worth nothing, then I might charge £2,000 to my profit and loss account each year to account for it. Each time I do so, I'll reduce the 'carrying value' of the asset in my balance sheet by the £2,000. The result is that after five years, the entire cost of the car has gone through the profit and loss account and the value of it in the balance sheet is zero. Which is what we want.

You should depreciate all your assets (or at least the ones that wear out) and there are a variety of ways to do it, mostly more complicated than the preceding example. However you do it, though, you will almost certainly not use the way the Inland Revenue works it out. So when you tweak your accounts to produce the figures for the tax return, the first thing you need to do is to add back your depreciation charge and do it again the Inland Revenue's way. In other words you need to work out your 'capital allowances'.

Assuming that you're a small or medium-sized business (which you almost certainly are), then for most assets that you buy, you're allowed to charge 40 per cent of their cost in the first year, as a capital allowance. After that, the 'value' (that is, the original cost less the 40 per cent) gets transferred to your general pool of assets. You can charge 25 per cent of the total value of this pool against your profits each year as a capital allowance.

Capital allowances - summary

		Capital allowances		Balancing charges
● Cars (Separate calculations must be made for each car costing more than £12,000 and for cars used partly for private motoring.)		**3.14** £		**3.15** £
● Other business plant and machinery		**3.16** £		**3.17** £
● Agricultural or Industrial Buildings Allowance (A separate calculation must be made for each block of expenditure.)		**3.18** £		**3.19** £
● Other capital allowances claimed (Separate calculations must be made.)		**3.20** £		**3.21** £
		total of column above		total of column above
Total capital allowances/balancing charges		**3.22** £		**3.23** £

There are different rules, though, for some things, depending on what type of investment the government is trying to encourage you to make. So, at the moment, you can charge as a capital allowance the entire cost of any investment in 'information and communications technology' in the first year. Effectively, then, you treat these goods as business expenses rather than assets. This makes it relatively attractive to blow a few bob on some computers. In Northern Ireland, this 100 per cent first-year capital allowance is extended to most things, to encourage investment in the region.

Cars don't benefit from the 40 per cent rate in their first year. Instead, you just charge 25 per cent of their value each year. Cars that cost more than £12,000 get increasingly less favourable treatment as they get more expensive, since the capital allowance is limited to £3,000 per vehicle. Presumably the theory is that a Ferrari isn't necessary to ferry you from job to job and, to the extent that it costs more than £12,000, it's really a private luxury that has nothing to do with your business. Fair enough.

Assets that you expect to have a working life of more than 25 years are called 'long-life assets', and you're only allowed a capital allowance of 6 per cent of their cost each year. There are also special rules for the cost of constructing buildings in 'Enterprise Zones', which the Government is trying to beef up. For 'short-life assets' that you expect to last less than five years (or which you expect to sell within five years), you can elect to treat them separately from your main pool of assets.

The flip side to capital allowances are 'balancing charges'. These basically come into play when you've written down too much for an asset. Let's say that you pay £10,000 for a bit of plant and machinery, and accordingly set £4,000 of its cost against your profit in the first year. Then, in the second year, you sell the plant for £8,000. That's £2,000 more than the asset's written-down value, so you'd have to take a balancing charge (which increases your profit) of £2,000. Of course, if you'd sold the plant for only £4,000, then you'd have an extra £2,000 capital allowance to take.

With all this in mind, you should be able to work out your capital allowances and balancing charges for the year and put them into boxes **3.14** to **3.23**. As is (sort of) apparent from the form, you need to keep separate 'pools' for:

● each car bought for over £12,000
● each asset used partly for business use and partly for private use
● each short-life asset that you've elected to treat separately
● everything else, which can go together in one big pool.

Boxes 3.24 to 3.26 – Income and expenses – annual turnover below £15,000

If your business has an annual turnover of below £15,000, then you get the easy option of filling in boxes **3.24** to **3.26** instead of the more long-winded boxes **3.27** to **3.65**. It's up to you to make the figures accurate, and to do that you should keep proper accounts, or at least detailed records; but subject to that, you simply enter the relevant numbers and move forward to **3.74**.

Income and expenses - annual turnover below £15,000		
*If your annual turnover is £15,000 or more, **Ignore** boxes 3.24 to 3.26. Instead fill in Page SE2*		
*If your annual turnover is below £15,000, **fill in boxes 3.24 to 3.26 instead of Page SE2**. Read the Notes, page SEN2.*		
● Turnover, other business receipts and goods etc. taken for personal use (and balancing charges from box 3.23)	3.24	£
● Expenses allowable for tax (including capital allowances from box 3.22)	3.25	£
		box 3.24 *minus* box 3.25
Net profit (put figure in brackets if a loss)	3.26	£

Boxes 3.27 to 3.65 – Income and expenses – annual turnover above £15,000

Where your turnover is more than £15,000, you have to construct the dummy profit and loss account that is boxes **3.27** to **3.65**. To start with, you need to tell the taxman about your VAT position. If you're not registered for VAT, then you don't need to fill in either **3.27** or **3.28**. However, if you are VAT registered, you need to tick box **3.27** if your expense figures include VAT, or box **3.28** if they don't.

Income and expenses - annual turnover £15,000 or more

You must fill in this Page if your annual turnover is £15,000 or more - read the Notes, page SEN2

If you were registered for VAT, do the figures in boxes 3.29 to 3.64, include VAT? **3.27** ☐ or exclude VAT? **3.28** ☐

Sales/business income (turnover)
3.29 £

	Disallowable expenses included in boxes 3.46 to 3.63	Total expenses
● Cost of sales	**3.30** £	**3.46** £
● Construction industry subcontractor costs	**3.31** £	**3.47** £
● Other direct costs	**3.32** £	**3.48** £

box 3.29 *minus* (boxes 3.46 + 3.47 + 3.48)
Gross profit/(loss) **3.49** £

Other income/profits **3.50** £

● Employee costs	**3.33** £	**3.51** £
● Premises costs	**3.34** £	**3.52** £
● Repairs	**3.35** £	**3.53** £
● General administrative expenses	**3.36** £	**3.54** £
● Motor expenses	**3.37** £	**3.55** £
● Travel and subsistence	**3.38** £	**3.56** £
● Advertising, promotion and entertainment	**3.39** £	**3.57** £
● Legal and professional costs	**3.40** £	**3.58** £
● Bad debts	**3.41** £	**3.59** £
● Interest	**3.42** £	**3.60** £
● Other finance charges	**3.43** £	**3.61** £
● Depreciation and loss/(profit) on sale	**3.44** £	**3.62** £
● Other expenses	**3.45** £	**3.63** £

Put the total of boxes 3.30 to 3.45 in **box 3.66 below**

Total expenses total of boxes 3.51 to 3.63 **3.64** £

boxes 3.49 + 3.50 *minus* 3.64
Net profit/(loss) **3.65** £

You then put your total sales, or turnover, in box **3.29** and all your expenses in boxes **3.30** to **3.63**. The awkward thing here is working out which expenses are allowable for tax purposes (that is, can be deducted from the profit figure before reaching the profit upon which tax is calculated), and which aren't.

It all comes down to the different way that you and the taxman see the separation of your business and personal expenditure. You might charge a cross-Channel jolly with a couple of 'business contacts' (aka mates) to your business expenses, but the taxman will think, quite reasonably, that this is really a personal expense and should come out of your post-tax income. There's a list on page 7 of the *Notes on Self-Employment* that will help you decide what's allowable and what's not. Any additional information that relates to these expense figures should go in box **3.116**.

The total expenses (*before* deduction of the disallowables) goes in box **3.64**, and the net profit before tax goes in **3.65** (if you've made a loss, then you should put brackets around the figure).

Boxes 3.66 to 3.73 –
Tax adjustments to net profit or loss

Boxes **3.66** to **3.72** are for the various deductions and add-ons that enable you to reach the figure for your business's taxable profit for the year (though there's some more tinkering to do in the next section before we get to the actual figure that you'll pay tax on).

Tax adjustments to net profit or loss

		boxes 3.30 to 3.45	
● Disallowable expenses	**3.66** £		
● Adjustments (apart from disallowable expenses) that increase profits. Examples are goods taken for personal use and amounts brought forward from an earlier year because of a claim under ESC B11 about compulsory slaughter of farm animals	**3.67** £		
● Balancing charges (from box 3.23)	**3.68** £		
		boxes 3.66 + 3.67 + 3.68	
Total additions to net profit (deduct from net loss)		**3.69** £	
● Capital allowances (from box 3.22)	**3.70** £		
		boxes 3.70 + 3.71	
● Deductions from net profit (add to net loss)	**3.71** £	**3.72** £	
		boxes 3.65 + 3.69 *minus* **3.72**	
Net business profit for tax purposes (put figure in brackets if a loss)		**3.73** £	

In box **3.66**, you put the total of the disallowable expenses from boxes **3.30** to **3.45**. Box **3.67** is a catch-all for any goods that you took out of the business for personal use (less any money you paid to the business for the goods), or other adjustments that will mean that your real business profits were higher than actually stated. Box **3.68** is for balancing charges and should just be the figure that you arrived at in box **3.23**. These are all the additions to your net profit figure and they should be totalled up and entered in box **3.69**.

Boxes **3.70** and **3.71** are then for figures that you're allowed to take away from your taxable profits. Capital allowances, that is the figure from box **3.22**, should be entered in box **3.70**. Box **3.71** is the catch-all for any other deductions you're allowed to make. This would include any income to your business that isn't taxable. If, for instance, you paid too much to your business for goods you took out (though why you should do this I don't know), then you'd put this amount in box **3.71**.

Once you've done that, you just put the total of boxes **3.70** and **3.71** in box **3.72** and the sum of **3.65** plus **3.69**, minus **3.72**, in box **3.73**, which is your 'net business profit for tax purposes'.

Boxes 3.74 to 3.93 –
Adjustments to arrive at taxable profit or loss

These boxes deal with adjustments for timing issues and prior losses you've made in your business. Start by entering the dates of the beginning and end of your basis period in boxes **3.74** and **3.75**. Basis periods were explained in the section on accounting periods, but basically it's just the period that covers all the figures you've been filling in.

Now copy the profit figure that you entered in box **3.26** (if your turnover is less than £15,000) or box **3.73** (if your turnover is more than £15,000) into box **3.76** (a loss should be entered in brackets). If you ticked box **3.10**, then the figure in **3.76** should be zero. If your basis period is not the same as the period covered by your accounts, you need to calculate the profit for your basis period by apportioning the profit from your different accounting periods. For instance, if your basis period includes three months from one twelve-month accounting period and nine months from a second, then you need to take a quarter (that is three-twelfths) of the first accounting period and three-quarters (that is nine-twelfths) of the second accounting period, and add them together. The difference between this figure and the figure you entered in box **3.76** should go in box **3.77**. (If the

---

Adjustments to arrive at taxable profit or loss

Basis period begins **3.74** ☐ / / and ends **3.75** ☐ / /

Profit or loss of this account for tax purposes (box 3.26 or 3.73) **3.76** £ ☐

Adjustment to arrive at profit or loss for this basis period **3.77** £ ☐

● Overlap profit brought forward **3.78** £ ☐ ● Deduct overlap relief used this year **3.79** £ ☐

● Overlap profit carried forward **3.80** £ ☐

Averaging for farmers and creators of literary or artistic works *(see Notes, page SEN8, if you made a loss for 2001-02)* **3.81** £ ☐

Adjustment on change of basis **3.82** £ ☐

---

figure in **3.76** is higher than this new figure, then the difference will be negative and the figure in **3.77** should be in brackets.)

Boxes **3.78** to **3.80** take care of any overlap relief that you're due. As explained in the section on accounting periods on pages 34–6, you might be allowed to claim a deduction for the tax paid on an 'overlap period' if you closed down or sold your business during the tax year, or if you changed your accounting date and your basis period is more than 12 months (thereby shortening the overlap period). So, with this in mind, **3.78** is for the overlap profit brought forward from your last tax return, **3.79** is for any overlap profit that you're allowed to deduct in this tax return and box **3.80** is for the overlap profit that you carry forward to the next tax year (for instance, if you've changed your accounting date and your overlap period has merely been reduced).

Feast and famine is the name of the game for farmers and market gardeners, but it can give them a headache in terms of wildly fluctuating profits. To help with this, they can sometimes average their profits over two years and that's where box **3.81** comes in. The helpsheet *IR 224: Farmers and market gardeners* explains more about this and other reliefs. The same goes for writers and artists and they have their own helpsheet *IR234: Averaging for creators of literary or artistic works.*

For certain professions and vocations, you may have previously used a 'cash' or 'conventional' basis for calculating your profits. You're no longer

Net profit for 2001-02 (if you made a loss, enter '0')		**3.83** £
Allowable loss for 2001-02 (if you made a profit, enter '0')	**3.84** £	
● Loss offset against other income for 2001-02	**3.85** £	
● Loss to carry back	**3.86** £	
● Loss to carry forward (that is allowable loss not claimed in any other way)	**3.87** £	
● Losses brought forward from earlier years	**3.88** £	
● Losses brought forward from earlier years used this year		**3.89** £
Taxable profit after losses brought forward		box 3.83 *minus* box 3.89 **3.90** £
● Any other business income (for example, Business Start-up Allowance received in 2001-02)		**3.91** £
Total taxable profits from this business		box 3.90 + box 3.91 **3.92** £
● Tick box 3.93 if the figure in box 3.92 is provisional		**3.93**

allowed to do this and, in making the switch to the 'true and fair view' basis, there may be an adjustment to make. This is what goes in box **3.82** and, to help you work it all out, there's the magnificently-titled helpsheet *IR 233: The 'true and fair' view for professions and the 'adjustment' on withdrawal of cash basis.*

Now, assuming you didn't enter anything in boxes **3.81** or **3.82**, you need to take your figure from **3.76** and make the adjustments, if any, that you've entered in boxes **3.77** and **3.79**. If this adjusted figure comes to a profit then you need to enter it in box **3.83** (and put a zero in **3.84**). If it comes to a loss, then you need to enter the loss in box **3.84** and put a zero in **3.83**.

If you have entered something in boxes **3.81** or **3.82**, you need to make the adjustments from these boxes as well as **3.77** and **3.79**. If you end up with a profit, enter it in box **3.83** and put a zero in box **3.84**. If you end up with a loss, put the loss in **3.84**, but put the total of your adjustments from boxes **3.81** and **3.82** in box **3.83**.

Just like it allows you deductions for business expenses, the Inland Revenue only aims to tax the overall profits you make, after taking away any losses. So, if your business makes a loss, you get to take it away from the business profits or other income or capital gains that you pay tax on. In fact, you can also take it away from business profits, other income or capital gains that you've made in earlier years and already paid tax on (thus reducing the tax you'd have to pay this year). If there are any losses left over after all of this, you can carry them forward and use them against profits, income or capital gains you make in the future. Fair enough! It can get very complicated, though. If you have significant losses from your business, and are unsure how to make use of them, then it will probably be worth talking to a tax adviser. Having said that, the various boxes stack up like this.

You should already have entered any allowable loss incurred for this tax year in box **3.84**. In **3.85** goes any of this loss that you want to set against other income and capital gains elsewhere in this tax return (you can't claim more losses, though, than you have profits, income or capital gains). If you want to use your loss from this tax return to offset profits, income or capital gains from earlier years, then this is called 'carry back' of losses, and the figure should go in box **3.86** (again, you can't claim to offset more losses than there are profits, income or capital gains). Any of the loss from **3.84** that doesn't get used up in boxes **3.85** and **3.86** should go in box **3.87** so you can 'carry it forward' to profits, income and capital gains you make in future years.

Box **3.88** is the figure for losses that you've 'brought forward' from previous years and then **3.89** is for the amount you're able to use this year. That'll be all of it if you've got enough profits, income and capital gains to use it up. If not, it will have to be carried forward to future years.

Box **3.90** is for your taxable profits after deducting the losses brought forward (in other words, box **3.83** minus box **3.89**). You then put other business income (for example, government incentives such as Enterprise Allowances or New Deal Payments) for the 2001/2 year into box **3.91**. Add **3.91** to **3.90** and you have your total taxable business profits for the 2001/2 year. This goes in box **3.92**. If it has been impossible to prepare exact figures for your business income and expenses before the latest date for sending in your tax return and you have used estimates instead, then the figure in **3.92** will be a provisional figure and you should tick box **3.93**.

National Insurance contributions

National Insurance contributions get split into different 'classes', and self-employed people have to make Class 2 contributions and, generally speaking, Class 4. You have to register your self-employment with the Inland Revenue (call the Self-Employment Services helpline on 0845 9154515), and can be fined if you don't. They should tell you all about it but, handy as ever, there is also an

Class 4 National Insurance contributions		
• Tick box 3.94 if exception or deferment applies	**3.94**	
• Adjustments to profit chargeable to Class 4 National Insurance contributions	**3.95**	£
Class 4 National Insurance contributions due	**3.96**	£

Inland Revenue leaflet on the subject: *National Insurance contributions for self-employed people: Class 2 and Class 4*. If you were a man aged over 65, or a woman aged over 60, or you were aged under 16 at the beginning of the tax year, then you're off the hook for both Class 2 and Class 4 National Insurance contributions. Otherwise…

Class 2 contributions are payable to the Inland Revenue National Insurance Contributions Office at a flat weekly rate for each week that you're self-employed (including holidays, but excepting complete weeks where you're off sick and/or receiving benefits). For the 2001/2 tax year, the rate is £2 per week for most types of business and it's generally paid by direct debit. The contributions count towards various social security benefits, like Incapacity Benefit, the Maternity Allowance and the State Retirement Pension. If your self-employed earnings are below a certain level (£3,995 for 2001/2), then you don't have to pay the Class 2 contributions. However, you can still elect to do so voluntarily, to keep building your social security entitlements.

Class 4 National Insurance contributions are payable as a percentage (7 per cent for 2001/2) of your business profits between the 'lower profits limit' (£4,535 for 2001/2) and the 'upper profits limit' (£29,900 for 2001/2). However, you have to make some adjustments to your business profits to reach the profit figure for National Insurance purposes. The good news is that if you're not calculating your own tax (see the comments about this on page 12), then you can leave box **3.95** blank and the Inland Revenue will work it out for you. If you do want to work out your tax, then there's a working sheet for the Class 4 National Insurance part of this in the Inland Revenue's *Notes on Self-Employment*.

If you've also been making Class 1 contributions, then you may be entitled to defer your Class 4 (and Class 2) National Insurance contributions. Apparently you can get out of paying them all together if you're a diver or diving supervisor 'working in connection with exploration or exploration activities on the UK continental shelf or in UK territorial waters', though we have absolutely no idea why this might be. Anyway, if you're out there, day in, day out, in the cold North Atlantic, or if you think for any other reason that you shouldn't be paying Class 4

National Insurance, then tick box **3.94**, leave box **3.95** empty and explain yourself in the additional information section (box **3.116**).

Subcontractors in the construction industry

Building subcontractors may receive some payments under the Construction Industry Scheme and these may already have had tax deducted from them. The deductions should be shown on the CIS25 vouchers that you get from your contractors. You should enter the amount of any deductions in box **3.97** and send your CIS25 vouchers in with your tax return.

Subcontractors in the construction industry		
● Deductions made by contractors on account of tax (you must send your CIS25s to us)	**3.97** £	
Tax deducted from trading income		
● Any tax deducted (excluding deductions made by contractors on account of tax) from trading income	**3.98** £	

Tax deducted from trading income

Enter in box **3.98** any tax that's already been deducted from your trading income. This might apply to certain non-resident entertainers and sports persons that carry out work in the UK and have tax deducted when they earn it.

Summary of balance sheet

If you don't have a balance sheet, or if your turnover was less than £15,000, then you don't have to fill in this section. Otherwise, you need to transfer the figures from your balance sheet into boxes **3.99** to **3.115**. The boxes may not exactly match the entries in your balance sheet, but it's a question of doing your best to squeeze it all into the most appropriate boxes. Remember that it's a balance sheet, so boxes **3.110** and **3.115** should be the same!

Additional information

This is for entering anything else you think the Inland Revenue might need. For the most part, we've already mentioned what sort of information should go in here. But if you think there's anything else the taxman needs to know, then stick it in! It's best to keep things brief though, otherwise you risk confusing matters.

Summary of balance sheet

Leave these boxes blank if you do not have a balance sheet

Assets

- Plant, machinery and motor vehicles — **3.99** £
- Other fixed assets (premises, goodwill, investments etc.) — **3.100** £
- Stock and work-in-progress — **3.101** £
- Debtors/prepayments/other current assets — **3.102** £
- Bank/building society balances — **3.103** £
- Cash in hand — **3.104** £

total of boxes 3.99 to 3.104
3.105 £

Liabilities

- Trade creditors/accruals — **3.106** £
- Loans and overdrawn bank accounts — **3.107** £
- Other liabilities — **3.108** £

total of boxes 3.106 to 3.108
3.109 £

Net business assets (put the figure in brackets if you had net business liabilities)

box 3.105 minus 3.109
3.110 £

Represented by

Capital Account

- Balance at start of period* — **3.111** £
- Net profit/(loss)* — **3.112** £
- Capital introduced — **3.113** £
- Drawings — **3.114** £

- Balance at end of period*

total of boxes 3.111 to 3.113 minus box 3.114
3.115 £

*If the Capital Account is overdrawn, or the business made a net loss, enter the figure in brackets.

Partnership

The Partnership supplementary pages are for those who… operate in partnership with others. But you knew that. Just like self-employment, though, it's not entirely straightforward to say who is, and who is not, in a partnership. The law says that a partnership is the relationship that exists between 'persons carrying on a business in common with a view to profit'. That really takes us back to the discussion at the beginning of the last chapter, on what constitutes self-employment. Similar factors will determine whether you're in a business or working for a company; the difference with a partnership is just that you're doing it with others, with a view to profit. Because you're all mutually doing it 'for profit', you all need to be taking on business risks instead of working for a salary.

Not surprisingly, then, the Partnership pages have a lot in common with the Self-Employment pages. Many of the issues, like accounting periods, overlap relief, expenses, losses, are basically the same, so, before reading this chapter, it would probably make sense to go back and read Chapter 3, Self-Employment.

What you'll need

In addition to the partners filling in their Partnership pages, every partnership has to complete its own Partnership tax return. This tax return will contain a 'Partnership Statement', which will have the information you need to fill in your Partnership pages. Needless to say, then, the first thing you'll need is your Partnership Statement. These come in two flavours: a 'full version' or a 'short version'.

You can use the short version of the Partnership Statement if your partnership's income is limited to trading income and interest on cash deposits (with tax already deducted). If you have other sources of partnership income for example, then you'll need to fill out the full Partnership Statement. Which Partnership Statement your firm uses will determine which set of Partnership supplementary pages you need, because there's a short and full version of these too. Whichever Partnership pages you get, you'll find it helpful to get hold of the Inland Revenue's guidance notes for that particular version. As ever, these are available from the orderline, on 0845 9000 404, or the Internet at **www.inlandrevenue.gov.uk/sa**.

The short Partnership pages

The short form pages begin with some basic details about your partnership, which you put in boxes **4.1** to **4.4**. Boxes **4.5** and **4.6** are then for the dates of your basis period (see Chapter 3, page 34). The remainder of that section, up to box **4.22**, refers to your partnership's trading or professional income and

---

Partnership details

Partnership reference number

4.1

Description of partnership trade or profession

4.2

- Date you started being a partner (if during 2001-02) **4.3** / /

- Date you stopped being a partner (if during 2001-02) **4.4** / /

Your share of the partnership's trading or professional income

Basis period begins **4.5** / / and ends **4.6** / /

- Your share of the profit or loss of this year's account for tax purposes (enter a loss in brackets) **4.7** £

- Adjustment to arrive at profit or loss for this basis period **4.8** £

- Overlap profit brought forward **4.9** £   Deduct overlap relief used this year **4.10** £

- Overlap profit carried forward **4.11** £

- Averaging for farmers and creators of literary or artistic works (see Notes, page PN3 if the partnership made a loss in 2001-02) or foreign tax deducted, if tax credit relief not claimed **4.12** £

- Adjustment on change of basis **4.12A** £

Net profit for 2001-02 (if loss, enter '0' in box 4.13 and enter the loss in box 4.14) **4.13** £

Allowable loss for 2001-02 **4.14** £

- Loss offset against other income for 2001-02 **4.15** £

- Loss to carry back **4.16** £

- Loss to carry forward
(that is, allowable loss not claimed in any other way) **4.17** £

- Losses brought forward from last year **4.18** £

- Losses brought forward from last year used this year **4.19** £

Taxable profit after losses brought forward
box 4.13 *minus* box 4.19
4.20 £

- Add amounts **not** included in the partnership accounts that are needed to calculate your
taxable profit (for example, Enterprise Allowance (Business Start-up Allowance) received in 2001-02) **4.21** £

Total taxable profits from this business
box 4.20 + box 4.21
4.22 £

Your share of the partnership taxed income

- Share of taxed income (liable at 20%) **4.70** £

Your share of the partnership trading and professional profits

from box 4.22

- Share of partnership profits (other than that liable at 20%) **4.73** £

Your share of the partnership tax paid

- Share of Income Tax deducted from partnership income **4.74** £

- Share of CIS25 deductions **4.75** £

- Share of tax deducted from trading income (not CIS25 deductions) **4.75A** £

boxes 4.74 + 4.75 + 4.75A
4.77 £

comes from your Partnership Statement. For the section on National Insurance contributions, you'll need to refer to what was said in Chapter 3, Self-Employment. The remaining boxes, which are confusingly numbered **4.70** to **4.77** (to try to match up with the full partnership pages) refer to the partnership's taxed income (from bank interest) and should be filled with figures from the Partnership Statement. The CIS25s referred to in box **4.75** are only relevant to subcontractors in the construction industry and are discussed in Chapter 3 (page 49).

The full Partnership pages

The full Partnership pages are essentially the same as the short form for the boxes up to **4.25** and after **4.70**, which cover partnership details, trading or professional income, National Insurance and taxed income (from bank interest). The difference is that there is a large section from box **4.26** to **4.69** asking about your share of other sources of untaxed income (and it's because you have these that you've had to go for the full version). With your full Partnership Statement in one hand and the Inland Revenue's *Notes on Partnership (Full)* in the other, it shouldn't be too much trouble to complete the puzzle. If you're in doubt about anything, try the Revenue's general advice line on 0845 9000 444.

Your share of the partnership's untaxed income		

Income Tax basis period begins **4.26** / / and ends **4.27** / /

■ *Income from UK savings*

- Allocated share of income **4.28** £
- Adjustment to income **4.29** £
- Adjusted income for basis period **4.30** £

■ *Income from foreign savings*

- Allocated share of income **4.31** £
- Adjustment to income **4.32** £
- Total foreign tax deducted, if tax credit relief not claimed **4.33** £
- Adjusted income for basis period **4.34** £

Untaxed income liable at 20%   box 4.30 + box 4.34 **4.35** £

■ *Other untaxed UK income*

- Allocated share of loss for 2001-02 **4.36** £
- Allocated share of income **4.37** £
- Adjustment to loss for basis period **4.38** £
- Adjustment to income **4.39** £
- Loss brought forward **4.40** £
- Loss carried forward **4.41** £

Taxable profit after adjustment and losses. Enter '0' if a loss **4.42** £

■ *Other untaxed foreign income*

- Allocated share of loss for 2001-02 **4.43** £
- Allocated share of income **4.44** £
- Adjustment to loss for basis period **4.45** £
- Adjustment to income **4.46** £
- Loss brought forward **4.47** £
- Total foreign tax deducted if tax credit relief not claimed **4.48** £

- Loss carried forward **4.49** £

Taxable profit after adjustment and losses. Enter '0' if a loss | **4.50** £

■ *Income from offshore funds*

- Allocated share of income **4.51** £

- Adjustment to income **4.52** £

- Total foreign tax deducted if tax credit relief not claimed **4.53** £

Taxable income after adjustment | **4.54** £

Your share of the partnership's untaxed income - continued

■ *Income from UK land and property*

- Allocated share of profit or loss for 2001-02 **4.55** £

- Adjustment to profit or loss for basis period **4.56** £

- Loss brought forward **4.57A** £

- Loss offset against total income (read the note on page PN6) **4.57B** £

- Loss carried forward **4.58** £

Taxable profit after losses. Enter '0' if a loss | **4.59** £

■ *Allowable loss on furnished holiday lettings*

- Allowable loss on furnished holiday lettings **4.60** £

- 2001-02 loss to set off against other income **4.61** £

- 2001-02 loss to carry back **4.62** £

- Loss to set against other property income (up to amount in box 4.59) **4.63** £

■ *Overlap relief - untaxed investment income*

- Overlap profit brought forward **4.64** £   Deduct overlap relief used this year **4.65** £

- Overlap profit carried forward **4.66** £

boxes 4.42 + 4.50 + 4.54 + 4.59 minus boxes 4.63 and 4.65

Untaxed income from this business (other than that liable at 20%) | **4.67** £

Your share of the partnership's taxed income

- Share of taxed income (income liable at 10%) **4.68A** £

- *Minus* foreign tax deducted on income within box 4.68A, if tax credit relief **not** claimed **4.69A** £

box 4.68A minus box 4.69A

Taxed income liable at 10% | **4.70A** £

- Share of taxed income (income liable at 20%) **4.68** £

- *Minus* foreign tax deducted on income within box 4.68, if tax credit relief **not** claimed **4.69** £

Land & Property

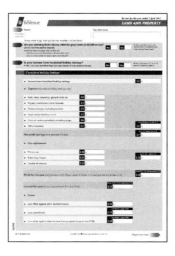

Broadly speaking, you get taxed on your income from property as though it's a business that you're running as a self-employed person. You take your income and deduct the allowable expenses to reach a figure for your profit. Of course the Inland Revenue throws in a few little wrangles to keep you on your toes, but the Land & Property supplementary pages really aren't too bad.

In fact, income that you might think comes from land may actually come from a pure business, making the Self-Employment pages more appropriate anyway. This might be the case if you contribute enough time and energy to your land to make it a 'trade', rather than simply organizing to rent out a room. Cleaning or cooking duties might, for instance, tip the balance, and something like a guest house would almost certainly be classed as a self-employed business rather than a simple property letting. There is more information on this in the Inland Revenue's helpsheet *IR223: Rent a Room for traders*.

One respect in which the letting of property differs from running a business as a trader is that you can only set any losses against your income from property – not against your other income, as you could do with business losses. Presumably it would be too easy to fudge this sort of thing, and claim that the costs of doing up the new extension to your house should really be tax-deductible because you failed to let it to anyone while the work was being done. This sort of argument doesn't wash with the taxman. He'll just turn around and say, if you let it in the future, you can set these expenses against the income. But otherwise, no!

The problem is in spotting whether something is being done for profit or for personal consumption. If you make a loss, which will be because the property is not let, the Inland Revenue will quite reasonably start with the view that the property is really there for personal consumption.

'Furnished holiday lettings' are one special instance where the taxman decides that your property letting is being done for profit and that you can, after all, set any losses against your other income for the year. Generally speaking, a furnished holiday letting is a UK property that is:

- furnished
- available for holiday letting to the public on a commercial basis for 140 days or more during the year
- actually let as holiday accommodation for 70 days or more during the year
- not normally occupied continuously for more than 31 days by the same person for at least seven months of the year.

One final special case is where you let furnished accommodation in your own home, but not to the extent that it becomes a self-employed business in its own right as described above. Where your total income from doing this doesn't exceed £4,250 in the tax year, you'll be exempt from paying tax under the 'Rent a Room' scheme. So, if you own your flat, but rent a room out to Bob your mate from University, then you won't have to pay tax on it, so long as the rent works out as less than... hold on a second, tap, tap, tap... £81.73 per week.

If you make more than £4,250 in the year from a 'Rent a Room' type letting, you have a choice. Either you can knock off the £4,250 from your gross rental income and pay tax on the rest, or you can just ignore the whole 'Rent a Room' thing and calculate the tax normally. The difference is that with 'Rent a Room', you don't get to deduct any expenses from your gross rental income, whereas you would if you did it normally. Which is better, then, depends on whether the expenses that you can deduct exceed the £4,250 that you'd be allowed to knock off under the 'Rent a Room' scheme.

If two people derive income from letting furnished accommodation in the same property then, assuming that it qualifies for 'Rent a Room' relief, they'll each be able to claim half the exemption – that is, £2,125.

What you'll need

As ever, you'll need the pages themselves and the Inland Revenue's *Notes on Land & Property*. There are also various helpsheets (we'll come to the more important ones as we go through, but you probably won't need them), which are listed at the start of the *Notes*. The other thing you'll need, of course, is a full record of the income you've received from your property over the tax year, and the expenses you've incurred in order to get that income.

A major difference between the Land & Property and Self-Employment pages is that you don't get to choose your 'basis period'. You have to use 6 April to 5 April and, if you actually produce accounts for another period, you'll need to apportion them to the right period. So, if you use 1 January to 31 December as your period, you'd have to take 270/365 of all the figures for one year and then 95/365 of all the figures for the next and add them together (the 95 is the number of days up to April 5). It's quite a faff, so you're probably better off using 6 April to 5 April in the first place.

Are you claiming 'Rent a Room' relief for gross rents of £4,250 or less?

The first section of the Land & Property pages just involves saying whether you come fully within the 'Rent a Room' relief, as described above. If you tick 'yes', then you've finished the Property pages. I did say it wasn't too bad!

> **Are you claiming Rent a Room relief for gross rents of £4,250 or less?**
> (Or £2,125 if the claim is shared?)
> Read the Notes on page LN2 to find out
> - whether you can claim Rent a Room relief; and
> - how to claim relief for gross rents over £4,250
>
> No ☐ Yes ☐
>
> If 'Yes', and this is your only income from UK property, you have finished these Pages

Is your income from furnished holiday lettings?

Question number 2 is almost as simple, though it doesn't have such far-reaching consequences. If you have income from furnished holiday lettings, then you need to fill in the next section. Otherwise, you can skip it.

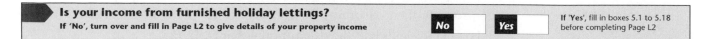

> **Is your income from furnished holiday lettings?**
> If 'No', turn over and fill in Page L2 to give details of your property income
>
> No ☐ Yes ☐
>
> If 'Yes', fill in boxes 5.1 to 5.18 before completing Page L2

Boxes 5.1 to 5.18 – Furnished holiday lettings

Boxes **5.1** to **5.9** just involve entering your various sources of income and expenses and should be pretty straightforward, assuming you've kept decent records. Where the property is owned jointly, you should only include your share of the income and your share of the expenses. For more details about the types of expenses that are allowable, have a look further down where we cover boxes **5.24** to **5.29**. Boxes **5.10** to **5.13** are for deductions for private use, capital allowances and balancing charges and, again, there's more further down (this time under boxes **5.32**, **5.33** and **5.36**).

Furnished holiday lettings

● **Income from furnished holiday lettings**   **5.1** £

■ *Expenses* (furnished holiday lettings only)

● Rent, rates, insurance, ground rents etc.   **5.2** £

● Repairs, maintenance and renewals   **5.3** £

● Finance charges, including interest   **5.4** £

● Legal and professional costs   **5.5** £

● Costs of services provided, including wages   **5.6** £

total of boxes 5.2 to 5.7

● Other expenses   **5.7** £   **5.8** £

box 5.1 minus box 5.8

Net profit (put figures in brackets if a loss)   **5.9** £

■ *Tax adjustments*

● Private use   **5.10** £

box 5.10 + box 5.11

● Balancing charges   **5.11** £   **5.12** £

● Capital allowances   **5.13** £

boxes 5.9 + 5.12 minus box 5.13

Profit for the year (copy to box 5.19). If loss, enter '0' in box 5.14 and put the loss in box 5.15   **5.14** £

boxes 5.9 + 5.12 minus box 5.13

Loss for the year (if you have entered '0' in box 5.14)   **5.15** £

■ *Losses*

● Loss offset against 2001-02 total income	**5.16** £	
● Loss carried back	**5.17** £	see Notes, page LN4
● Loss offset against other income from property (copy to box 5.38)	**5.18** £	see Notes, page LN4

Boxes **5.16** to **5.18** then deal with any allowable losses. Since losses from furnished holiday lettings can be offset against your other losses, the rules are the same as for the losses of self-employed traders and were covered in Chapter 3, on pages 44–7. You might also like to look at the Inland Revenue helpsheet *IR227: Losses*. When you've filled these in, move on to boxes **5.19** to **5.48** on the next page.

Boxes 5.19 to 5.48 – Other property income

The first few boxes in this section, **5.19** to **5.23**, are for entering your sources of property income. If the property is jointly owned, then you should only include your share of the income. The slightly tricky one here is box **5.22A**, though it's quite unusual and unlikely to apply. A reverse premium is where someone pays you money to encourage you to buy a property to rent to them (or, in fact, to someone else). If you received such a payment, then well done, but as far as the Inland Revenue is concerned it's effectively just part of the rent that you get, so it gets included in box **5.22A**.

Boxes **5.24** to **5.29** are for you to enter the expenses you incurred in letting out the property. If you own the property jointly, then you should only include your share of the expenses. If your total property income, before expenses, was

Other property income

■ *Income*

● Furnished holiday lettings profits	**5.19** £ copy from box 5.14	
● Rents and other income from land and property	**5.20** £	Tax deducted **5.21** £
● Chargeable premiums	**5.22** £	
● Reverse premiums	**5.22A** £	boxes 5.19 + 5.20 + 5.22 + 5.22A **5.23** £

less than £15,000 in the year then you can leave them blank and just enter your total expenses in box **5.29**, 'Other expenses', and transfer it over to box **5.30**.

On the whole, you can include any expenses incurred that relate to the sole purpose of earning your rental income. What you can't claim are expenses relating to your own personal use of the property, or capital costs, such as those incurred in buying the property you intend to let (or, indeed, any losses you make in selling it). If, for instance, you rented out the property for only part of the year and used it yourself for the rest, then you'd only be allowed to deduct expenses that related to the rental period. You can deal with this in one of two ways. Either enter only the rental portion of the year's expenses in boxes **5.24** to **5.29**, or enter the full amount in those boxes, but add back the expenses that related to your personal use in box **5.32**, which we'll come to in a moment.

Box **5.24** is for any rent you pay to others for the property you let out, as well as ground rents, water rates, community charge and insurance on the property or its contents. You can also deduct the cost of any insurance you pay against loss of rents, but if you make any claims, you'd have to include them as income in box **5.20**.

Box **5.25** is for repairs and maintenance. These are expenses that are required to keep your property in its current state. They might include minor building work or wear and tear on furnishings (unless you claimed the equivalent as a capital allowance in box **5.37**, see page 63). They might also include the cost of replacement furnishings, but you'd have to deduct any money you get from selling or scrapping the original item. If you do work on the property that amounts to improvements, additions or alterations, then it's treated as a capital cost, like the cost of buying the property in the first place, and is not allowable.

■ *Expenses* (do not include figures you have already put in boxes 5.2 to 5.7 on Page L1)

● Rent, rates, insurance, ground rents etc.	**5.24** £	
● Repairs, maintenance and renewals	**5.25** £	
● Finance charges, including interest	**5.26** £	
● Legal and professional costs	**5.27** £	
● Costs of services provided, including wages	**5.28** £	
● Other expenses	**5.29** £	total of boxes 5.24 to 5.29 **5.30** £
Net profit (put figures in brackets if a loss)		box 5.23 *minus* box 5.30 **5.31** £

Box **5.26** is for any interest charged on a mortgage or other loan that you used to buy the property. You can also deduct expenses you incurred in arranging the loan.

Legal and professional costs are included in box **5.27**. These involve fees paid to property agents for managing the property, collecting rents, producing inventories and such like. You can also include legal fees incurred in the ongoing management of the property, such as the renewal of a lease (so long as it's for less than 50 years) or the eviction of a bad tenant. What you can't deduct is the legal and professional fees associated with the original purchase of the property or for improvements, such as architect's fees on an extension.

If you provide services to your tenant, such as gardening, porterage or cleaning, then you can enter the cost of these in box **5.28**. Of course, to the extent that you make use of the same services, then you're not allowed a deduction. For instance, if you share a gardener equally with your tenant, then you could only claim for half of his wages as a letting expense. You can accommodate this either by including only half of the gardener's expense in box **5.28**, or by including the whole amount but adding back the extent of your personal use in box **5.32**.

Box **5.29** is for any other expenses. One example might be the cost of advertising for new tenants (unless this has been included already as a professional fee in box **5.27**).

Now, tot up all the expenses and put the total in box **5.30**, then take this away from the income in box **5.23** and place the resulting net profit figure in box **5.31**.

Boxes **5.32** to **5.39** are for various adjustments. They start with boxes **5.32** and **5.33**, which go to increase the amount of your rental profits. Box **5.32** is where you put the amount of expenses incurred for your own personal use, to the

• Private use	**5.32** £			
				box 5.32 + box 5.33
• Balancing charges	**5.33** £			**5.34** £
• Rent a Room exempt amount	**5.35** £			
• Capital allowances	**5.36** £			
• Tick box 5.36A if box 5.36 includes a claim for 100% capital allowances for flats over shops	**5.36A**			
• 10% wear and tear	**5.37** £			
				boxes 5.35 to box 5.38
• Furnished holiday lettings losses (from box 5.18)	**5.38** £			**5.39** £

extent that they were included in the figures in boxes **5.24** to **5.29**, as already discussed. Box **5.33** is for any balancing charges. These are the flip side of capital allowances and are covered when we look at those under box **5.36**. If you're renting out residential property, though, they won't apply. The total of boxes **5.32** and **5.33** goes in box **5.34**.

Boxes **5.35** to **5.38** are for adjustments that go to reduce your rental profits, starting with box **5.35**, which is for the 'Rent a Room' exemption we discussed at the beginning of this chapter.

Boxes **5.36** and **5.37** are for capital allowances and the '10 per cent wear and tear allowance'. Where you're renting out residential property, you're not allowed to make deductions for the depreciation of your property or its contents or for capital allowances (if you think you're not renting out residential property and might be entitled to capital allowances, you should start by talking to your local tax office, but you will probably also need a tax adviser). A clue to an exception to this is given by box **5.36A**, for '100% capital allowances for flats over shops'. In fact, the incentive is for the 'cost of the renovation or conversion of vacant or underused space above shops and other commercial premises to provide flats for rent.' Full details are in the Inland Revenue leaflet *IR250: Capital Allowances and Balancing Charges in a Rental Business*.

Generally though, with residential property you can either just deduct the cost of repair, maintenance and replacement as described for box **5.25** (but remember you can't deduct the cost of original purchases or improvements) or you can elect to make use of the '10 per cent wear and tear allowance'. In practice, it's almost always best to use the 10 per cent allowance.

With the 10 per cent wear and tear allowance, the Inland Revenue simply deems that an amount equal to 10 per cent of your rental income just about covers the cost of wear and tear. For these purposes, the rental income is the rent that you receive after deducting costs and charges that would normally be borne by the tenant, but are in fact borne by you. So, if you pay your tenant's council tax, then you must deduct this from your rental income to arrive at the figure from which you take 10 per cent to put in box **5.37**.

Box **5.38** is for any losses from furnished holiday lettings that you're electing to deduct from your other property income, and should just be lifted from box **5.18**. The figures in boxes **5.35** to **5.38** get added together and entered in box **5.39**. Box **5.40** is then for your adjusted profit and results from adding together boxes **5.31** and **5.34**, and then deducting box **5.39**. If you made a loss, put a zero in box **5.39** and enter the amount of your loss in box **5.41**.

		boxes 5.31 + 5.34 *minus* box 5.39
Adjusted profit (if loss enter '0' in box 5.40 and put the loss in box 5.41)		**5.40** £

	boxes 5.31 + 5.34 *minus* box 5.39	
Adjusted loss (if you have entered '0' in box 5.40)	**5.41** £	

• Loss brought forward from previous year	**5.42** £

	box 5.40 *minus* box 5.42
Profit for the year	**5.43** £

■ *Losses etc*

- Loss offset against total income (read the note on page LN8)   **5.44** £
- Loss to carry forward to following year   **5.45** £
- Tick box 5.46 if these Pages include details of property let jointly   **5.46**
- Tick box 5.47 if **all** property income ceased in the year to 5 April 2002 **and** you don't expect to receive such income again, in the year to 5 April 2003   **5.47**

In box **5.42**, you should enter the amount of any loss brought forward from the 2000/1 tax year. This will be the figure in box **5.45** of the Land and Property pages of your 2000/1 tax return (but excluding any figure in box **5.46** of those pages). This can then be deducted from the figure in **5.41** to give you your total taxable property profits for the 2001/2 tax year, which should go in box **5.43**. If you end up with a loss, then you need to put a zero in box **5.43** and put the amount of the net loss in box **5.45** to carry forward to next year.

Box **5.44** relates to losses that can be set against your total income for the year. This might be the case where you've made a loss on furnished holiday lettings or agricultural land or where the loss arises as a result of certain claims to capital allowances. If you think this might be relevant to you, start by looking at page 8 of the Inland Revenue's *Notes on Land & Property*. However, it doesn't make a lot of sense and the chances are you'll need to see a tax adviser.

Finally, tick box **5.46** if you've included, in boxes **5.1** or **5.20**, any income from property that is jointly owned; and tick box **5.47** if you stopped getting property income in the tax year and you don't expect it to start again in the next tax year.

Foreign

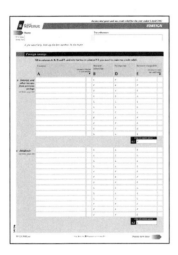

You only need to worry about the Foreign supplementary pages if you have income or gains overseas. For most people who fill in UK tax returns, this isn't likely to be very much, if any. That's just as well, because things can get very messy. We've all heard of people with offshore this and tax haven that, but for most of us it's like the Ferraris that tend to go with this sort of thing: exciting, alluring but very unlikely to have much to do with our lives. The truth is that overseas taxation is pretty mundane and murky, and you're more likely to be caught up in it on account of a two-year placement in Germany.

The problem introduced by having overseas income and gains is best explained by an example. Millicent lives and works in the UK, teaching at a school in Eastbourne as it happens, but has inherited a property on the Costa del Sol that she rents out to holidaymakers. She produces a tax return and the Inland Revenue, given half a chance, would like to get their hands on tax relating to all her income, here *and overseas*. The thing is, though, that the Spanish tax office also, quite reasonably, thinks it should get some tax on the income that Millicent makes from the property, since it is, after all, in their country.

So, it looks as though Millicent stands to get taxed twice on her rental income, and that's not really very fair. The good news is that something has been done about this. Since the UK and Spain are on friendly terms, and have tax systems of which the other broadly approves, they've entered into a 'double taxation treaty'. By the terms of this treaty, they decide how to divide up the tax that Millicent has to pay, the theory being that for every Millicent, there's probably a Madelena with a property in Brighton, so it all evens out.

With your typical tax haven, the UK isn't going to be so approving of its tax system, largely because they don't charge much. So there won't be a double taxation treaty, and if you're UK resident, you'll have to pay UK tax on your tax haven income as well as the teeny bit of tax to your tax haven. Now we're back on to tax havens again, which I was hoping to avoid, but hopefully it's becoming clear that exactly how you get taxed on overseas income and gains depends mainly on your residence status, whether there's a tax treaty between the UK and that country, and what, exactly, it says.

What the UK taxes and when

Broadly speaking and subject to those double tax treaties, the UK Inland Revenue likes to take its slice of the following:

- Any income arising in the UK, whether or not it belongs to a UK *resident*
- Any income arising outside the UK that belongs to someone *resident* in the UK
- Any capital gains arising anywhere in the world that belong to individuals *resident* or *'ordinarily resident'* in the UK.

As well as the concepts of *residence* and *ordinary residence*, which determine what gets taxed, there's something called *domicile*, which can have an effect on when you get taxed on overseas income and capital gains (we'll come to the definitions of these things in a little while). Basically (who am I trying to kid?), if you're not *domiciled* in the UK or if you're a citizen of the Commonwealth or the Republic of Ireland, then you pay any UK tax on your non-UK income or gains only when you actually bring the money into this country. This is called the 'remittance basis'. Otherwise, you pay tax on the income or gains as and when they arise, which is called the 'arising basis'.

So, in the absence of a double taxation treaty, you pay UK tax on overseas income, but after you've deducted any foreign tax paid on it. In most cases, where there *is* a tax treaty, you pay UK tax on your foreign earnings, but then you get to deduct any overseas tax that you've paid from your UK tax bill, by claiming 'tax credit relief'. This will normally result in paying less tax.

Who needs to complete the Foreign pages?

The Foreign supplementary pages, which are the main focus of this chapter, are for people resident in the UK who have overseas income, or who are resident or ordinarily resident in the UK and have overseas capital gains.

If, however, you think you're like Madelena and not UK resident, but still need to fill in a UK tax return on account of income from your property in Brighton, then you need to fill out the relevant pages of the tax return for that income (for example the Land & Property supplementary pages) and then complete the Non-Residence supplementary pages, which we'll get to in Chapter 9.

Chapter 9 is also the place where we'll look more closely at the meanings of *residency* and *ordinary residency* (and, for that matter, *domicile*). So, if you're not sure where you stand with regard to these things, then you'd better start there.

What you'll need

It's hard to say what exactly you'll need for the Foreign pages, since the documents you get will vary from country to country. What it comes down to, though, is having details of the income and gains that you've made overseas and the documents showing any tax that you've paid there. We'd also strongly advise that you get hold of the Inland Revenue's *Notes on the Foreign Pages*.

Filling in the Foreign pages

Once you've worked out your residency and domicile (see Chapter 9 if necessary) and established, for instance, whether your foreign income will be taxed on the arising or the remittance basis (look at the section 'What the UK taxes and when' earlier in this chapter), then you're 90 per cent of the way to filling in the Foreign supplementary pages. So much so that I'm not going to go through it box by box. Apart from anything else, there are too many possibilities and we'd be here forever. But if you have your status sorted out, and you have the details of your overseas income or gains to hand, then things shouldn't be too bad.

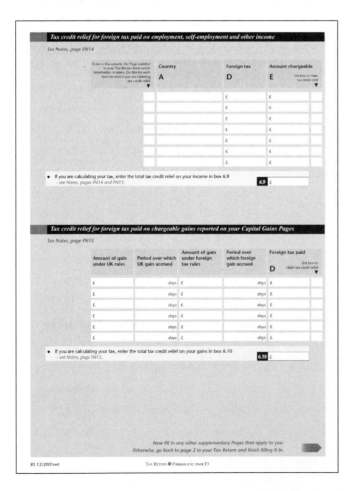

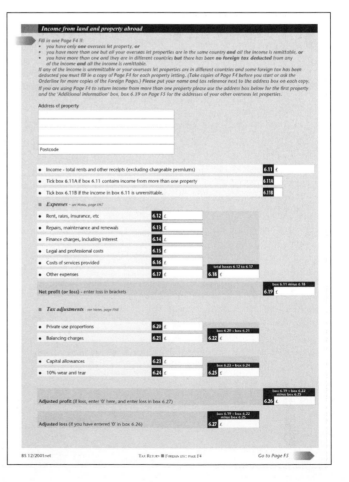

The pages are split into four sections:

- Income from foreign savings
- Foreign savings income taxed on the remittance basis and foreign income from overseas pensions or social security benefits, from land or property abroad, chargeable premiums or income/benefits received from overseas trusts, companies and other entities (a bit of a mouthful that)
- Tax credit relief for foreign tax paid on employment, self-employment and other income
- Tax credit relief for foreign tax paid on chargeable gains reported in your Capital Gains pages.

There is an additional section at the back to give more information about any property you have abroad.

Notice that there isn't a section for earnings from employment, self-employment and partnerships overseas. Instead, if any of these apply to you, you need to fill in the Employment, Self-Employment or Partnership supplementary pages as appropriate. You then need to fill out the bit on page three of the Foreign pages to get the 'tax credit relief' on those earnings. Similarly, capital gains from overseas transactions should be entered in the Capital Gains Tax pages and the tax credit relief claimed in the Foreign pages.

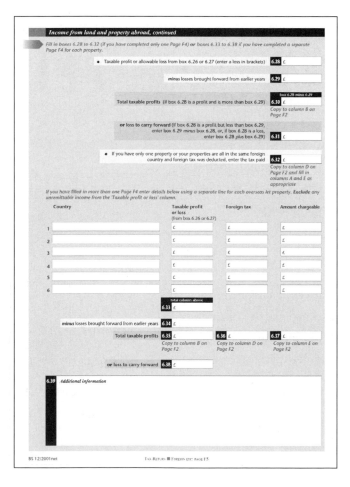

For other types of foreign income, such as interest on foreign savings, dividends, rents and pension income, it's a question of entering it in the relevant bit of the Foreign pages. The guidance *Notes* do a pretty good job of explaining what to put in the various boxes, so it probably doesn't help much for me to repeat it here. Of course, if you have any queries that the *Notes* don't answer, the Inland Revenue's general advice helpline might be able to point you in the right direction even if they can't answer the question.

Trusts etc

The word 'Trusts' is scary enough for most people, but add the word 'etc' to it and it suggests a whole new underworld of legalese and arcane nonsense. Sure enough, if you look too far below the surface here, things can get very nasty. There are some definite positives, though. First of all, the Trust pages are really just a page (though there's a whole page given to you for additional information, whatever that might be). So if it's a bit scary, at least it's not going to be scary for box after box and page after page. Another nice thing about trusts is that they have trustees and personal representatives. They'll quite often be solicitors or accountants, so there should be someone to answer questions or even tell you what to do. Perhaps the best thing, though, is that anything you need to enter in this section should be very repetitive (except, we hope, the bit about deceased persons), so that once you've done it for one year, you can just keep filling in the same boxes year after year (or until the Chancellor decides to change things again anyway).

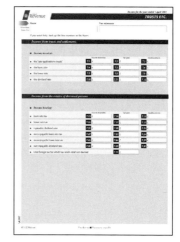

What you'll need

To fill in these pages, you'll need the Trust pages themselves, as well as the Inland Revenue's *Notes on the Trusts* pages (though these are pretty hard to follow). You should also have the vouchers, and any other documents, that detail the money you've received from the trust or estate (an R185 in the case of a 'discretionary trust'). Most importantly, you'll probably need a phone and the phone number of trustees or personal representatives, so you can ask them what's going on. If you put all the relevant information in last year's tax return and nothing much has changed, then you'll also find it very useful indeed to have a copy of last year's return to use for reference.

Boxes 7.1 to 7.12 –
Income from trusts and settlements

A trust (which, for present purposes, is near enough the same as a settlement) is a mechanism whereby certain people, called trustees, hold assets on behalf of other people, called the beneficiaries. The extent of each beneficiary's interest in the trust will depend on the exact terms of the trust, and this is what will make the biggest difference to how trust income is taxed.

What's known as a 'bare trust', where the beneficiary is absolutely entitled to the contents of the trust to the extent that he could make the trustees hand them over, is ignored for tax purposes; the income and gains are treated as the normal income and gains of the beneficiary. So, if what you've got is a bare trust, then you don't need to worry about the Trust supplementary pages. Instead, fill in the pages that are relevant for that type of income or gain, as though the trust wasn't there.

Other trusts are constructed so that people have differing rights over the income or gains. Perhaps the trust is for someone's grandchildren and we don't yet know how many there are going to end up being; or maybe the trustees have discretion as to who to pay money to within a certain class of possible beneficiaries. One way or another, we can't say for sure who it all belongs to and this is where the Trusts supplementary pages come in.

The first example in the previous paragraph would be a case where you're absolutely entitled to *income* (because it gets split between the existing grand-children), but you're not absolutely entitled to *capital* (because you don't yet know how many ways to split it). In this, or any other case where you have an absolute right to the income, but not the capital:

● *Don't* enter any 'scrip dividends' in the Trust pages. These should go in boxes **10.21** to **10.23** of the main bit of the tax return (see page 112, in Chapter 10 for more about this).

● *Don't* enter any foreign income in the Trust pages. This should go in the Foreign supplementary pages. See Chapter 6.

● *Don't* enter any trust income that you received gross (i.e. before tax) in the Trust pages. This should go in the bit of your tax return that's relevant to the particular type of income.

● *Do* enter any income that you received from the trust after some tax had been deducted. This will be at different rates, depending on the nature of the income, and you need to fill in a different line depending on what rate of tax

Income from trusts and settlements

■ *Income taxed at:*

	Income receivable	Tax paid	Taxable amount
● the 'rate applicable to trusts'	7.1 £	7.2 £	7.3 £
● the basic rate	7.4 £	7.5 £	7.6 £
● the lower rate	7.7 £	7.8 £	7.9 £
● the dividend rate	7.10 £	7.11 £	7.12 £

has been deducted. Your trustees should be able to tell you what has happened. In fact, they should provide you with a little voucher giving the exact amounts.

Where you don't have an absolute right to the income or gains from a trust, perhaps because the terms of the trust give the trustees discretion over who to give it to, then it depends if the trustees are resident in the UK or not. Residence is explained in Chapter 9. If your trustees are UK resident, then they should pay the income after deducting tax at the 'rate applicable to trusts', so you'll need to fill in boxes **7.1** to **7.3**. You should get a voucher from the trustees giving you the relevant numbers. If your trustees are not resident in the UK, then the money is considered to be foreign rather than trust income. You therefore need to fill in the Foreign pages, rather than the Trusts pages.

In certain cases, for instance where someone has put money into a trust (or settlement), but they themselves (or their spouse or child under 16) still stand to gain from it, the Inland Revenue may ignore the trust and treat the income and gains as still belonging to the person who set it up. If you've set up a trust or settlement, then the chances are that you took advice at the time about how the Inland Revenue would view it, but if you're in any doubts, you should get hold of helpsheet *IR270: Trusts and settlements – income still treated as the settlor's.*

Boxes 7.13 to 7.31 – Income from the estates of deceased persons

If you've received income from a deceased person's estate during the tax year, as opposed to distributions of the estate's capital, then some part of what you've received may need to be entered in these boxes. This area can get very complicated but, on the whole, the personal representatives of the estate (in most cases, the 'executors') should be able to tell you what to do. In fact, they should give you a voucher detailing the figures that need to go in the various boxes. If you have further doubts about it, try looking at the Inland Revenue's *Notes to the Trusts* pages. Assuming that this doesn't make things clearer, then you, or the personal representatives, will probably need to take some advice to find out what's going on.

Income from the estates of deceased persons

■ *Income bearing:*

	Income receivable	Tax paid	Taxable amount
● basic rate tax	7.13 £	7.14 £	7.15 £
● lower rate tax	7.16 £	7.17 £	7.18 £
● repayable dividend rate	7.19 £	7.20 £	7.21 £
● non-repayable basic rate tax	7.22 £	7.23 £	7.24 £
● non-repayable lower rate tax	7.25 £	7.26 £	7.27 £
● non-repayable dividend rate	7.28 £	7.29 £	7.30 £
● total foreign tax for which tax credit relief not claimed	7.31 £		

Capital Gains

At its simplest, capital gains tax, or CGT, is a tax you pay if you make a gain from selling something you own. If we didn't get taxed on this, you see, we'd all just cook up schemes for turning our income into capital gains. That would mean we'd just kept reinvesting our profits instead of taking them out and spending them and, apart from reducing the amount of tax the government gets, that might destabilize the economy. So the original idea behind CGT was to make it all the same to you and me whether we take our investment returns in the form of income or as capital gains. This would be a relatively simple thing to achieve, but successive governments have decided, in their own sweet way, that there are areas where they'd actually like us to invest our money, and there are ways that they'd like us to do it. Hence, there are reliefs and exemptions all over the shop. On their own, they wouldn't be so bad – but taken together, they're an absolute horror.

Anyway, horror or no horror, you'll have to fill in the Capital Gains Tax supplementary pages if you answered 'yes' to any of the three parts of question 8 on page 2 of the tax return. Popping back there for a moment, they were:

- If you have disposed of your only or main residence do you need the Capital Gains Tax pages?
- Did you dispose of other chargeable assets worth more than £15,000 in total?
- Were your total chargeable gains more than £7,500 or do you want to make a claim or election for the year?

The first question seems more like an exam question than anything else. You'd be forgiven for responding, 'Well I don't know, you're the taxman.' The reason it's phrased in that slightly funny way is that they presume, quite reasonably, that you'll know whether you need the pages or not. After all, you really should have established the tax situation before you sold the property. The good news is that you have to do quite a lot not to qualify for tax relief on your primary residence, like not live there or run a business from the home or have grounds adding up to more than half a hectare. Anyway, if private residence relief is something you'd like to know more about, then you'll be needing helpsheet *IR283: Private residence relief.*

The second and third questions also hide one or two confusions. To start with, you should be thinking of the value of the assets you disposed of, rather than what you actually got for them. You should also exclude any exempt assets (see page 78). If you're not domiciled in the UK and are chargeable on the 'remittance basis', then you should only take account of disposals to the extent that you've brought ('remitted') the proceeds into the UK during the tax year. Have a look at Chapter 9, Non-Residence etc for more about this.

The other point is that you need to fill in the Capital Gains Tax supplementary pages if there's something you want to tell the taxman, even though you don't have any gains. For example, if you want to claim a loss to carry forward to future years you'll need to fill out the pages. There are a whole host of other reliefs and claims that may need to be claimed via your tax return. Some of them are listed on page 85.

You see, I said it was a horror. We're barely a page into the chapter and we've already talked about chargeable assets, disposals, private residence relief and even something touting itself as the 'remittance basis'. We'd better go back and do some groundwork.

Gains, losses and disposals

Any transaction that can produce a capital gain (or loss) is known as a 'disposal', and selling something is not the only way that this can happen. Any situation where you transfer all or part of your interest in an asset to someone else can potentially be caught. This might include an exchange of all or part of an asset, or where you've received a capital sum (as opposed to income) resulting from your ownership of an asset. However, there are certain exceptions to this where, for instance, you have shares in a company that gets taken over and you receive shares in the acquiring company as the price for your shares. In this case, and in some cases where a company 'reorganizes' its shares, it's treated as though your shares have just become the new shares without any 'disposal' taking place. (For more about this, get hold of the Inland Revenue helpsheet *IR285: Share reorganizations, company takeovers and Capital Gains Tax*.)

You can even find yourself with a capital gains tax bill if you *give* something away. Although, technically speaking, you haven't received any money for it, in certain circumstances you'll be deemed to have effectively sold the thing to the person you were giving it to (for its market value), and made a gift of the cash. In other circumstances, for example where you give something to your spouse, you'll be deemed to have transferred the asset to the receiver of the gift at the same price as it cost you (so you make no gain or loss); so that when they come to sell it, they'll make a gain (or loss) that relates back to what you paid for it in the first place.

Where tax is potentially payable on a capital gain, it gets called a 'chargeable gain'. Similarly, where you make a loss that you're allowed to set off against your gains, it's called an 'allowable loss'.

Calculating chargeable gains

You calculate your chargeable gain (or allowable loss) by taking the price you got for your asset and deducting the cost of the asset in the first place (including any costs associated with the purchase like, for instance, stamp duty), the cost of any improvements (for instance, the cost of renovating a damaged antique table) and the cost of selling (like broker's commission). You then get to take various reliefs, like 'indexation allowance' and 'taper relief', into account (we'll come to these in a moment). Here's an example of how all this might work in practice. There are, by the way, several useful worked examples of how CGT works on pages 20–22 of the Inland Revenue's *Notes on Capital Gains*. There is also a working sheet for you to work out your own gains on page 23 of those notes.

Example 1

Let's say that you bought an antique chest of drawers on 25 October 1994 for a price of £2,500. You then spent £200 on 17 July 1996, dealing with some woodworm in the drawers. On 12 December 2001, you took it along to Antiques Roadshow and were told that it was a very special example of the eighteenth-century work of Colin the Carpenter from Crewe. Beautiful curves, wonderful clawed feet etc, etc, insurance value £20,000. But sod that for a game of soldiers – the very next day, you sell it at auction for £18,000. The auctioneer charges you 10 per cent (that's £1,800 if you don't have your calculator). You have a chargeable gain of…

FIGURE 1

	£
Sale proceeds	18,000
minus sale costs	1,800
	— — —
Net sale proceeds	16,200
minus purchase price	2,500
	— — —
	13,700
minus expenditure on the asset	200
	— — —
Net gain	13,400

Not bad. We'll complete the story with our chest of drawers, though, when we take a look at indexation and taper relief in a few pages time.

What if you had two chests of drawers and sold one? That's pretty straightforward, because the two chests can be easily told apart, so you'll always know which one you're selling and when you bought it. But some types of assets, like shares, for example, can't be distinguished so easily; and that confuses things.

Say you first bought shares in Tesco in 1994, then increased the holding in 1999, before offloading half of them in 2001. Which ones did you sell and how much did they cost? For reasons known only to someone in a dark office at Her Majesty's Treasury, how this sort of thing is treated depends on when exactly the different bits were bought. Sometimes you're treated as selling some of each, and sometimes the most recent ones you bought. Also, if you buy the same shares again within 30 days of selling them, you're treated as though you never sold them in the first place. There are also some extra nuances for holdings in unit trusts and other investment funds, particularly when they've been acquired under a monthly savings scheme. Rather than going into all the detail here (and there is a fair bit of it), if you have issues with any of this, then you'll want to get hold of the Inland Revenue helpsheet: *IR284 – Shares and Capital Gains Tax*.

Exempt assets

Some things don't get taxed at all, mostly because it's either too awkward to work it all out (and keep tabs on us) or the government's trying to be nice (and/or to encourage us to do certain things). The most common asset types where you don't get charged capital gains tax are listed in the table on page 78.

- Private cars
- Your home (so long as it's your prime dwelling)
- 'Personal belongings' worth less than £6,000 when you sell them
- National Savings Certificates, Premium Bonds and British Savings Bonds
- UK Government Bonds (otherwise known as 'gilts')
- Anything held inside an Individual Savings Account (ISA) or their fore-runner, Personal Equity Plans (PEPs)
- Bonuses on Tax Exempt Special Savings Accounts (TESSAs)
- Personal injury compensation (after all, what would be the 'acquisition cost'!)
- Foreign currency for personal (or family) use
- Life assurance policies or deferred annuity contracts (unless purchased from a third party)
- Betting, lottery or pools winnings
- Save As You Earn (SAYE) terminal bonuses
- Compensation for certain mis-sold pensions
- Shares issued after 18 March 1986 where you have relief under the business expansion scheme

Small receipts

In some situations, you might receive a sum of money in respect of an asset that's 'small' in relation to the value of that asset. For instance, you might get a small insurance payment on account of minor damage to a painting. In this situation, you wouldn't need to account for capital gains tax. You would, however, have to deduct the 'small receipt' (for example, the insurance payout) from the expenditure on the asset that you deduct from the sale proceeds, if and when you eventually sell it.

For these purposes, small is considered to be an amount that does not exceed the original cost of the asset (plus improvements) **and** is less than £3,000 or 5 per cent of the asset's value. If you have a receipt that doesn't fit this description, but which you think should be considered small in the circumstances, then you'll need to have it out with your local tax office.

Indexation allowance

As discussed at the beginning of this chapter, the idea behind capital gains tax is to tax you on the gains you make on assets that you dispose of. However, the aim is to tax you on the *real* increase in your asset's value, not the part of the increase that can be put down to inflation. Back in the 1970s and 1980s, the inflation was normally the biggest bit, so the 'indexation allowance' was introduced to try to remove the inflation from your capital gain.

Later on in the 1980s, they decided that so much of gains during the 1970s were down to inflation that it would be easier simply to ignore all gains that took place before 31 March 1982. So all assets acquired before 31 March 1982 are deemed to have been acquired at this point, for their value on that date (or their value when acquired if that's greater, which is pretty unlikely). Now that inflation has all but disappeared (at least for the time being), indexation allowance has been scrapped, as from April 1998. Instead, we've got 'taper relief' (which is designed to encourage us to hold onto our assets for the long term, and will be discussed in a moment). The effect of all this is:

- Assets acquired on or after 1 April 1998 don't have anything to do with indexation allowance
- Assets acquired before 6 April 1998 get an indexation allowance designed to adjust your gain for the effect of inflation up to 6 April 1998
- Assets acquired before 31 March 1982 are deemed to have a cost equal to their value at that date (or their true cost if that is higher).

The way it works is that the government, between March 1982 and April 1998, produced a set of figures every month that you could use to work out your indexation allowance. Of course, since 1998, those figures haven't changed, so you can get hold of up-to-date sets relatively easily. For starters, they're on page 16 of the Inland Revenue's *Notes on Capital Gains*. Basically, all you have to do is find the figure that corresponds to the month that you acquired your asset, then multiply your gain by that number to give you your indexation allowance (that is the bit of your gain that can be put down to inflation). You then deduct your indexation allowance from your net gain to give you your 'net chargeable gain after indexation'. The same rules apply to any money spent on improving your asset. So, going back to our chest of drawers, figure 2 (page 80) sets out how to work out the gain after indexation.

	£
Sale proceeds	18,000
minus sale costs	1,800
	— — —
Net sale proceeds	16,200
minus purchase price	2,500
	— — —
	13,700
minus indexation allowance on Purchase price (£2,500 x 0.120*)	300
	— — —
	13,400
minus expenditure on the asset	200
	— — —
	13,200
minus indexation allowance on expenditure (£200 x 0.067*)	13
	— — —
Net chargeable gain after indexation	13,187

* The figures respectively for October 1994 and July 1996 from page 16 of the Inland Revenue's *Notes on Capital Gains*.

FIGURE 2

Note that the most the indexation allowance can do is reduce a potential gain to zero. You can't use it to create an allowable loss. There is more detail on the Indexation Allowance in the Inland Revenue's *Notes on Capital Gains*, starting on page 14.

Taper relief

Taper relief was introduced by Gordon Brown in the 1998 Budget at the same time that the indexation allowance disappeared, though its purpose is not so much to account for the effect of inflation but to encourage us to hold our investments for the long term. The way it works is that the amount of your gain that actually gets charged to capital gains tax reduces for each whole year that you hold the asset after 5 April 1998 (although for non-business assets it doesn't actually get going until the third year is up). The percentages of the gain that's chargeable is shown in figure 2 and you can follow our chest of drawers example through to its conclusion in figure 3. There's more detail on Taper Relief in the Inland Revenue's *Notes on Capital Gains* starting on page 17 and in the helpsheet *IR279: Taper Relief.*

FIGURE 3

NON-BUSINESS ASSETS

Number of whole years that the asset is held after 5 April 1998	Percentage of gain that's chargeable
1	100%
2	100%
3	95%
4	90%
5	85%
6	80%
7	75%
8	70%
9	65%
10 or more	60%

BUSINESS ASSETS

Number of whole years that the asset is held for after 5 April 1998	Percentage of gain that's chargeable
1	87.5%
2	75%
3	50%
4 or more	25%

	£
Sale proceeds	18,000
minus sale costs	1,800
	— — —
Net sale proceeds	16,200
minus purchase price	2,500
	— — —
	13,700
minus indexation allowance on Purchase price (£2,500 x 0.120)	300
	— — —
	13,400
minus expenditure on the asset	200
	— — —
	13,200
minus indexation allowance on expenditure (£200 x 0.067)	13
	— — —
Net chargeable gain after indexation	13,187
multiply by taper relief of 95%	12,528
(for an asset held for 3 whole years after 5 April 1998)	
Total chargeable gain after indexation and taper relief	12,528

FIGURE 4

Personal exemption

For the 2001/2 tax year, the 'personal exemption' for capital gains tax is £7,500. This means that after taking off any indexation and taper relief, you don't pay tax on your first £7,500 of chargeable gains. The personal exemption tends to rise over the years. There's some guidance on how to make use of your personal exemption at the end of this chapter, starting on page 93.

Losses

As already explained, allowable losses can be set off against any chargeable gains you make during the tax year. Any losses that are left over can then be carried forward to be used in future years. It gets complicated, though, where losses from different years interact with each other and the personal exemption. The three main rules to remember are:

- Losses from the current year are set off in priority to losses brought forward from a previous year
- Losses from the current year are set off to reduce gains all the way to zero
- Losses brought forward are used to reduce gains to the personal exemption

We can use an example to illustrate this. Imagine that you had the following gains and losses in the 1999/0, 2000/1 and 2001/2 tax years:

	1999/0	2000/1	2001/2
Gains	£10,000	£20,000	£25,000
Losses	£30,000	£2,500	£0

In the 1999/0 tax year, you must use all of your current year losses to reduce the gain to zero if possible. So you use £10,000 of the losses against the £10,000 gains and have £20,000 of losses to carry forward to the next year.

In the 2000/1 tax year, you must use all of your current year losses, of £2,500, to reduce the gain to zero if possible. In this case the current year losses are only enough to reduce your gain to £17,500. However, you also have the losses brought forward, and these can be used to reduce the gains as far as your personal exemption. For 2000/1 the personal exemption was £7,500, so you use £10,000 (£17,500 minus £7,500) of your brought-forward losses to get you down to the personal exemption. You're still left with £10,000 of losses to carry forward to next year.

In the 2001/2 tax year, you don't have any current year losses, so you move straight to the losses brought forward. Of these there are £10,000, which reduces the gain of £25,000 down to £15,000. You can attack this with taper relief and then the personal exemption but, except perhaps in the case of business assets, you'll have some tax to pay.

If this doesn't sound confusing enough, it gets a whole lot worse when you take account of taper relief. The trouble is that in relation to this, not all gains are equal. Depending on how long you've held the asset, more or less of the gain might be chargeable to tax. On that basis, you get to choose which of your gains you cancel out with any losses that you have. So, if you have two gains and one of them is, say, 85 per cent chargeable to tax while the other is 100 per cent chargeable to tax, you'd want to wipe out the 100 per cent one first.

There are also certain special rules that cover how particular losses are set against certain types of gain. Basically, you need to be a bit careful where gains and losses arise out of trusts, or where you've made a loss on a disposal to a 'connected person' (broadly speaking, family members, business partners, companies you control or trusts you've set up). In these cases, you should start by looking at page 10 of the Inland Revenues *Notes on Capital Gains*, but you're probably best to seek advice.

Other reliefs

In addition to the above, there are a whole host of additional reliefs that the government allows you. Most of them are designed to encourage investment in one area or another. If you're entitled to them, you'll probably know about them, since that's probably part of the reason that you made that particular investment in the first place. If you want to know more, then page 18 of the Inland Revenue's *Notes on Capital Gains* has brief details of them. For the full monty, though, you'd need to get hold of the specific helpsheets. There's a list of the main reliefs, together with the name of the helpsheet where there is one, in the table on page 85.

What you'll need

OK, so if you're still with me after all that, we can move on to the actual Capital Gains Tax pages. To fill them in, you'll need, of course, the Capital Gains pages themselves and, if your capital gains situation is anything other than very straightforward, you should get hold of the Inland Revenue's *Notes on Capital Gains*.

Beyond this, all you really need are the details of any transactions you've made during the year that have resulted in a chargeable gain or an allowable loss. That's generally pretty easy, because it will have happened recently.

TABLE 4: HELPSHEETS ON CAPITAL GAINS

RELIEF	DESCRIPTION	HELPSHEET
Roll-over relief	Gains on business assets can be deferred ('rolled over') when replaced	IR290: Business asset roll-over relief
Gifts hold-over relief	Gains can be deferred where certain assets are given away	IR295: Relief for gifts and similar transactions
Dependent relative relief	Relief for gains on a home you have provided to a dependent relative	IR283: Private residence relief
Halving relief	Relief for half of a gain deferred from before 31 March 1982	IR280: Rebasing – assets held at 31 March 1982
Enterprise Investment Scheme	Gains deferred when you subscribe for EIS shares and relief against gains on disposal	IR297: Enterprise Investment Schemes and Capital Gains Tax
Venture Capital Trusts	Gains deferred when you subscribe for VCT shares and relief against gains on disposal	IR298: Venture Capital Trusts and Capital Gains Tax

What's more difficult is laying your hands on the details of your purchase of the relevant asset, so that you can actually work out the size of the gain or loss. Needless to say, you'll need these details too. Where you absolutely can't lay your hands on them, then it's a question of making your best guess about what you paid and explaining, in the additional information box, how you arrived at the estimate and why you don't have the detailed records. Of course, the Inland Revenue can then challenge you if they don't agree with you.

One of the main things that incurs capital gains tax for most people are their dealings in financial investments, like unit trusts (outside of an ISA) or direct shareholdings in companies. If you habitually use the same broker to do all this for you, then they'll probably come up with a nice summary of all your gains and losses at the end of the tax year. If you get one of these, then hang on to it!

It will save a lot of trouble. If you don't get a nice statement of your investment gains and losses, then you'll need the 'contract notes' that you should have received with each purchase and sale.

Boxes F1 to F7 – The first page

Straight away, you'll see why we needed to go through some of the jargon. The first page needs to be completed 'if all your transactions were in quoted shares or other securities unless taper relief is due on any of them, or any were held at 31 March 1982, or you are claiming a relief, for example, Enterprise Investment Scheme referral relief'. Otherwise, you have to fill out the rest of the form instead. Note that page 1 can't be used in combination with the alternative boxes on pages 2 and 3.

'Quoted shares or other securities' are basically things that are traded on some form of stock exchange, as well as unit trusts and open-ended investment companies (OEICs). So, if dealing in these was all you got up to during the year, then page 1 might be for you – *unless* you're claiming taper relief (which means that you'd need to have held the shares or whatever for three whole years, assuming they're non-business assets) and *unless* you held the assets on 31

A Enter details of quoted shares or other securities disposed of	B Tick box if estimate or valuation used	C Enter the date of disposal	D Disposal proceeds	E Gain or loss after indexation allowance, if due (enter loss in brackets)	F Further information, including any elections made
1		/ /	£	£	
2		/ /	£	£	
3		/ /	£	£	
4		/ /	£	£	
5		/ /	£	£	
6		/ /	£	£	
7		/ /	£	£	
8		/ /	£	£	

Total gains **F1** £ — Total your gains in column E and enter the amount in box F1

Total losses **F2** £ — Total your losses in column E and enter the amount in box F2

Net gain/(loss) **F3** £ (box F1 minus box F2) — If your net gains are below £7,500 **or** you have a net loss, there is no liability; copy box F3 into box F7 and complete Page CG8. Otherwise, carry on to box F4

minus income losses set against gains **F4** £

F5 £ (box F3 minus box F4) — If your gains are now below £7,500, there is no liability; copy box F5 to box F7 and complete Page CG8. Otherwise, carry on to box F6

minus losses brought forward **F6** £ — Enter losses brought forward up to the **smaller** of either the total losses brought forward or the figure in box F5 **minus** £7,500

Total taxable gains **F7** £ (box F5 minus box F6) — Copy this figure to box 8.7 on Page CG8 (if F7 is blank because there is no liability, leave 8.7 blank).

Note:
This Page is only for transactions in quoted shares or other securities.
See the definition on page CGN2 of the Notes on Capital Gains.

March 1982 and *unless* you're claiming for some other relief. Note that you can still use page 1 if you're just using indexation allowance but, if you're doing that, then you'll have held the asset before 6 April 1998 and will, presumably, be after some taper relief.

Anyway, if you fit the bill, fill in the details of your transactions (and if you don't, move on to page 2). If you need more space, you can photocopy the page and attach it as a schedule. Having done that, you need to tot up the gains and put the answer in box **F1**, tot up the losses and put the answer in box **F2** and take **F2** away from **F1** to give you your net gain for the year in **F3**. If this is less than the personal exemption (of £7,500 for the 2001/2 tax year), then you can simply transfer the figure from **F3** into **F7** and move on to page 8 of the Capital Gains Tax pages (see pages 90–92 of this book).

Box F4 is for certain income losses that you can set against capital gains. These are quite unusual and include certain types of trading loss. Where these arise, they've generally been covered elsewhere in the book, so you should know if they apply to you. If you've got some unusual income losses and have any doubts, you'll need to speak to your tax office. Anyway, anything that you can put in **F4** gets deducted from **F3**, to give you your total net chargeable gains, which goes in **F5**.

If **F5** is now less than £7,500, you can just copy the figure to box **F7** and move on to page 8. Otherwise, you need to enter any losses brought forward into **F6**, *but only as much of them as are needed to get you down to £7,500.* Excess losses that aren't needed in box **F6** can be carried forward to next year. Once you've filled in box **F7**, you can skip straight to page 8.

Boxes 8.1 to 8.4 – Pages 2 and 3

If you weren't able to get away with the simple form on page 1, you'll need to fill in the details of your various transactions on pages 2 and 3. Because taper relief is different for business and non-business assets, a distinction needs to be drawn between the two. The first eight rows are for assets that were either wholly used for business purposes *or* wholly used for non-business purposes (you'll need to put a 'bus' in column **I** on page 3 if it was a business asset). The final two rows, **9** and **10**, are for assets that were used partly for business and partly for personal use. If you enter anything in these two rows, for columns **H** to **M** you need to break the asset down, pro rata, into its different bits. Any losses you made should be detailed in rows **13** to **16**.

Otherwise, the boxes are fairly self-explanatory. In column **AA**, you need to say what type of asset it was. Where it isn't a quoted share or other security (broadly speaking anything traded on a stock exchange or unit trusts or open-ended investment companies), and you've therefore entered 'U', 'L' or

Your 2001-02 Capital Gains Tax liability

A Brief description of asset	AA* Type of disposal. Enter Q, U, L or O	B Tick box if estimate or valuation used	C Tick box if asset held at 31 March 1982	D Enter the later of date of acquisition and 16 March 1998	E Enter the date of disposal	F Disposal proceeds	G Enter details of any elections made, reliefs claimed or due and state amount (£)
Gains on assets without mixed (business and non-business) use							
1				/ /	/ /	£	
2				/ /	/ /	£	
3				/ /	/ /	£	
4				/ /	/ /	£	
5				/ /	/ /	£	
6				/ /	/ /	£	
7				/ /	/ /	£	
8				/ /	/ /	£	
Gains on assets with mixed (business and non-business) use (see the notes on page CGN4)							
9				/ /	/ /	£	
10				/ /	/ /	£	

* Column AA: for transactions in
- quoted shares or other securities, (see the definition on page CGN2 of the Notes) enter **Q**
- other shares or securities, enter **U**
- land and property, enter **L**
- other assets (for example, goodwill), enter **O**   *Complete Pages CG4 to CG6 for all U, L and O transactions*

Losses

Description of asset	Type of * disposal. Enter Q, U, L or O	Tick box if estimate or valuation used	Tick box if asset held at 31 March 1982	Enter the later of date of acquisition and 16 March 1998	Enter the date of disposal	Disposal proceeds	Enter details of any elections made, reliefs claimed or due and state amount (£)
13				/ /	/ /	£	
14				/ /	/ /	£	
15				/ /	/ /	£	
16				/ /	/ /	£	
							Total losses of

TAX RETURN ■ CAPITAL GAINS: PAGE CG2

'O', then you'll need to fill in the 'further information' section on pages 4, 5 and 6.

Column **G** is for you to enter details of any elections or reliefs that you're claiming to reduce the amount of your gains (if you need more room, then

	H Chargeable Gains after reliefs but before losses and taper	I Enter 'Bus' if business asset	J Taper rate	K Losses deducted			L Gains after losses	M Tapered gains (gains from column L x % in column J)
				K1 Allowable losses of the year	K2 Income losses of 2001-02 set against gains	K3 Unused losses b/f from earlier years		
	£		%	£	£	£	£	£
	£		%	£	£	£	£	£
	£		%	£	£	£	£	£
	£		%	£	£	£	£	£
	£		%	£	£	£	£	£
	£		%	£	£	£	£	£
	£		%	£	£	£	£	£
	£		%	£	£	£	£	£
	£	Bus	%	£	£	£	£	£
	£		%	£	£	£	£	£
	£	Bus	%	£	£	£	£	£
	£		%	£	£	£	£	£
Total	8.1 £ Total column H				8.5 £ Total column K2	8.6 £ Total column K3		8.3 £ Total column M

	Losses arising	

11 **Attributed gains from UK resident trusts** *(enter the name of the Trust on Page CG7)* £

12 **Attributed gains from non UK resident trusts** *(enter the name of the Trust on Page CG7)* £

Total of attributed gains 8.4 £

	£
	£
	£
	£
year 8.2 £	

box 8.3 + box 8.4

Total taxable gains (after allowable losses and taper relief) £

Copy to box 8.7 on Page CG8 and complete Pages CG4 to CG6 for all U, L and O transactions

Copy to box 8.10 on Page CG8 and, unless you need only complete the totals boxes (see page CGN5), complete column K1

you should use 'additional information' on page 7). You need to enter the appropriate percentage of taper relief that applies in column **J** (see page 80 of this book).

Column **K** is where you set out the amount of any losses that you're choosing to set against each of your gains. You'll want to use up your losses on those gains that attract the least taper relief first of all. **K1** is for any losses from this year, **K2** is for any 'income losses' (see the comments on box **F4** on page 87 of this book) and **K3** is for losses brought forward from previous years.

When you've filled in the details of your transactions, you need to total the columns where indicated and put your total taxable gains in the (surprisingly) un-numbered box at the bottom right of page 3.

Pages 4 to 7

Pages 4, 5 and 6 are for further details of transactions that you listed on pages 2 and 3, but which weren't to do with 'quoted shares or other securities'. Page 4 is for 'other shares or securities' (broadly speaking ones that aren't quoted on a stock exchange of some sort), page 5 is for Land & Property and page 6 is for 'other'. Page 7 (box **8.22**, in fact) is for any additional information, like descriptions of reliefs that wouldn't fit in column **G** of page 2.

Page 8, boxes 8.7 to 8.9 – Chargeable gains and allowable losses

The first two questions on page 8, relating to estimates of value and reliefs, are straightforward. The third question, 'are you claiming, and/or using, any clogged losses?', is not. The good news is that clogged losses are pretty unusual. They generally arise where you make a loss on a disposal to a 'connected person' and can then only be used to reduce gains on disposals to the same 'connected person'. There's a more complete explanation on page 10 of the Inland Revenue's *Notes on Capital Gains*. If you think you might have clogged losses, start there and perhaps talk to your tax office, but some professional advice might be in order.

The remaining questions in this section are straightforward, until we get to box **8.9**. If you think that you've received anything from a non-resident or dual-resident trust, and that **8.9** might therefore be relevant to you, then you'll

---

Chargeable gains and allowable losses

Once you have completed Page CG1, or Pages CG2 to CG6, fill in this Page.

Have you 'ticked' any row in Column B, 'Tick box if estimate or valuation used' on Pages CG1 or CG2 or in Column C on Page CG2 'Tick box if asset held at 31 March 1982'? **NO** ☐ **YES** ☐

Have you given details in Column G on Pages CG2 and CG3 of any Capital Gains reliefs claimed or due? **NO** ☐ **YES** ☐

Are you claiming, and/or using, any 'clogged' losses (see Notes, page CGN10)? **NO** ☐ **YES** ☐

Enter the number of transactions from Page CG1 or column AA on Page CG2 for:

- transactions in quoted shares or other securities **box Q** ☐
- transactions in other shares or securities **box U** ☐
- transactions in land and property **box L** ☐
- other transactions **box O** ☐

Total taxable gains (from Page CG1 **or** Page CG3) **8.7** £ ☐

Your taxable gains *minus* the annual exempt amount of £7,500 (leave blank if '0' or negative) box 8.7 minus £7,500 **8.8** £ ☐

Additional liability in respect of non-resident or dual resident trusts (see Notes, page CGN6) **8.9** £ ☐

---

want to get hold of the helpsheet *IR301: Capital gains on benefits from non-resident and dual-resident trusts* which, as you might imagine, goes into it. Otherwise, move on.

Page 8, boxes 8.10 to 8.21 – Capital losses

Having established your total taxable gains for the year, the final step is to detail all your losses. The first section deals with the losses you made in this tax year. Start by moving your loss figure from either box **8.2** (on page 3) or box **F2** (if you filled out page 1) into box **8.10**. Then enter, in box **8.11**, the total value of this year's losses that you've used up this year (that is, the total of column **K1** on page 3 or the smaller of boxes **F1** and **F2** on page 1).

Box **8.12** is for personal representatives and box **8.13** is only relevant if you've incurred a loss on unlisted shares or an Enterprise Investment Scheme. Start by looking at pages 11 and 9, respectively, of the Inland Revenue's *Notes on Capital Gains* if you think any of this might apply to you. Finally, you need to put a note of the value of this year's losses that you haven't used in box **8.14**.

Capital losses

(If your loss arose on a transaction with a connected person, see Notes page CGN13, you can only set that loss against gains you make on disposals to that same connected person.)

■ **This year's losses**

- Total (from box 8.2 on Page CG3 or box F2 on Page CG1)

  8.10 £

- Used against gains (total of column K1 on Page CG3, or the smaller of boxes F1 and F2 on Page CG1)

  8.11 £

- Used against earlier years' gains (generally only available to personal representatives, see Notes, page CGN11)

  8.12 £

- Used against income (only losses of the type described on page CGN9 can be used against income)

  8.13A £ — amount claimed against income of 2001-02

  8.13B £ — amount claimed against income of 2000-01

  box 8.13A + box 8.13B **8.13** £

- This year's unused losses

  box 8.10 *minus* (boxes 8.11 + 8.12 + 8.13) **8.14** £

■ **Earlier years' losses**

- Unused losses of 1996-97 and later years

  8.15 £

- Used this year (losses from box 8.15 are used in priority to losses from box 8.18) (column K3 on Page CG3 or box F6 on Page CG1)

  8.16 £

- Remaining unused losses of 1996-97 and later years

  box 8.15 *minus* box 8.16 **8.17** £

- Unused losses of 1995-96 and earlier years

  8.18 £

- Used this year (losses from box 8.15 are used in priority to losses from box 8.18) (column K3 on Page CG3 or box F6 on Page CG1)

  box 8.6 *minus* box 8.16 (or box F6 *minus* box 8.16) **8.19** £

■ **Total of unused losses to carry forward**

- Carried forward losses of 1996-97 and later years

  box 8.14 + box 8.17 **8.20** £

- Carried forward losses of 1995-96 and earlier years

  box 8.18 *minus* box 8.19 **8.21** £

The second section deals with losses brought forward from previous years. These need to be split into losses from the year 1996/7 and later, and losses from before 1996/7. Otherwise, the boxes are pretty self-explanatory.

Using your personal exemption

As we saw earlier in this chapter, you can make a certain amount of capital gains before you pay any CGT. It's called the personal exemption and for the 2001/2 tax year it amounted to £7,500. Crucially, though, you can't carry unused personal exemption forward to next year. This means it can be worth creating a small gain each year, just to use the exemption, since it might reduce the chances of there being a gain in future years that's bigger than your exemption, and that you therefore have to pay tax on.

This used to be called 'bed and breakfasting', because people would sell enough shares in, say, Tesco to make a gain up to their personal exemption – and then buy the same shares back the very next morning. Bingo! You've increased the base cost of your portfolio, so there's less potential CGT to pay in the future, but you haven't paid any tax. Gordon Brown decided that this 'bed and breakfasting' nonsense was all a bit silly so, in the 1998 budget, he tried to do away with it. Unfortunately, as so often happens when the government tinkers with a perfectly good scam, they ended up just creating a more complicated but perfectly good scam.

What Gordon said was that if you re-buy the same shares within a 30-day period, it's treated as though you never actually sold them at all, so a traditional 'bed and breakfast' would be treated as though it never happened. This is where you can try your skills as a tax adviser. Can you see a way around this? There are quite a few.

First of all, you can just wait the 30 days: not so much a 'bed and breakfast' as a 'long-term holiday let'. Sure, the shares might go up in the meantime, which would be a bit of a pain, but they might go down, too. Some years you'll win and some years you'll lose, but over a lifetime's saving and investing, it should make little difference. Except to say that you'll have that bit of money not in shares for a month each year and, as we'll see in Chapter 17, it's generally best for your long-term investments to be kept in shares. Still, it might be worth it to save on a bit of CGT, depending on costs and other factors mentioned below.

You can avoid these problems, though, if you feel that your portfolio of shares needs rebalancing. The various shares in your portfolio will fare differently from each other over the years: some will do well and some will do badly. This can cause problems, because the ones that do well will begin to account for more and more of your portfolio. In other words, over the years, your portfolio will gradually tend to become more concentrated in a few shares, or even sectors, thereby increasing your risks. So, you may have the opportunity to kill two birds with one stone. You can sell a slice of the investment that's getting too dominant in your portfolio and reinvest the money at the other end, or in something entirely new. This way, you adjust the balance of your portfolio and get to use your personal exemption at the same time.

Marriage also brings with it the opportunity to play games with the taxman. If, for instance, you have your investments neatly spread between you (as you probably should – see Tax Saving Tips in Chapter 20), then there should be plenty of scope for swapping shareholdings. The process has been dubbed, rather unimaginatively, 'bed and spousing' and it essentially works like this: 'You sell your Tesco and I'll buy them back, while I'll sell my Glaxo and you can buy them back.' Note that you'd have to sell them to, and buy them back from, the stock market, because if you buy and sell them to and from each other directly, it won't trigger a capital gain.

Perhaps the handiest trick of all is the 'bed and ISA'. The Inland Revenue sees your Individual Savings Account as a separate entity from you, so you can sell some shares, creating the gain, and then use that money to make your ISA subscription for the year. Then, with the money safely tucked up inside the ISA, you can go ahead and buy back the same shares inside the ISA that you just sold outside of it.

Of course, stockbrokers love all this 'bed and whatever' stuff since to do it means giving them commission and their gain is your loss. You therefore need to balance up the benefit of a potential future CGT saving against the cost of buying and selling the relevant shares. This involves a lot of guesswork, but it's probably safe to say that it's not worth doing unless you can create gains of up to most of the personal exemption in any one year. Otherwise, you could as easily wait until next year, when you're likely to be that bit closer to the full exemption, but still below it.

It's also worth making sure you get plenty of 'bang for your buck'. In other words, you want to create a large gain from selling a small value of shares (thus paying the least commission, depending on how your stockbroker works this out, and stamp duty). That, in turn, would mean selling the shares that have the biggest gain as a proportion of their value. This fits in neatly with the idea of rebalancing your portfolio by selling a slice of shareholdings that have become uncomfortably large in relation to the rest.

A further confusing factor is taper relief, since the shares with the largest gain, before taper relief, are likely to be the ones you've held the longest, and which therefore attract the greatest amount of relief. The only answer to this is to go through the painstaking process of working out the gains you could make from selling different bits of your various shareholdings and calculating the cost of doing it. There's an added complication in that having sold old shares and bought new shares, you'll start the taper relief clock ticking again.

So, on top of the sums, there are several subjective judgments that come into play and you have to think forward to where you, or rather your investments, might be in a few years' time. Of course you could pay someone to make these decisions for you. But with a hundred other clients to deal with, are they really going to put as much thought into it as you can? And if they do, how much will they have to charge you for the time?

Non-Residence etc

The Non-Residence etc supplementary pages are for people with UK tax to pay, and tax returns to complete, on account of having income or gains in the UK, but who aren't *resident*, *ordinarily resident* or *domiciled* in the UK during the tax year. There's also something called *split-year treatment* that you might have a claim to if you had *dual residency* during the year, and for that you'd need to fill in these pages.

The reason these issues of residence matter is that they determine how much the UK will tax you. Broadly speaking, the UK aims to take its slice of the following:

● Any income arising in the UK, whether or not it belongs to a UK *resident*.
● Any income arising outside the UK that belongs to someone *resident* in the UK.
● Any capital gains arising anywhere in the world that belong to individuals *resident* or *ordinarily resident* in the UK.

The foreign income and gains referred to in the second and third bullet points are what the Foreign supplementary pages are all about (see Chapter 6). UK income and gains are dealt with by filling in the relevant supplementary pages, and then filling in the Non-Residence pages, if appropriate. So, if you live in Spain but own a property in Brighton and receive an income from renting it out, then you'd tell the Inland Revenue about the income in the Land & Property pages and then tell them about your living in Spain in the Non-Residence pages. So, before we get on to the tax return itself, we'd better have a look at the meaning of *domicile*, *residence* and *ordinary residence*.

Domicile, residence and ordinary residence

Confusingly as ever, what you and I would think of simply as residence is, in fact, split into three different categories: domicile, residence and ordinary residence and it's possible to fit into several combinations of these categories.

Domicile is only relevant in a few situations, so we'll get it out of the way first. It can basically be thought of as a very long-term form of residence, and it's the hardest thing to shift. It isn't concerned with your to-ings and fro-ings over different tax years, nor even with your nationality; but rather with where you plan to live your life. It has to do with your state of mind. You can go overseas for a few years and lose your UK residence, but if you plan eventually to return to the UK to live out your remaining years, then your domicile would remain with the UK throughout.

You start out life with what's known as a domicile of origin (normally inherited from your father). This will stick with you unless and until you make a major decision to move to another country and remain there: essentially a full-blown emigration. You then pick up the domicile of your adopted country. You can never be without a domicile and you can never have more than one at a time.

The effect of a non-UK domicile is that you'll only pay tax on capital gains to the extent that they're actually brought into the country (the 'remittance basis'), as opposed to when you actually made the gain (the 'arising basis'). If you have any doubts about your domicile status, then you should probably speak to your local tax office. They'll then ask you to complete a questionnaire and make a decision.

There is also no strict definition of residence and ordinary residence, but the way they're applied is much more matter of fact. To start with, if you're in the UK for half the tax year or more (183 days in fact), the Inland Revenue will take the view that you're UK resident. For purposes of the calculation, days entering and leaving the country are generally not included. On top of this, the Inland Revenue will also consider you UK resident if you visit the UK regularly over four years and, *on average*, spend a quarter of each year here (91 days in fact). From the fifth year, you'll start being UK resident.

Ordinary residence sort of sits in between residence and domicile. You can probably most easily think of it as being the place where you tend to be resident, even if you're technically not resident for the odd year. So, if you're normally UK resident, but happen to be away for most of one tax year, you'll still be ordinarily resident in the UK for that year even if you lose your UK residence. Similarly, you can be UK resident for a tax year without being ordinarily resident, if you tend to be resident abroad but happen to be here for most of one particular year.

The 183 and 91 day rules, if you pass them, will make sure you're included as UK resident, but just because you don't pass them, it doesn't necessarily mean that you won't be UK resident. If you don't pass the tests and think you might not be resident, the first thing to do is answer the questionnaire in the Inland Revenue's *Notes on Non-Residence* supplementary pages. These are designed to establish your residence status. If you don't agree with the answer, or want further information on this for any other reason, then you'll want to get hold of the Inland Revenue leaflet *IR20: Residents and non-residents: liability to tax in the United Kingdom* (it also covers domicile). I can't say it's a great read, but it is at least relatively understandable. If things still aren't adding up, you should call the Inland Revenue's Residence Advice and Liability (RAL) office. Their helpline number is 0151 472 6196.

What you'll need

The first thing you'll need is a record of all your movements, into and out of the UK, over the past year. If you expect residence (etc) to be an issue, then it'll be well worth keeping some sort of diary. Otherwise, you're stuck with piecing it all together from your passport and the spent boarding cards that are still sitting in the bottom of your bits and bobs drawer because they seem a bit too important to throw away.

The other thing you'll definitely need is the Inland Revenue's *Notes on Non-Residence*. As well as attempting to explain some of the theory behind the taxation of non-residents, the notes incorporate some relatively straightforward questions for you to answer to determine your residence status.

Filling in the Non-Residence pages

The pages start by asking you to declare your residence (etc) status. 'I am…'. No beating around the bush then. We've gone into more detail about what the different terms mean on page 97, and it's worth starting off with a look at that, but really it's best to keep things simple and follow through questions 1 to 18 in the *Notes*. Answering these questions will tell you which of boxes **9.1** to **9.8** to tick.

If you're claiming to be non-resident, and have ticked box **9.2**, then you may

Residence status

I am *(please tick appropriate box)*

- resident in the UK **9.1**
- ordinarily resident in the UK **9.3**
- not domiciled in the UK (and it is relevant to my Income Tax or Capital Gains Tax liability) **9.5**
- claiming personal allowances as a non-resident **9.7**

- not resident in the UK **9.2**
- not ordinarily resident in the UK **9.4**
- claiming split-year treatment **9.6**
- resident in a country other than the UK (under a double taxation agreement) at the same time as being resident in the UK **9.8**

Information required if you claim to be non-resident in the UK for the whole of 2001-02

- Are you in any of the following categories:

    - a Commonwealth citizen (this includes a British citizen) or an EEA (European Economic Area) national?

    - a present or former employee of the British Crown (including a civil servant, member of the armed forces etc)?

    - a UK missionary society employee?

    - a civil servant in a territory under the protection of the British Crown?

    - a resident of the Isle of Man or the Channel Islands?

    - a former resident of the UK and you live abroad for the sake of your own health or the health of a member of your family who lives with you?

    - a widow or widower of an employee of the British Crown?

    Yes **9.9**   No **9.10**

- How many days have you spent in the UK, excluding days of arrival and departure, during the year ended 5 April 2002? *Enter the number of days* **9.11** *days*

- Were you resident in the UK for 2000-01? Yes **9.12** No **9.13**

- How many days have you spent in the UK up to 5 April 2002, excluding days of arrival and departure, since 5 April 1998 or, if later, the date you originally left the UK ? *Enter the number of days* **9.14** *days*

- What is your country of nationality? **9.15**

- In which country are you resident? **9.16**

still be entitled to the allowances you would get if you were UK resident. If you want to claim the allowances, you need to tick box **9.7**. Boxes **9.9** to **9.16** then press for the information necessary to support your claim for allowances. The circumstances in which you're entitled to allowances are set out on page 7 of the *Notes*, but it gets pretty complicated, because it depends a lot on the tax treaties

Information required if you claim to be not ordinarily resident in the UK for the whole of 2001-02

- Were you ordinarily resident in the UK for 2000-01? Yes **9.17** [ ] No **9.18** [ ]

- When you came to the UK, did you intend to stay here for at least three years? Yes **9.19** [ ] No **9.20** [ ] Not applicable **9.21** [ ]

- If you have left the UK, do you intend to live outside the UK permanently? Yes **9.22** [ ] No **9.23** [ ] Not applicable **9.24** [ ]

Information required if you claim split-year treatment

- Date of your arrival in the UK **9.25** [Day / Month / Year]

- Date of your departure from the UK **9.26** [Day / Month / Year]

Information required if you claim to be not domiciled in the UK

- Have you submitted full facts to the Inland Revenue (for example, on forms DOM1 or P86) regarding your domicile in the six years ended 5 April 2002? Yes **9.27** [ ] No **9.28** [ ]

- If you came to the UK before 6 April 2001, has there been a relevant change in your circumstances or intentions during the year ended 5 April 2002? Yes **9.29** [ ] No **9.30** [ ] Not appropriate **9.31** [ ]

Information required if you are resident in the UK and you also claim to be resident in another country for the purposes of a Double Taxation Agreement

- In which country as well as the UK were you regarded as resident for 2001-02? **9.32** [ ]

- Were you also regarded as resident in the country in box 9.32 for 2000-01? Yes **9.33** [ ] No **9.34** [ ]

Information required if you are not resident or are resident in another country for the purpose of a Double Taxation Agreement and are claiming relief under a Double Taxation Agreement

- Amount of any relief you are claiming from UK tax if you are not resident in the UK or are dual resident **9.35** £ [ ]

You must fill in and send me the claim form in *Help Sheet IR302: Dual residents* or *Help Sheet IR304: Non residents - relief under Double Taxation Agreements* as applicable. These are available from the Orderline.

that the UK has signed up to with the different countries (also known as double taxation agreements). For example, if you are a Commonwealth citizen, a national of the European Economic Area or a resident of the Isle of Man or the Channel Islands, then you'll get the allowances, no problem. If you're a *national* of Bulgaria or a *resident* of Mauritius, then you'll also get the allowances but, for Macedonia, you'd have to be both a *national* and a *resident*. In these latter cases, you may need to support your claim with a certificate from the relevant tax authority to demonstrate residence and/or a passport (or other acceptable document) to demonstrate nationality. The situation with regard to certain former Soviet Union and Yugoslav states is, apparently, unclear. That's politics, I suppose.

The remaining boxes are pretty self-explanatory, if a little obscure. The best thing is not to worry too much about where they're coming from and stick to answering the questions. If you're claiming to be not ordinarily resident, then you need to back this up by providing the information in boxes **9.17** to **9.18**. If you're claiming split year treatment then it's boxes **9.25** and **9.26**, and if you're claiming not to be domiciled in the UK, you need to complete boxes **9.27** to **9.31**. If you are claiming to be resident in the UK, but also resident in another country for the purposes of a double taxation agreement, then you need to complete boxes **9.32** to **9.34**. Finally, **9.35** is for the amount of any relief you're claiming from UK tax, under a double taxation agreement, if you are not resident in the UK or are dual resident. If you have anything to put in **9.35**, then you'll also need to complete the claim form in *IR302: Dual residents* or *IR304: Non-Residents – relief under Double Taxation Agreements*.

Tax liability

All this matters because your residence (etc) status determines what you pay tax on, and therefore which other sections of the tax return you need to complete. To work this out, have a look at the tables on pages 8-12 of the Inland Revenue *Notes on Non-Residence*. Where you come across the word 'liable', you'll have another section of the tax return to fill in somewhere. In some cases, you'll find that you're 'liable on the remittance basis'. This means that you're potentially liable to tax for sums that were *received* into the UK during the year, regardless of when the income or gain actually arose. This contrasts with the normal 'arising basis', where it matters when the income arises rather than whether it was brought into the UK or not.

The Main Body of the Tax Return

So, after going around all the houses, of share schemes, trusts, foreign income and goodness knows what else (I hope it hasn't been too bad), we can finally get back to the main body of the tax return. This really is the home stretch, so pin your ears back and prepare for the final push.

What you'll need

The main theme of this section is income from UK savings and investments, so this is where you'll need to record any interest on cash deposits, dividends from shares and income received from pensions and the like. For each source of income, you should receive some sort of certificate or voucher setting out the amount of the income and the amount of the tax that's already been deducted before the income reached you.

So, for a cash savings account you should get a 'Statement of Income Received' and a 'Certificate of Tax Deducted'. Similarly, if you hold shares directly in a company, you should receive a 'Dividend Voucher' for the dividends paid during the year. YOU NEED TO HANG ON TO THESE THINGS! It's nigh-on impossible to fill in the tax return without them. You can get hold of replacements, but that might mean a lot of phone calls to a lot of people that haven't the first idea what you're on about. So you really need to have a special drawer somewhere where, without fail, you put these things as and when they arrive.

You will, of course, also need the tax return and the Inland Revenue guide to filling it in, available on the Internet at **www.inlandrevenue.gov.uk/sa/** or the orderline on 0845 9000 404. It might also help to get hold of the Inland Revenue helpsheet *IR110: A guide for people with savings*. It's on the Inland Revenue website at **www.inlandrevenue.gov.uk/pdfs/ir110.pdf**, or available from the orderline.

Did you receive any income from UK savings and investments?

At the top of page 3 of your tax return is what looks like a pretty simple question. 'Did you receive any income from UK savings and investments?' If you've kept all of your income statements, if any, then it *is* relatively simple, but there

BOX 1: INCOME FROM UK SAVINGS AND INVESTMENTS

Income from UK savings and investment *includes*:

- Interest from UK banks, building societies or deposit takers, including any interest on current accounts
- Interest distributions from UK authorized unit trusts or UK open-ended investment companies
- FIRST Option Bonds and Fixed Rate Savings Bonds
- Other income from National Savings (other than exclusions listed in box 2)
- Other savings and investment income, including purchased life annuities and relevant discounted securities
- Dividends from UK companies, UK authorized unit trusts or UK open-ended investment companies
- Other distributions
- UK scrip dividends
- Any interest, dividends, bonuses and other income from an invalid or voided Tax Exempt Special Savings Account (TESSA), Personal Equity Plan (PEP) or Individual Savings Account (ISA). Your TESSA operator, PEP manager, or ISA manager will give you details of the income to be included in your tax return
- If you are the beneficiary of a bare trust (one in which you have an immediate absolute title to (a share of) the capital and income), enter your (share or) income here. You should not include it in the Trusts etc pages. You may need to ask the trustees for details of your (share of) income
- Accrued income on the transfer of securities

Income from UK savings and investment *excludes*:

● Premium Bond, National Lottery and gambling prizes

● Interest, dividends and bonuses from a Tax Exempt Special Savings Account (TESSA) unless your TESSA closed before the five years were up – for details ask the orderline (0845 9000 404) for the leaflet *IR114: TESSA – tax-free interest for taxpayers*

● Interest, dividends and bonuses from an Individual Savings Account (ISA) – for details ask the orderline (0845 9000 404) for the leaflet *ISA/1: The answers on ISAs – your guide*

● Dividends and other income from a Personal Equity Plan (PEP), or interest paid on cash held in a PEP unless you draw more than £180 interest – for details ask the orderline for the leaflet *IR89: Personal Equity Plans*

● Interest and terminal bonuses under Save As You Earn schemes

● The first £70 of interest from a National Savings Ordinary Account

● Accumulated interest on National Savings Certificates, including index-linked certificates

● Interest on National Savings Children's Bonus Bonds

● Interest on Ulster Savings Certificates (if you normally live in Northern Ireland and lived there when you bought the certificates or when they were repaid)

● Interest awarded by a UK court as part of an award of damages for personal injury or death. If the interest is awarded by a foreign court, ask your Inland Revenue office about Statutory Concession A30

● Dividends on ordinary shares in a Venture Capital Trust where shares are within the limit of £100,000 acquired per tax year – for details ask the orderline for leaflet *Venture Capital Trusts (VCTs) – A brief guide*

● Adoption allowances paid under the provisions of the Adoption Allowance Regulations 1991 or schemes approved by the Secretary of State for Scotland under Section 51 Adoption (Scotland) Act 1988

● **If you are a trustee**, untaxed interest paid direct by the payer, acting through your authority, to beneficiaries who are entitled under trust to income as it arises.

BOX 2: INCOME FROM UK SAVINGS AND INVESMENT – EXCLUSIONS

are a few confusions. First of all, there are quite a few things that give you income but which don't have tax charged on them – such as premium bonds, certain National Savings products, ISAs and Tessas. The Inland Revenue has a list of things you should and shouldn't include as 'income from UK savings and investments' on page 8 of the *Notes* for the main body of the tax return. For convenience, we've reproduced them on pages 103 and 104.

Even these lists use some pretty funny language, though, so if you're at all unsure about whether you have any income to mention here, it's probably best to skip the question at the top of page 3 for the time being. Instead, we can go through the section box by box. If we end up by not filling anything in, then we can go back and answer 'no' to the question. Of course, if you're absolutely sure you didn't have any of this type of income, then forget I mentioned it, tick the 'no' box and move directly to Question 11 on page 4.

There are also various types of income that should be included elsewhere in the tax return. For instance, income from UK pensions and retirement annuities should be included in boxes **11.11** and **11.12** (See page 113). Gains made on UK life insurance policies, life annuities or capital redemption policies go in boxes **12.1** to **12.8** (see page 117).

If you received cash or shares as a 'building society windfall' when it was taken over or something, then depending on the circumstances, you might have to pay tax on the proceeds. If the payment is liable to income tax, then it should go in boxes **10.2** to **10.4**. If it's capital gains tax, then you may need to complete the Capital Gains Tax supplementary pages. Go back and have another look at question 8 on page 2 of the tax return. The building society itself should be able to tell you how the payment is treated. Otherwise, try the Inland Revenue's general tax helpline on 0845 9000 444.

One further point to mention before we get into the thick of it, is about the savings of any children that you have. If you have given money to your children (under the age of 18), which produces more than £100 income (before tax) in a tax year, then the *whole* of that income should be included on the tax return as *your* savings income.

Boxes 10.1 to 10.26 – Income from UK savings and investments

Boxes **10.1** to **10.4** cover interest earned on accounts with 'UK banks, building societies and other deposit takers'. These types of accounts tend to pay interest after deducting tax at the basic rate, but if you're a non-taxpayer, then you can fill out a form called an 'R85' to register to have the interest paid without tax being deducted. You can get these from banks and the Inland Revenue but, if you're a non-taxpayer, it's rather odd that you're filling out a tax return. Anyway, assuming that your accounts pay interest after tax has been deducted, you're going to be interested in boxes **10.2** to **10.4**. So, from your bank statements or any 'certificates of interest received', add up the totals and enter them in the boxes. But you knew that anyway.

For each type of income that goes in boxes **10.2** to **10.14**, you have to show the income before tax has been deducted, the amount of tax deducted and the income after tax has been deducted. Generally the income certificate or statement that you receive from the financial organization paying the interest will

---

Q10 **Did you receive any income from UK savings and investments?** **NO** [ ] **YES** [ ]

If yes, fill in boxes 10.1 to 10.26 as appropriate. Include only your share from any joint savings and investments.

■ *Interest*

● Interest from UK banks, building societies and deposit takers - *if you have more than one bank or building society etc account enter **totals** in the boxes.*

- enter any bank, building society etc interest that **has not** had tax taken off. (Most interest is taxed by your bank or building society etc. so make sure you should be filling in box 10.1, rather than boxes 10.2 to 10.4)

Taxable amount
10.1 £ [ ]

- enter details of your **taxed** bank or building society etc interest. *The Working Sheet on page 10 of your Tax Return Guide will help you fill in boxes 10.2 to 10.4.*

Amount **after** tax deducted	Tax deducted	Gross amount **before** tax
10.2 £ [ ]	**10.3** £ [ ]	**10.4** £ [ ]

● Interest distributions from UK authorised unit trusts and open-ended investment companies (dividend distributions go below)

Amount **after** tax deducted	Tax deducted	Gross amount **before** tax
10.5 £ [ ]	**10.6** £ [ ]	**10.7** £ [ ]

● National Savings (other than FIRST Option Bonds and Fixed Rate Savings Bonds and the first £70 of interest from a National Savings Ordinary Account)

Taxable amount
10.8 £ [ ]

● National Savings FIRST Option and Fixed Rate Savings Bonds

Amount **after** tax deducted	Tax deducted	Gross amount **before** tax
10.9 £ [ ]	**10.10** £ [ ]	**10.11** £ [ ]

● Other income from UK savings and investments (except dividends)

Amount **after** tax deducted	Tax deducted	Gross amount **before** tax
10.12 £ [ ]	**10.13** £ [ ]	**10.14** £ [ ]

Tax is deducted from interest on savings at the rate of 20 per cent or, in the language of vulgar fractions, they take away one fifth, or 1/5. If they take away one-fifth, or 1/5, then you're left with four fifths, or 4/5.

So, if you know the amount of interest before tax is deducted, the 'gross' interest, then you need to take one fifth of it (in other words divide by 5) to get the amount of tax deducted. The amount of interest that's left after deducting the tax, the 'net' interest, will be the other four-fifths of the gross interest (in other words, divide by 5, then multiply by 4).

If you know the amount of net interest, to work out the tax deducted and the gross interest you need to do everything in reverse. This means multiplying by 5/4 instead of 4/5. So, to get the gross interest from the net interest, you need to multiply the latter by five-fourths (in other words, divide by four and multiply by 5). The amount of tax that's been deducted is the extra quarter that's been added on, in other words, one quarter of the net tax.

Let's say we have gross interest of £50. To get the tax deducted we take one fifth of it, or £10. That leaves us with the other four-fifths, the net interest of £40 (which we can also get by dividing the £50 by 5 and multiplying by 4).

If we have net interest of £40, then to get the gross interest, we need to take five-fourths of it (in other words, divide by 4 and then multiply by 5). That gives us £50. The amount of interest deducted will be the extra quarter that's been added on, or £10.

show all three figures, but if not, you can work them out for yourself as shown in the box above. There is also a useful working sheet for boxes 10.2 to 10.4 on page 10 of the Inland Revenue's *Tax Return Guide*.

If you have any UK authorized unit trusts or open-ended investment companies (OEICs) that pay interest, then you need to enter these in boxes **10.5** to **10.7**. Note that these boxes are only for funds that pay interest. That will mean funds that have cash and/or bonds as their primary investment.

If you have a unit trust or OEIC that invests predominantly in shares, then it will pay dividends to you rather than interest, and it'll be boxes **10.18** to **10.20** that you're after. You can tell if something is a unit trust because your investment should be defined as a number of 'units'. If it's available to the general public in this country, then it should be 'authorized'. You have to be slightly careful, though, because some investment managers will operate their own in-house unit trusts for clients that may not be authorized (they should explain it to you if this is the case). OEICs have shares and are rather more difficult to spot. If you're not sure what you've got, then probably the easiest thing to do is to phone up the managers of the fund and ask them.

Bear in mind that you might be getting interest even though you don't receive anything. This is because you might have invested in 'accumulation units', as opposed to 'income units'. If so, then your interest will get rolled up in the value of your units instead of being paid out to you. All of this should be spelt out clearly (in a manner of speaking) in the tax voucher you receive from the unit trust or OEIC.

National Savings is a bit fiddly because some products are tax-free, while some aren't. In the tax-free category come Premium Bonds, Index-Linked and Fixed Rate Savings Certificates and Children's Bonus Bonds. You also don't have to pay tax on the first £70 of interest in a National Savings Ordinary Account. To confuse matters further, the Inland Revenue likes you to distinguish between interest from 'National Savings FIRST Option and Fixed-Rate Savings Bonds' (which goes in boxes **10.9** to **10.11**) and other taxable National Savings products (which goes in boxes **10.8**). If you're not sure whether your National Savings product is taxable, then try calling them up on 0845 964 5000. They've also got quite a fancy website, at **www.nationalsavings.co.uk**, in case you're a bit shy.

Boxes **10.12** to **10.14** sound like a catch-all, but the Inland Revenue is quite specific about what should be entered (the full low down is on pages 11 and 12 of the *Tax Return Guide*).

Interest not included in boxes 10.1 to 10.11
You should enter any interest earned on government bonds (also known as gilts), other loan stocks (such as 'corporate bonds') or loans to an individual or organization. You should also enter any interest earned from credit unions or friendly societies.

Where tax has been deducted on these types of payments, include the details in all three boxes, as you did for boxes **10.2** to **10.11**. It's quite possible, though, that some of these payments will come to you without the deduction of any tax. In this case, you should put the total received in both box **10.12** and **10.14** and leave **10.13** blank.

Relevant discounted securities and gilt 'strips'
Boxes **10.12** to **10.14** are also for gains that are deemed to count as interest on 'relevant discounted securities'. These are things that, instead of or as well as paying

interest, give you the bulk of your investment return by giving you more back after a number of years (when the security redeems) than you put in (hence the term discount because you buy them at a discount to what they will be worth).

For instance, if you buy something for £70 and will get £100 for it in 7 years' time, then it will be a relevant discounted security and, even though you haven't technically received interest on it, the Inland Revenue will deem you to have done so. If you think of it, you have effectively got interest (at the rate of 5.2 per cent per year in fact), because you've had the £30 on your investment of £70. It's just that you've received the interest all at once. Of course, you could say the same thing about a share or a house. At least you hope to sell them for more than you put in. The difference is in the certainty with which the greater amount will be available and when. If you think you might have a relevant discounted security, you should start by asking the company that provides it about its tax status.

With a relevant discounted security, you get taxed in the year you get the money from it, on the difference between what you get for it and what you paid for it. This figure should go in box **10.14**. Gilt strips, a form of Government bond, are an exception to this rule. With these, you pay tax on the amount that they've increased in value each tax year, and that amount goes in box **10.14**.

If you happen to get a loss from the disposal of a relevant discounted security (which is generally as difficult as it would be unfortunate), then you can set that loss against your taxable income for the year, by entering details in box **15.8** on page 5 of the tax return.

Transfer of income from securities
Well, we really are getting into the nitty-gritty now. It has been known for people to sell or transfer their right to the income from something to try to avoid the tax. Well, if you do this, the income is still deemed to be yours and it goes in box **10.14**.

Purchased life annuities
Annuities provide you with an income for life and you tend to get them with money built up in pension schemes or from retirement annuity contracts or trust schemes. Where this is the case, the income should go in boxes **11.10** to **11.14**. You can, however, buy an annuity with money that doesn't come from a pension. It would be unusual, since they generally don't make the best investments, but they can make sense in some circumstances. Anyway, if you've got an annuity that didn't come from a pension or a retirement annuity contract or

trust, then the annuity provider will provide you with a certificate detailing the figures that need to go in boxes **10.12** to **10.14**.

Accrued income

If you buy an interest-bearing security, such as government bonds (gilts), corporate bonds or 'permanent interest-bearing securities' (PIBS), then when you buy (and sell) them, the price may or may not include the interest that they've become entitled to since the last interest payment (known as accrued interest). In other words, the price may or may not have an element of interest rolled into it. Since the Inland Revenue is only aiming to charge you tax on interest that accrues while you actually own the security, there may be an adjustment to make when you buy or sell securities with or without accrued interest. The good news is that you don't have to worry about any of this so long as you never owned more than £5,000 worth, by nominal value, of interest-bearing securities in 2001/2 or 2000/1 tax years.

If you did have more than £5,000 worth at any stage in those two years, then the adjustment is the amount by which the price was increased or reduced as a result of the accrued interest, but it can break both ways. If you buy securities without accrued interest or sell them with accrued interest, there's a charge to income tax. If you buy securities with the accrued interest or sell them without the accrued interest, then there's a relief against income tax.

For each kind of security, you need to combine the charges and reliefs to produce a net figure. Where the net figure is a charge to income tax, then you need to combine the total amount in box **10.14**. Where the reliefs exceed the charges for a kind of security, deduct the excess from the 'gross' interest received from that kind of security and enter the reduced amount of interest in box **10.14**. The figure in box **10.13** should not be changed. There's more about this on pages 11 and 12 of the *Tax Return Guide*.

Boxes 10.15 to 10.26 – Dividends

For basic-rate, starting-rate and non-taxpayers, the taxation of dividends is very straightforward. You simply get your dividend from the company and pay no further tax on it. For higher-rate taxpayers, the basic situation is also pretty simple: you have to pay tax of 25 per cent of the net dividends that you receive. Unfortunately, though, that's just too easy, so the Inland Revenue makes you calculate something that it calls a tax credit (though that description stretches the truth somewhat) and fill in an extra couple of boxes. For various peculiar reasons, the tax credit is calculated as one-ninth of the dividend payment that you receive. So, if you imagine that you receive a dividend of £90, then the tax credit will be one-ninth of that, or £10. The dividend plus the tax credit will therefore be £100. The latter two figures are really just there to cause trouble though. You have to enter them in the boxes, but the bottom line is that a higher-rate taxpayer that receives a £90 dividend has to cough up £22.50, that is 25 per cent of the £90, in tax.

Dividends and other qualifying distributions from UK companies
Boxes **10.15** to **10.17** are for dividends and 'other qualifying distributions' from UK companies (if you get dividends from foreign companies, then you need to fill in the Foreign pages – see Chapter 6). Straightforward dividends should be accompanied by a 'dividend voucher'. This shows the amount of the dividend and tax credit. The total of your dividends goes in box **10.15**, the total tax credits go in **10.16** and you add those two boxes together to get the figure for box **10.17**.

'Other qualifying distributions' refers to things that companies sometimes do that don't necessarily look much like dividends, but which the Inland Revenue thinks are similar enough and therefore treats as such. The *Notes* say that a qualifying distribution is a distribution that isn't a non-qualifying distribution – and then goes on to describe non-qualifying distributions. Part of that description states that 'a non-qualifying distribution is... a bonus issue by a company of securities or redeemable shares (except a bonus issue giving rise to a qualifying distribution)'. On any basis, the definitions are not ideal.

You can try to make sense of them if you like, but really the best thing to do is look at the documentation that the company sends out with these deals. Somewhere there should be a section called 'Taxation to UK Residents' or some such, and it should tell you what to do. If you don't have the relevant documents or can't work them out, call up the company and ask for the investor relations department or, failing that, the company secretary's office. They should be able to tell you how the distribution is classified. If your distribution is 'qualifying' then you should enter the information in boxes **10.15** to **10.17** and give details

■ *Dividends*

● Dividends and other qualifying distributions from UK companies | Dividend/distribution **10.15** £ | Tax credit **10.16** £ | Dividend/distribution **plus** credit **10.17** £

in the additional information section (box **23.5**). Something along the lines of 'B Share issue by Pink Elephants PLC on 25 October 2001' should do the trick.

Dividend distributions from UK authorized
unit trusts and open-ended investment companies

You should receive a dividend voucher from your unit trust or OEIC manager that sets out the dividend and tax credit. These go in boxes **10.18** and **10.19** and the totals in these boxes are added together to get the figure for box **10.20**. If you haven't got a dividend voucher, then you'll need to phone up and ask for one. If you're not sure whether what you've got is a 'UK authorized unit trust or open-ended investment company', then see the comments on page 109 about boxes **10.5** to **10.7**. Ultimately, though, the easiest way to check is to phone up the managers and ask.

Note that if you have accumulation units (that is, your income gets automatically rolled up into new units), then you still have to pay income tax on the income that has accumulated. As before, the details of the net dividend and the tax credit should be on your dividend voucher. If you've bought new units during the year, there will probably be something on your dividend voucher called 'equalisation'. Note that this is not income and shouldn't be declared here. (Instead, it should be deducted from the purchase price of your units for capital gains tax purposes.)

Dividend distributions from UK authorised unit trusts and open-ended investment companies	Dividend/distribution	Tax credit	Dividend/distribution **plus credit**
	10.18 £	**10.19** £	**10.20** £

Scrip dividends from UK companies

Scrip dividends are where you opt for extra shares in a company instead of the cash dividend. Note that this is different from a 'dividend reinvestment plan', where you do actually get the cash dividend – it's just that it gets used immediately to buy extra shares. Scrip dividends are quite unusual these days, but if you get one, it should come with a dividend voucher showing what the 'appropriate amount in cash' of the dividend is, as well as the tax credit. These amounts should be entered in boxes **10.21** and **10.22**. Add them together to get the total to be entered in box **10.23**.

Scrip dividends from UK companies	Dividend	Notional tax	Dividend **plus notional tax**
	10.21 £	**10.22** £	**10.23** £

Non-qualifying distributions and loans written off

As mentioned under 'qualifying distributions' above, the definition of non-qualifying distributions is not ideal. The best thing to do is to check the documentation that the company sent out about the deal. If that doesn't make sense, then call the company up and ask for the investor relations department or the company secretary's office. They should be able to tell you how the distribution should be treated.

			Notional tax		Taxable amount	
● Non-qualifying distributions and loans written off	**10.24** £		**10.25** £		**10.26** £	

Boxes 11.1 to 11.13 – UK Pensions, retirement annuities and social security benefits

In the same way as before, this section starts off by asking a seemingly simple question: 'Did you receive a taxable UK pension, retirement annuity or Social Security benefit?' On the whole, it should *be* pretty simple, too, but there can be confusion if you get some of the more unusual Social Security benefits. Again, though, the Inland Revenue *Notes* provide a helpful list of things to include and exclude. These are reproduced in the boxes on pages 114–15. Some of the more esoteric items are rather complicated, but hopefully if they apply to you, they'll leap off the page and everything will be crystal clear. In any case, we haven't really the space to go into it all here. If you think something applies to you and it's not making sense, a quick call to the helpline (0845 9000 444) or your local tax office should give you the answers.

So, having said all that, you should be in a position to put a tick in either the 'yes' or the 'no' box. If you're a 'no', you can move straight along to question 12. If you're a 'yes', then you need to spell it all out in boxes **11.1** to **11.4**. These are pretty self-explanatory and the various figures should be included in the statements you get from each source of income.

The State Retirement Pension that goes in box **11.1** should include the basic old age pension, plus any additional 'State Earnings Related Pensions' (SERPS), graduated pension and age addition if you are over 80. You should also include any incapacity addition or addition for a dependent adult. The Christmas Bonus and Winter Fuel Payment are not taxable and should not be included. Your local benefits office should be able to produce a form (the BR735) detailing your benefits through the tax year.

Taxable UK pensions, retirement annuities and Social Security benefits *include*:

- State Retirement Pension
- Widow's Pension or Bereavement Allowance
- Widowed Mother's Allowance or Widowed Parent's Allowance
- Industrial Death Benefit Pension (but not Child Allowance)
- Jobseeker's Allowance
- Invalid Care Allowance
- Statutory Sick Pay and Statutory Maternity Pay paid by the Inland Revenue
- Taxable Incapacity Benefit
- Other pensions or retirement annuities paid by someone in the UK. These include pensions or annuities
  - From a former employer
  - From your late husband's or wife's employer
  - From personal pension plans
  - From Free-Standing Additional Voluntary Contributions (FSAVC) schemes
  - For injuries at work or for work-related illnesses
  - From service in the armed forces
  - From retirement annuity contracts or trust schemes (but not purchased life annuities)
- Income withdrawals from personal pension plans where the purchase of an annuity has been deferred

ALLOWABLE BENEFITS

If you were receiving the Jobseeker's allowance at the end of the tax year, then the Department of Social Security (DSS) should give you a form P60U, by 31 May following the end of the tax year, telling you the figure to go in box **11.5**. If you received the Jobseeker's allowance during the year, but stopped getting it before the end of the tax year, then you should have been given a P45U providing the information for box **11.5**.

Statutory Sick Pay and Statutory Maternity Pay will generally have been paid by your employer and, in which case, will need to be included in the relevant section of the Employment pages (see Chapter 1). Otherwise, the total for the year needs to go in box **11.7**.

If you received Incapacity Benefit during the year, then the Department for Works and Pensions will give you a form (a P60(IB) or P45(IB) depending on whether you're still getting it at the end of the tax year). This will tell you the amount to put in boxes **11.8** and **11.9**.

NON-ALLOWABLE BENEFITS

Taxable UK pensions, retirement annuities and social security benefits *exclude*:

- Additions to your State Pension or Social Security benefits that you get because you have a dependent child. These **are not taxable**. But include additions for adult dependents; these **are taxable**
- Jobfinder's grant
- New Deal training allowance – if, instead of a training allowance, you received a wage from a New Deal employment, it should be included in box 1.8 of the Employment Pages for that employment
- Employment Zone payments
- Maternity Allowance, which is **not taxable**. (Statutory Maternity Pay is taxable. Include Statutory Maternity Pay paid by the Department of Social Security in box 11.7 and Statutory Maternity Pay paid by your employer in boxes 1.8 to 1.10 on the Employment Pages)
- War Widow's pension, and some pensions paid to other dependents of deceased Forces and Merchant Navy personnel, are not taxable. Sometimes these are not paid, or are reduced, because you get another State pension or benefit such as a pension from overseas. Where this happens, it reduces the taxable amount of the other pension or benefit you receive. Ask the orderline (0845 9000 404) for helpsheet *IR310: War Widow's and dependent's pensions*, which tells you how to work out the taxable amount
- Pensions for wounds or disability in military service or for other war injuries
- Pensions or benefits you get under the rules of another country (even if they are paid to you by the Employment Service or the Department For Works and Pensions on behalf of that other country). These overseas pensions go on the Foreign pages, available from the oderline (0845 9000 404)
- Refunds of surplus funds from additional voluntary contributions. These go in boxes 12.10 to 12.12
- Purchased life annuities. These go in boxes 10.12 to 10.14.

Boxes **11.10** to **11.13** are for any non-state pensions that you receive from companies and financial institutions in the UK. This will include 'occupational' pensions paid by your, or your spouse's, former employer, as well as income from annuities resulting from personal pension schemes, Free-Standing Additional Voluntary Contribution schemes and retirement annuity contracts. If you have deferred taking an annuity under one of these schemes and, in the meantime, are making income withdrawals (also known as 'income draw-

Q11 **Did you receive a taxable UK pension, retirement annuity or Social Security benefit?** *Read the notes on pages 13 to 15 of the Tax Return Guide.* **NO** **YES** If yes, fill in boxes 11.1 to 11.14 as appropriate.

■ *State pensions and benefits* Taxable amount for 2001-02

● State Retirement Pension - *enter the **total** of your entitlements for the year* **11.1** £

● Widow's Pension or Bereavement Allowance **11.2** £

● Widowed Mother's Allowance or Widowed Parent's Allowance **11.3** £

● Industrial Death Benefit Pension **11.4** £

● Jobseeker's Allowance **11.5** £

● Invalid Care Allowance **11.6** £

● Statutory Sick Pay and Statutory Maternity Pay paid by the Inland Revenue **11.7** £

Tax deducted / Gross amount **before** tax

● Taxable Incapacity Benefit **11.8** £ **11.9** £

■ *Other pensions and retirement annuities*

● Pensions (other than State pensions) and retirement annuities - *if you have more than one pension or annuity please give details of each one in box 11.14* Amount **after** tax deducted **11.10** £ Tax deducted **11.11** £ Gross amount **before** tax **11.12** £

11.14

● Deduction - *see the note for box 11.13 on page 15 of your Tax Return Guide* Amount of deduction **11.13** £

down'), then you should include this income here also. The information for these boxes will be included in the P60 that you should have received from the payer of your pension before 31 May following the end of the tax year.

Box **11.13** has the appealing title 'deduction' but is, unfortunately, only going to be relevant to those who have pensions that relate to some form of service to overseas governments. If that's you, then start by looking at page 15 of the *Tax Return Guide*.

Boxes 12.1 to 12.12 – Gains on UK life policies or refunds of surplus funds from AVCs

Again, we start off with a question. This time it's 'Did you receive any gains on UK life policies or refunds of surplus funds from AVCs?' If the answer to this might be 'yes', then hopefully you'll know all about it. On the other hand, if you haven't any idea what this question's about, there's a fair chance that you're a 'no'.

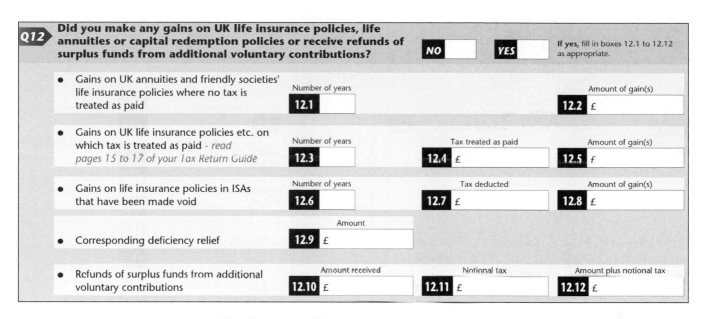

The first part of the question – gains on UK life policies – refers to 'chargeable events' affecting life insurance policies (and 'life annuities' and 'capital redemption policies'). Chargeable events basically occur when value flows out of your policy. This might happen on the death of the life insured, or on a part surrender, sale or gift of the policy, or on the payment of a cash bonus. When these things happen, they might give rise to a taxable gain. In this case, you should be sent a 'chargeable event notice' by the insurance company telling you the figures to go in boxes **12.1** to **12.9**. The *Tax Return Guide* goes into some detail about all this on pages 15–17. There is also the Inland Revenue helpsheet *IR320: Gains on UK life insurance policies.*

The second part of the question, refunds of surplus funds from AVCs, relates to the overfunding of Additional Voluntary Contribution schemes (AVCs). AVCs are essentially a means by which you can top up your company pension. The trouble is that you can top them up too much, and since the government limits how much you can put into pensions, a surplus may be repaid to you when you stop work. In which case, you should have received a certificate from your pension provider showing the figures to go in boxes **12.10** to **12.12**.

Boxes 13.1 to 13.6 –
Other taxable income not entered elsewhere

Terrified that they might not have wrung every last penny of tax out of you, the Inland Revenue closes off the business end of your tax return with the ultimate

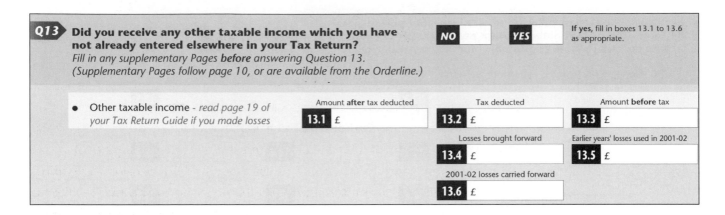

in vague 'you tell me' questions. 'Did you receive any other taxable income which you have not already entered elsewhere in your tax return?' This question essentially places the onus on you to make sure you do your best to declare everything.

Just to help you along, the *Notes* provide (on pages 17 and 18) a few examples of 'other income' that might have slipped through the net elsewhere: things like 'profits from isolated literary or artistic activities' and 'sale of patent rights if you received a capital sum'. Did you take £20 from your mate for posting flyers about her business through a thousand letterboxes? This is your chance to come clean. Of course, if something amounts to a trade, then the correct place for it would be the Self-Employment, Partnership or Land & Property supplementary pages. This 'other income' section is really for one-offs. If you're not sure where you stand, then the helpline (0845 9000 444) is a good place to start, as would be your local tax office.

Where you have expenses that 'had to be spent solely to earn the income' and which were not spent 'for private or personal reasons' and which were 'not spent on something that you intend to keep for a while (such as a computer)', you can deduct them from your gross income in arriving at your taxable income. Of course it's possible that your 'isolated artistic activity' wasn't the greatest success, and you ended up getting less for it than you paid for the paint. In this case, you'll need to record your losses in boxes **13.1** to **13.6**. These can be set against some types of income in the 'other income' section or, if there is no such 'other income', then they can be carried forward to be used against similar income in the future. If you think you have anything to go in this section, then you should start by getting hold of the Inland Revenue helpsheet *IR325: Other taxable income.*

Boxes 14.1 to 14.17 –
Relief for pension contributions

Where you make contributions to an occupational pension scheme, that is, via your employer, then the tax relief on your contributions is dealt with at source by your payroll people. It therefore doesn't need mentioning here. Instead, this bit is for pension contributions that you make off your own bat, out of your own taxed income (or taxable income/earnings if you're self-employed).

You can only contribute so much of your earnings to a pension, depending on your age, and the relevant amounts are shown in the box below. The picture is complicated, though, by the ability to shuffle contributions between different years. For the complete picture, get hold of Inland Revenue helpsheet *IR330: Pension payments*.

Boxes **14.1** to **14.5** are for payments made to retirement annuity contracts taken out before 1 Jully 1988. The gross amount of qualifying payments in the tax year (that is, those that come within the limits) go into box **14.1**. Box **14.2** is for payments for which you've already claimed relief in an earlier year and **14.3** is for payments that you are now carrying back to a previous year. **14.4** is for payments, made between 5 April 2002 and the date you send in your tax return, for which you want to claim relief now. Page 20 of the *Tax Return Guide* and the helpsheet *IR330: Pension Payments* explain when, and to what extent, you can carry your retirement annuity payments forward and back. Box **14.5** is for your total relief claimed on retirement annuity contracts, which you get by deducting boxes **14.2** and **14.3** (but not **14.4**) from **14.1**.

	Age at beginning of tax year	Maximum percentage of earnings that you can contribute to a pension	Maximum percentage of earnings that you can contribute to a retirement annuity contract
MAXIMUM PENSION CONTRIBUTIONS	35 or less	17.5%	17.5%
	36-45	20.0%	17.5%
	46-50	25.0%	17.5%
	51-55	30.0%	20.0%
	56-60	35.0%	22.5%
	61-74	40.0%	27.5%

Q14 **Do you want to claim relief for your pension contributions?** NO [ ] YES [ ] If yes, fill in boxes 14.1 to 14.11 as appropriate.

Do not include contributions deducted from your pay by your employer to their pension scheme or associated AVC scheme, because tax relief is given automatically. But **do include** *your contributions to personal pension schemes and Free-Standing AVC schemes.*

■ *Payments to your retirement annuity contracts - only fill in boxes 14.1 to 14.5 for policies taken out before 1 July 19*
 See the notes on page 19 of your Tax Return Guide.

| Qualifying payments made in 2001-02 | **14.1** £ | 2001-02 payments used in an earlier year | **14.2** £ | Relief claimed box 14.1 *minus* (boxes 14.2 and 14.3, but not 14.4) |
| 2001-02 payments now to be carried back | **14.3** £ | Payments brought back from 2002-03 | **14.4** £ | **14.5** £ |

■ *Payments to your personal pension (including stakeholder pension) contracts - enter the amount of the payment you made with the basic rate tax added (the* **gross** *payment). See the note for box 14.6 on page 21 of your Tax Return Guide.*

Gross qualifying payments made in 2001-02	**14.6** £	
2001-02 gross payments carried back to 2000-01	**14.7** £	Relief claimed box 14.6 *minus* box 14.7 (but not 14.8)
Gross qualifying payments made between 6 April 2002 and 31 January 2003 brought back to 2001-02 - *see page 22 of your Tax Return Guide*	**14.8** £	**14.9** £

■ *Contributions to other pension schemes and Free-Standing AVC schemes*

● Amount of contributions to employer's schemes **not deducted** at source from pay **14.10** £

● Gross amount of Free-Standing Additional Voluntary Contributions paid in 2001-02 **14.11** £

Boxes **14.6** to **14.11** are for payments to personal pensions, which includes the new 'stakeholder pensions'. New rules on pensions make it possible for people to contribute up to £2,808 to a personal pension, *even if they're not working*. And you'll still get tax relief, taking your contributions up to £3,600 even if you're not paying tax. If you are working, you can contribute more: up to the limits in the box on page 119 in fact. We say more about pensions in Chapter 17 and there's a lot of detail on pages 20 to 22 of the *Tax Return Guide*. Anyway, for present purposes, start with the total amount of the qualifying payments in box **14.6**, fill in the boxes **14.7** and **14.8** for 'carry-back' (see helpsheet *IR330: Pension payments*), and do the sum for the final box in each section.

Boxes **14.10** and **14.11** are for top-up contributions to an occupational pension scheme via Additional Voluntary Contributions (AVCs) and Free-Standing Additional Voluntary Contributions (FSAVCs). In the case of AVCs, your contributions will almost certainly be made out of your pay packet, and tax relief will therefore be given at source. In which case, there will be nothing to go in box **14.10**. However, in certain circumstances, like a lump sum contribution, the AVC contribution might be made out of taxed income and you'll need to claim relief by entering the amount in box **14.10**. Contributions to an

FSAVC, on the other hand, will be made out of your taxed income and you will not have received tax relief at source. You'll therefore need to enter the gross amount of your contributions to FSAVCs in box **14.11**.

Boxes 15.1 to 15.12 – Other reliefs

So you're asked the question, 'Do you want to claim any of the following reliefs?' and the answer can only be, 'Er, well, yes, maybe, what have you got?' So you've got to go down the list one by one. Unfortunately, and you probably won't be surprised to hear this, most of them only apply in unusual situations.

Box **15.1** is to claim relief for interest on 'qualifying loans'. These would be loans to buy shares in, or otherwise fund a close company (see page 19 for what these are), or to buy an interest in a partnership, or to buy plant and machinery for your work. For more information, try the encouragingly-named helpsheet *IR340: Interest eligible for relief on qualifying loans.*

Box **15.2** is for maintenance payments or alimony paid to support your child or former spouse, but it will only apply in a few cases. First of all, it's only relevant if you or your former spouse was born before 6 April 1935. The payments also have to be made in accordance with some form of binding agreement or court order and your former spouse must not have remarried. There are a number of other requirements, but if this is beginning to sound familiar, then you should go to page 23 of the *Tax Return Guide* and get hold of helpsheet *IR121: Income tax and pensioners.*

Subscriptions for shares in Venture Capital Trusts (VCTs) may qualify for tax relief up to a total of £100,000. VCTs are funds that invest in certain types of generally small and generally very risky, up and (hopefully) coming companies. If you've put money into these things, then you should put the amount,

Q15	**Do you want to claim any of the following reliefs?**		
	If you have made any Gift Aid payments or other annual payments, after basic rate tax, answer 'Yes' to Question 15 and fill in boxes 15.5 and 15.9, as appropriate.	NO YES	If yes, fill in boxes 15.1 to 15.12, as appropriate.

		Amount of payment
●	Interest eligible for relief on qualifying loans	**15.1** £

		Amount claimed up to £2,070
●	Maintenance or alimony payments you have made under a court order, Child Support Agency assessment or legally binding order or agreement - if **you** were born after 5 April 1935, enter your former spouse's date of birth in the 'Additional information' box, box 23.5 - one of you must have been 65 or over on 5 April 2000 for you to claim the relief - *see page 23 of your Tax Return Guide*	**15.2** £

		Amount on which relief is claimed
●	Subscriptions for Venture Capital Trust shares (up to £100,000)	**15.3** £

	Amount on which relief is claimed
• Subscriptions under the Enterprise Investment Scheme (up to £150,000)	**15.4** £

	Total amount of payments made
• Gift Aid and payments under charitable covenants	**15.5** £

	One-off payments
• Enter in box 15.6 the total of any 'one-off' payments included in box 15.5	**15.6** £

	Amount of relief claimed
• Gifts of qualifying investments to charities	**15.7** £

	Amount of payment
• Post-cessation expenses, pre-incorporation losses brought forward and losses on relevant discounted securities, etc. - *see page 24 of your Tax Return Guide*	**15.8** £

up to £100,000, in box **15.3**. There's more information in the Inland Revenue leaflet *Venture Capital Trusts (VCTs), a brief guide.*

Some share subscriptions may be entitled to income tax relief under the Enterprise Investment Scheme (EIS). If so, you should have received a form EIS3 or EIS5, and the amount of relief you're claiming should go in box **15.4**. You'll also need to put details of the investment in box **23.5**, Additional Information'. There's more information in helpsheet *IR341: Enterprise Investment Scheme – income tax relief.*

Box **15.5** is for gifts made to charity under 'Gift Aid', or charitable covenants entered into before 6 April 2000. These payments are treated as having been made out of your income after basic rate tax has been deducted, so that the charity can reclaim the basic rate tax and you've effectively made a tax-free gift that's larger than the money you actually handed over. If you pay tax at the higher rate, though, you can get relief against your own income tax, the effect of which is to save you tax and make your gift, in pre-tax terms, that little bit smaller (because you're getting the tax relief rather than the charity). Either way, you should enter the amount of any of these payments made during the tax year in box **15.5**. If any of the payments included in box **15.5** was 'one-off' in nature, then it helps the Inland Revenue to get you tax code right for the future if you enter the amount of the 'one-off payments' in box **15.6**. There's more information about this in various Inland Revenue leaflets: *IR342: Charitable giving; IR65: Giving to charity by individuals; and IR64: Giving to charity by businesses.*

Gifts to charity can also be made in the form of shares or other 'qualifying investments'. If you made such gifts to charity during the year, then include the value of the gifts made in box **15.7**. More details about this can be found in *IR342: Charitable giving* and *IR178: Giving shares and securities to charity.*

If you ran a business and incurred expenses after you ceased trading ('post-cessation expenses'), then you may be entitled to income tax relief on account of them. Similarly, if you have a business that has losses carried forward (see pages 46–7) and you then turn it into a company (pre-incorporation losses), you might be entitled to set those losses against your income from that company. If you think this might apply to you, then start by looking at page 22 of the Inland Revenue's *Tax Return Guide*. Beyond that, you might need to talk to a tax adviser. Any post-cessation expenses and pre-incorporation losses that you're allowed to use should be entered in box **15.8**. This is also the box to enter any losses made on 'relevant discounted securities' (see the comments on these things on page 108–9).

Payments received under annuities and covenants 'entered into for full value for genuine commercial reasons in connection with the payer's trade or profession' are entitled to relief from higher rate tax, and should be entered in box **15.9**, excluding the amount of any basic rate tax that's treated as having been deducted.

If you make payments to a trade union or friendly society entitling you to some form of pension, life assurance or funeral benefits, then you can claim tax relief *on half of the part of the payment that pays for those benefits*. Your trade union or friendly society should be able to tell you how much of your payments can be claimed for. This figure should be entered into box **15.10**.

Where you are required to make payments to a scheme that provides a pension or other financial support for your spouse or children in the event of your death, you might be entitled to tax relief. Generally this will be dealt with at source by your payroll people at work, and you won't need to claim. However, in some circumstances, where for instance you've had to make a lump sum contribution, you might need to make a claim for relief. If this is the case, then your employer should be able to give you the figure to go in box **15.11**.

If in the past you've received a 'bonus issue of shares or securities' and these are subsequently redeemed (that is, cancelled by the company in return for a

		Payments made
● Annuities and annual payments	**15.9**	£
		Half amount of payment
● Payments to a trade union or friendly society for death benefits	**15.10**	£
● Payment to your employer's compulsory widow's, widower's or orphan's benefit scheme *- available in some circumstances – **first** read the notes on page 25 of your Tax Return Guide*	**15.11**	Relief claimed £
		Relief claimed
● Relief claimed on a qualifying distribution on the **redemption** of bonus shares or securities.	**15.12**	£

cheque sent to you – hopefully you'll know about it if it happens), then the money you receive from them is treated as a 'qualifying distribution' and taxed accordingly (by being entered in box **10.17** – see page 111). However, you get tax relief for the upper dividend rate tax that you paid when the shares or securities were issued in the first place, and this needs to be entered in box **15.12**. If you're in this particular boat, then the documentation provided by the company should help. If necessary, call up the investor relations department or company secretary's office and ask them what's going on.

Boxes 16.1 to 16.18 – Allowances

When it comes to allowances, again it's a question of, 'Well, what have you got?' Allowances basically 'allow' you an amount of income that you can receive free of tax, or on which you pay a specially low rate of tax. Everyone receives the 'personal allowance', which was worth £4,535 in the 2001/2 tax year, and means that you can essentially knock that amount off your income before you work out the tax due on the rest (if you're above the age of 65, then it may also increase as you get older depending on your income). Since everyone gets the personal allowance, you don't have to claim it, but there are three others: the blind person's allowance, the married couple's allowance and the Children's Tax Credit. There's also something called 'transfer of surplus allowance', which involves shuffling the allowances between husband and wife.

Blind person's allowance
If you're registered as blind with your local authority, then you will qualify for the blind person's allowance. If you live in Scotland or Northern Ireland, you don't get registered, but the test is the same, which is that you are 'so blind that you are unable to perform any work for which eyesight is essential'. There are more details on this in the leaflet *IR170: Blind Person's Allowance* and this is available on the Inland Revenue's website which, incidentally, has won a 'web-sight'

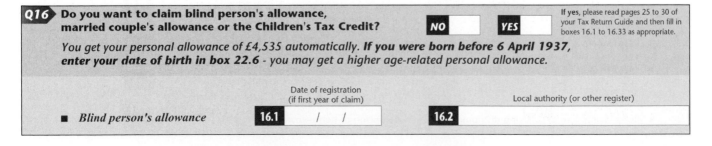

award for accessibility from the Royal National Institute for the Blind (RNIB). If you suffer from poor eyesight, you should contact the RNIB on 0207 388 1266, or on the Internet at www.rnib.com, for information and guidance about your tax return and state benefits.

Married couple's allowance

The married couple's allowance is only available if you, or your spouse, were born before 6 April 1935 (it was removed in 2000, but they wanted to keep it for people that were over 65 at that point). If this is you, then you'll need to fill in boxes **16.3** to **16.13**; otherwise move on to box **16.14**. In the 2001/2 tax year, the allowance gave you a band of £5,365 on which you get tax relief of 10 per cent. The allowance may reduce depending on your income and may increase if either spouse is over the age of 75.

Full details of the Married Couple's Allowance can be found on pages 26 and 27 of the *Tax Return Guide.* It's more than a little fiddly, but the boxes on the

---

■ *Married couple's allowance -* *In 2001-02 married couple's allowance can only be claimed if either you, or your husband or wife, were born* ***before 6 April 1935****. So you can only claim the allowance in 2001-02 if either of you had reached* ***65 years of age before 6 April 2000****. Further guidance is given beginning on page 26 of your Tax Return Guide.*

If **both** you and your husband or wife were born after 5 April 1935 you cannot claim; **do not** complete boxes 16.3 to 16.13.

If **you can claim** fill in boxes 16.3 and 16.4 if you are a married man or if you are a married woman and you are claiming half or all of the married couple's allowance.

- Enter your date of birth (if born before 6 April 1935) **16.3** / /

- Enter your spouse's date of birth (**if born before 6 April 1935 and** if older than you) **16.4** / /

Then, if you are a married man fill in boxes 16.5 to 16.9. If you are a married woman fill in boxes 16.10 to 16.13.

- Wife's full name **16.5**　　　　　　　　　　　　　　　　● Date of marriage (if after 5 April 2001) **16.6** / /

- Tick box 16.7 if you or your wife have allocated half of the minimum amount of the allowance to her **16.7**

- Tick box 16.8 if you and your wife have allocated all of the minimum amount of the allowance to her **16.8**

- Enter in box 16.9 the date of birth of any previous wife with whom you lived at any time during 2001-02. *Read 'Special rules if you are a man who married in the year ended 5 April 2002' on page 27 before completing box 16.9.* **16.9** / /

- Tick box 16.10 if you or your husband have allocated half of the minimum amount of the allowance to you **16.10**

- Tick box 16.11 if you and your husband have allocated all of the minimum amount of the allowance to you **16.11**

- Husband's full name **16.12**　　　　　　　　　　　　　　　　● Date of marriage (if after 5 April 2001) **16.13** / /

---

tax return are relatively straightforward if you follow the instructions. Boxes **16.3** and **16.4** are for the dates of birth of you and/or your spouse. Then, if you're the man, you need to fill in boxes **16.5** to **16.9** with your wife's name, the date of the marriage (if after the beginning of the tax year) and whether any elections have been made. If you're the woman, you need to fill in boxes **16.10** to **16.13** with the same information.

Children's Tax Credit
Boxes 16.14 to 16.26 are for the Children's Tax Credit, which is a tax relief for people that have at least one child under the age of 16 living with them. The precise rules state that the child is either your own, a stepchild, an adopted child, or a child that you look after at your own expense (meaning that you must meet half of the child's maintenance costs for the period that he or she is living with you). The child must also be under 16 at the start of the tax year and must live with you for at least part of the year. Where it is only for part of the year, then you have to reach agreement with whoever else the child lived with about how to share the relief (if you can't reach an agreement, then someone at the Inland Revenue will decide for you).

The credit can only be claimed for one child (except sometimes in the case of seperated couples) and it gives relief on up to £5,200 of income at the rate of

---

■ ***Children's Tax Credit*** *– even if you have already completed a separate Children's Tax Credit (CTC) claim form and received the relief in your tax code, you should still fill in boxes 16.14 to 16.26, as directed. Any reference to 'partner' in this question means the person you lived with during the year to 5 April 2002 – your husband or wife, or someone you lived with as husband or wife. Guidance for claiming CTC is on pages 27 to 29 of your Tax Return Guide. Please read the notes before completing your claim, particularly if either you, or your partner, were liable to tax above the basic rate in the year to 5 April 2002.*

- Enter in box 16.14 the date of birth of a child living with you who was born on or after 6 April 1985. *It generally makes sense to claim for the youngest child*

  16.14 [/ /]

- Tick box 16.15 if the child was your own child or one you looked after at your own expense. If not, you cannot claim CTC – go to box 16.27, if appropriate, or Question 17.

  16.15 [ ]

- Tick box 16.16 if the child lived with you **throughout** the year to 5 April 2002.

  16.16 [ ]

  If you ticked box 16.16 and
  - you were a lone or single claimant, you have finished this question; go to Question 17,
  - you have a partner, go to box 16.18.

- If the child lived with you for only **part of the year** you may only be entitled to a proportion of the CTC. Enter in box 16.17 your share in £s that **you have agreed** with any other claimants that you may claim for this child. But leave boxes 16.17 to 16.25 blank if you separated from, or started living with, your partner during the year to 5 April 2002. Special rules apply to work out your entitlement; ask the Orderline for *Help Sheet IR343: Claiming Children's Tax Credit when your circumstances change* which explains how to complete box 16.26.

  16.17 £ [   ]

If you lived with your partner (for CTC this means your husband or wife, or someone you lived with as husband and wife) for the whole of the year to 5 April 2002, fill in boxes 16.18 to 16.25 as appropriate.

- Enter in box 16.18 your partner's surname   **16.18**

- Enter in box 16.19 your partner's National Insurance number   **16.19**

- Tick
  - box 16.20 if **you** had the higher income in the year to 5 April 2002,   **16.20**

  or

  - box 16.21 if **your partner** had the higher income in that year   **16.21**

- Tick box 16.22 if either of you were chargeable to tax above the basic rate limit in the year to 5 April 2002.   **16.22**

If you ticked boxes 16.20 and 16.22 your entitlement will be reduced – see page 29 of your Tax Return Guide; your partner cannot claim CTC - go to box 16.28, or Question 17 as appropriate.

If you ticked boxes 16.21 and 16.22 your partner's entitlement will be reduced; you cannot claim CTC – go to box 16.27, or Question 17, as appropriate.

*If **neither** of you were chargeable above the basic rate and **you** had the lower income **and***
- *you don't want to claim half of the entitlement to CTC, and*
- *you didn't make an election for CTC to go to the partner with the lower income*

you have finished this part of your Return - go to boxes 16.27 or 16.28, or Question 17, as appropriate (your partner should claim CTC if they have not already done so).

Otherwise, tick one of boxes 16.23 to 16.25

- I had the higher income and I am claiming all of our entitlement to CTC   **16.23**

- We are both making separate claims for half of our entitlement to CTC   **16.24**

- We elected before 6 April 2001, or because of our special circumstances, during the year to 5 April 2002 (see page 29 of your Tax Return Guide), for the partner with the lower income to claim all of our entitlement to CTC   **16.25**

- If you separated from, or starting living with, your partner in the year to 5 April 2002, enter in box 16.26 the amount of CTC you are claiming *(following the guidance in Help Sheet IR343)*   **16.26** £

10 per cent for the 2001/2 tax year, so the most you can save is £520. However, the amount of relief you get is reduced by £2 for every £3 of income you have that's chargeable to higher rate tax. This means that if you have income of more than about £41,735, then you won't get anything.

The credit can be claimed by single parents and married or unmarried couples. In the case of couples, there are rules about who claims it, to make sure that it gets reduced according to the highest earner's income. So, if either, or both, of the couple pays tax at above the basic rate limit, then the higher earner has to claim it. If neither partner pays tax above the basic rate limit, then the credit normally goes to the higher earner, although you can share it equally or elect for the lower earner to get the whole lot (if the partner that's getting the credit doesn't have enough income to make use of it all, then the surplus can be transferred to the other). Boxes **16.18** to **16.26** are designed to sort this all out. Full details of the Children's Tax Credit are given on pages 27 to 29 of the *Tax Return Guide*, along with various examples of how it works.

Transferring or using unused allowances

All or part of your blind person's allowance, married couple's allowance and/or children's tax credit can be transferred to your spouse if you didn't have enough income during the tax year to use it up, and if you lived with your spouse, or partner in the case of Children's Tax Credit, for at least part of the year. To take advantage, you need to tick whichever of boxes **16.27** and **16.30** is relevant and give details of your spouse's name, address, tax reference code, National Insurance number and Tax Office in the additional information section in box **23.5** on page 9 of the tax return. If you're calculating your own tax, then you also need to enter the transferred amounts in boxes **16.31** and **16.33**.

■ *Transfer of surplus allowances* - *see page 29 of your Tax Return Guide before you fill in boxes 16.27 to 16.33.*

- Tick box 16.27 if you want your spouse to have your unused allowances   **16.27** ☐

- Tick box 16.28 if you want to have your spouse's unused allowances   **16.28** ☐

- Tick box 16.29 if you want to have your partner's unused CTC   **16.29** ☐

- Tick box 16.30 if your surplus CTC should be transferred to your partner   **16.30** ☐

Please give details in the 'Additional information' box, box 23.5, on page 9 - *see pages 29 and 30 of your Tax Return Guide for what is needed.*

If you want to calculate your tax, enter the amount of the surplus allowance you can have.

- Blind person's surplus allowance   **16.31** £

- Married couple's surplus allowance   **16.32** £

- Surplus CTC   **16.33** £

Question 17 – student loan repayments

Repayments of 'Income Contingent Student Loans' (introduced in 1998) are collected by the Inland Revenue, and the amount of the repayments depend on

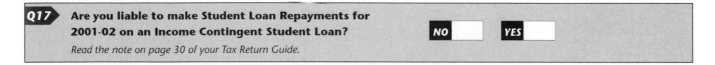

Q17   **Are you liable to make Student Loan Repayments for 2001-02 on an Income Contingent Student Loan?**   NO ☐   YES ☐
Read the note on page 30 of your Tax Return Guide.

your income. If you are due to make repayments on one of these loans for the 2001/2 tax year, then you'll need to tick the 'yes' box to question 17 and, if you're calculating your own tax, you'll need to work out the amount of the repayment and enter it in box **18.2A** (see page 150 in Chapter 11).

Question 18 – Calculating your tax

Calculating your tax is optional. So long as you get your tax return in by 30 September, the Inland Revenue will do it for you in time for you to make your first payment on 31 January. However, if you miss 30 September, you'll need to work the tax out yourself to make sure you know the amount to pay on 31 January in order to avoid paying extra because you're late.

Calculating your tax is an immensely contorted exercise and no fun at all, but then do you trust the Inland Revenue to get it right? Do you trust yourself? Of course, if you're doing your tax return online, then the calculation will be done automatically. It's not a bad option, but a little late now if you've been doing it on paper so far. Anyhow, if you need, or want, to calculate your own tax, then you'll need to hop over to Chapter 11, which is dedicated to the whole

Q18 Do you want to calculate your tax and any Student Loan Repayment?	**NO**	**YES**	Use your Tax Calculation Guide then fill in boxes 18.1 to 18.8 as appropriate.

• Unpaid tax for earlier years **included in your tax code for 2001-02**	**18.1**	£
• Tax due for 2001-02 included in your tax code for a later year	**18.2**	£
• Student Loan Repayment due	**18.2A**	£
• Total tax, Class 4 NIC and Student Loan Repayment due for 2001-02 **before** you made any payments on account *(put the amount in brackets if an overpayment)*	**18.3**	£
• Tax due for earlier years	**18.4**	£
• Tax overpaid for earlier years	**18.5**	£
• Your first payment on account for 2002-03 *(include the pence)*	**18.6**	£
• Tick box 18.7 if you are claiming to reduce your 2002-03 payments on account, make sure you enter the **reduced** amount of your first payment in box 18.6 and say why you are claiming in the 'Additional information' box, box 23.5, on page 9	**18.7**	
• Any 2002-03 tax you are reclaiming now	**18.8**	£

sordid business. When you've done the sums, you can come back and fill in boxes **18.1** to **18.8**.

Question 19 – Claiming repayments

If you've paid too much tax, you can either just let it stand against your next tax bill, or you can claim it back as a repayment. The Inland Revenue itself says it prefers not to bother with amounts of less than £10, but you can challenge that should you wish. Anyway, if you want to claim a repayment, you'll need to answer yes to question 19 and fill in boxes **19.1** to **19.12**.

Q19 **Do you want to claim a repayment if you have paid too much tax?** *(If you tick 'No' or the tax you have overpaid is below £10, I will use the amount you are owed to reduce your next tax bill.)*

NO ☐   **YES** ☐   **If yes,** fill in boxes 19.1 to 19.12 as appropriate.

Should the repayment be sent:

- to your bank or building society account? *Tick box 19.1 and fill in boxes 19.3 to 19.7*   **19.1** ☐

or

- to your nominee's bank or building society account? *Tick box 19.2 and fill in boxes 19.3 to 19.12*   **19.2** ☐

*We prefer to make repayment direct into a bank or building society account. (But tick box 19.8A **or** box 19.8B if you would like a cheque to be sent to you or your nominee.)*

Name of bank or building society
19.3

Branch sort code
19.4

Account number
19.5

Name of account holder
19.6

Building society reference
19.7

If you would like a cheque to be sent to:

- you, at the address on page 1, *tick box 19.8A*   **19.8A**

or

- your nominee, *tick box 19.8B*   **19.8B**

Agent's reference for you (if your agent is your nominee)
19.9

I authorise
Name of your nominee/agent
19.10

Nominee/agent address
19.11

Postcode

to receive on my behalf the amount due

19.12 *This authority must be signed by you. A photocopy of your signature will not do.*

Signature

Question 20 - 2001/2 Tax already refunded

If you've had any of your 2001/2 tax bill refunded to you already, for whatever reason, by the Inland Revenue or the Benefits Agency, then you need to answer 'yes' to this question and put the amounts in box **20.1**.

Q20 Have you already had any 2001-02 tax refunded or set off by your Inland Revenue office or the Benefits Agency (in Northern Ireland, the Social Security Agency)?
Read the notes on page 30 of your Tax Return Guide

| NO | | YES | | If yes, enter the amount of the refund in box 20.1. |
| | | | | **20.1** £ |

Questions 21 and 22 - Name, address and other personal details

Phew! They're getting easier now. We're very definitely on the home straight. Have a quick look at the front page of the tax return and check your name and address. If they're wrong at all, then they like you to physically correct them on the front page.

Q21 Is your name or address on the front of the Tax Return *wrong*?   NO ☐   YES ☐   If yes, please make any corrections on the front of the form.

Q22 Please give other personal details in boxes 22.1 to 22.7. *This information helps us to be more efficient and effective.*

Please give a daytime telephone number - this will help us if we need to contact you about your Tax Return.
22.1

Your agent's telephone number
22.2

and their name and address
22.3

Postcode

Your first two forenames
22.4

Say if you are single, married, widowed, divorced or separated
22.5

Your date of birth
22.6   /   /

Your National Insurance number
(if known and not on page 1 of your Tax Return)
22.7

Question 23 - Other information

Tick any relevant boxes from box **23.1** to **23.4**, as described. The one that's most likely to affect you is box **23.1**. If you pay tax through PAYE and the amount you

Q23 **Please tick boxes 23.1 to 23.4 if they apply. Provide any additional information in box 23.5 below (continue on page 10, if necessary).**

Tick box 23.1 if you do **not** want any tax you owe for 2001-02 collected through your tax code.

23.1 ☐

Tick box 23.2 if this Tax Return contains figures that are provisional because you do not yet have final figures. Page 31 of your Tax Return Guide explains the circumstances in which Tax Returns containing provisional figures may be accepted and tells you what you must enter in box 23.5 below.

23.2 ☐

Tick box 23.3 if you are claiming relief now for 2002-03 trading, or certain capital, losses. Enter in box 23.5 the amount and year.

23.3 ☐

Tick box 23.4 if you are claiming to have post-cessation or other business receipts taxed as income of an earlier year. Enter in box 23.5 the amount and year.

23.4 ☐

owe for 2001/2 is less than £2,000, then you may be able to have it collected through your tax code for 2003/4, but you'll have to get this tax return in by 30 September 2002. If you can do it, this saves trouble and also means you don't have to find a lump sum for 31 January. However, box **23.1** is there for you to tick if, for some reason, you *don't* want to take advantage of this. There is further explanation about the other boxes on page 26 of the Inland Revenue's *Tax Return Guide*.

Question 24 – Declaration

So, finally we get to the bottom line. In certain circumstances, like if you're mentally incapable, someone else can sign the form for you and that's what box **24.2** is about. But since you've been reading this book and filling in the return, we'll assume that's not the case. So, tick the boxes to show which parts of the tax return you have filled in and are sending back and read the declaration in box **24.1**: 'The information I have given in this Tax Return is correct and complete to the best of my knowledge and belief.' If something's wrong, you can't hang it on a professional adviser or friend that helped you fill the form in and you certainly can't hang it on us! You have to check the form yourself and make sure it all stacks up 'to the best of your knowledge and belief'. So, when you're happy that all's well, stick in the date and sign the blasted thing.

It'll be tempting to stuff it in the envelope and send it back to the Inland Revenue as soon as you can but, before you do that, **take a copy of it**. Whether you have to sneak it into work or take it round the corner to copy shop, you'll find life much easier next year.

Calculating and Paying the Tax

It's all very well filling in the boxes, as we've been doing for countless chapters, but at some stage someone's actually got to do some adding up, even multiplying – and, we hope, some subtracting and dividing. Otherwise, we'll never know how much to write our cheques for. That might suit us, but it doesn't suit the Inland Revenue so well, and one way or another, they'll make sure the sums are done. They're even prepared to do it for you, but to do this they really need you to send in the tax return by the 30 September following the end of the tax year. If you're late, they'll still work out the tax for you, but they can't promise it will be done before 31 January (again following the end of the tax year), at which point they'll start charging you interest on anything that you owe.

So, first of all, you need to decide if you want to do the calculating yourself. If you don't (and who can blame you?), you'll want to try to get the return in by the end of September, so that the Inland Revenue has time to do the sums before 31 January and you can be sure of not paying any interest. If you miss this date, the Inland Revenue suggests that you at least have a stab at the amount due, and pay them that, so that there will be less interest to pay if they can't get the right number worked out before the end of January. Whether you feel up to this, of course, is for you to decide.

If you do fancy testing yourself with some gentle arithmetic (go on, make sure you can still do it), or if you simply don't trust the Inland Revenue to get it right, then the 30 September deadline doesn't matter so much. You effectively get the extra four months that the Inland Revenue expect to take to work it out for yourself. The date that will matter more is the 31 January. Don't delay, though, since, assuming that you've got tax to pay, you'll be liable to a £100 fine (plus any interest of course) if you miss this date as well (and it goes up by more later on).

The easiest way to calculate your own tax is to do the form over the Internet as discussed on page 11. This way, the clever software will do the sums at the click of a mouse button and, bingo, it spits out a number that you need to write on a cheque. You can't say fairer than that. If you're distrustful of the 'ether' and prefer paper (it's that white stuff that you used to write on with a magic stick), then you'll need one of the Inland Revenue's two *Tax Calculation Guides*. The simple one, running to a mere 17 pages, should have been sent to you along with your tax return and it should do for most people. There is, however, a *Comprehensive Tax Calculation Guide* and you'll need this if you're complicated. For the purposes of calculating your tax, you'll be complicated if:

You have any of the following kinds of income
- Scrip dividends or non-qualifying distributions (see pages 112–13 of this book)
- Gains on UK life policies (see pages 116–17 of this book)
- Taxable lump sums (see page 24 of this book)

OR

You have filled in any of the following supplementary pages
- Share Schemes (see Chapter 2)
- Lloyd's Underwriters
- Partnership – Full (See Chapter 4)
- Foreign (see Chapter 6)
- Trusts etc. (see Chapter 7)
- Capital Gains (see Chapter 8)
- Non-Residence etc. (see Chapter 9)

OR

You have claimed one of the less common reliefs in question 15 on page 5 of the main body of your tax return (boxes **15.1, 15.9, 15.11** or **15.12**).

The comprehensive guide doesn't so much introduce more complexity (well no more than the extra boxes, and pages, in the tax return did anyway); it's just that much longer (32 pages instead of 17, in fact). For the purposes of this chapter, we're going to steer clear of it, for fear of confusing the vast majority of people who have no interest in it.

The Inland Revenue, bless it, is keen to collect our tax. Not surprisingly, then, it has gone to considerable effort to make the calculation guide as clear as possible. Credit where credit's due, because on the whole they've been very successful. The guide starts off by explaining the steps in the process – reproduced below.

STEP BY STEP GUIDE

Step 1 – brings together all the **non-savings** income you've entered on your Return

Step 2 – totals the deductions and allowances you've claimed on the Return (all UK residents are entitled to the 'personal allowance' of £4,535)

Step 3 – adds savings and dividend income to get your **total income**, takes away your deductions and allowances to get to your **taxable income**, and then works out the tax due, so far

Step 4 – takes off further allowances, deductions and tax paid at source – then works out your total income tax, Class 4 National Insurance contributions (if you're self-employed or in partnership) and any Student Loan repayments – to give you the figure to enter in box **18.3** on page 8 of your Return

Step 5 – works out what you have to pay for 2001/2 by 31 January 2003, or what we have to pay you

Step 6 – works out any 2002/3 payments on account you may have to make on 31 January and 31 July 2003

Pages 13 to 17 may not apply – they contain working sheets for the age-related allowances (**briefly**, if you're over 65), the married couple's allowance, the Children's Tax Credit and the collection of Student Loans

So that you don't have to juggle too many bits of paper, we've basically reproduced the various steps of the Inland Revenue's *Tax Calculation Guide* for 2001/2 in this chapter, although we've added some extra explanation and hopefully made it a bit easier to follow. Where a box ends up with an important number in it, we've labelled the box so that we can easily tell you where to find that number later. The box numbering might look a little arbitrary, but we've kept to the same numbers as the Inland Revenue's *Calculation Guide* so that you can cross-refer to that if you want to. The box numbers in the guide all start with a 'w' to distinguish them from the boxes in the actual tax return (we think the 'w' is short for worksheet, but we can't be sure). There are some gaps in the numbering, because we've only used the labelling where necessary.

If you're doing a return for any tax year other than 2001/2, you'll need to use the Inland Revenue's own *Calculation Guide* because things might have changed. Even so, we hope our explanation of the various steps will help you. So, with your pen in your hand and your completed tax return handy, let's push on.

Step 1 – Add together non-savings income from your tax return

Here's where we introduce each source of **non-savings** income. The first is Employment income and it gets made up from a whole raft of different boxes in your tax return. Enter the figures from your tax return in Table 11.1:

	Tax Return Box	Column A	Tax Return Box	Column B
TABLE 11.1 – EMPLOYMENT INCOME	1.8		1.31	
	1.9		1.32	
	1.10		1.33	
	1.12		1.34	
	1.13		1.35	
	1.14		1.36	
	1.15		1.37	
	1.16		1.38	
	1.17			
	1.18			
	1.19			
	1.20			
	1.21			
	1.22			
	1.23			
	1.27			
	1.28			
	Total		Total	
	Total Column A minus Total Column B (this number goes into Table 11.3)			

Your income, if any, from UK pensions also comes from a number of boxes and you can work this out in Table 11.2.

Tax Return Box	Column A	Tax Return Box	Column B	
11.1		11.13		**TABLE 11.2 – INCOME FROM UK PENSIONS ETC**
11.2				
11.3				
11.4				
11.5				
11.6				
11.7				
11.9				
11.12				
Total		Total		
Total Column A minus Total Column B (this number goes into Table 11.3)				

You can now enter your income from the various (non-savings) sources in table 11.3 (most likely it will only be one or two boxes).

Source of income	Amount	Box Label	Comment	
Employment			From the bottom line of Table 11.1 on page 137 of this book	**TABLE 11.3 – SOURCES OF NON-SAVING INCOME**
Ministers of religion			Box 1M.51 minus box 1M.45 from the Ministers' pages	
Self-Employment			Box 3.92 on the Self-Employment pages	
Partnership			Box 4.73 on the Partnership pages	
UK Land & Property			Box 5.43 on the Land & Property pages	
UK Pensions etc.			From the bottom line of Table 11.2 above	
Other income			Box 13.3 minus box 13.5 from the main body	
Total		**w1**	**This figure gets taken to Table 11.6 on page 142**	

The total at the bottom of Table 11.3, in the box labelled 'w1' gets taken into the calculation in Step 3, where we bring all our income together.

Step 2 – Add together deductions and allowances

You can add up your deductions and allowances in Table 11.4.

Most people won't have any deductions. The first couple of boxes, labelled 'losses', are only for people who filled in the Self-Employment, Partnership or Land & Property supplementary pages and have made losses. If you have filled out those supplementary pages and have losses to bring into account in this tax return (from boxes **3.85**, **4.15**, **5.16** and **5.44**), then enter them here.

The fourth box, 'Pensions Payments' only relates to contributions to retirement annuity contracts and to an employer's pension scheme that have not been deducted at source from your pay. Payments to personal pensions (including 'stakeholders') and 'Free Standing Additional Voluntary Contributions' (FSAVCs) get included later on (in table 11.5). There's more about this on pages 119–21 of this book. Anyway, if you've entered figures in boxes **14.5** and **14.10**, then enter them here.

The next box, 'other deductions', is for anything you've entered in boxes **15.2** (some maintenance or alimony payments), **15.7** (gifts of qualifying investments to charity), **15.8** (post-cessation expenses, pre-incorporation losses brought forward and losses on relevant discounted securities) and **15.10** (payments to a trade union or friendly society for death benefits).

There's probably not much going on with allowances, either, because most people will only have something to go in the first box, 'personal allowance'. In fact, everyone is entitled to the personal allowance and we're all entitled to the same amount, so we've put it in for you.

If you or your spouse were aged over 65 at the end of the tax year, then you may also have something to put in the box labelled 'age-related allowance'. To work out the figure, though, you have to go to page 13 of the Inland Revenue's *Tax Calculation Guide* and go through an absurdly convoluted calculation process. We haven't repeated it here, but if you follow the instructions carefully, then you should get there in the end!

	Amount	Box Label	Comment
Deductions			
Losses from Self-Employment			Box 3.85 on the Self-Employment pages
Losses from Partnership			Box 4.15 on the Partnership pages
Losses from Land & Property			Box 5.16 *plus* 5.44 on the Land & Property pages
Pension payments			Box 14.5 *plus* 14.10 from the main body
Other deductions			Box 15.2 *plus* 15.7 *plus* 15.8 *plus* 15.10 from the main body
Allowances			
Personal allowance	4,535		Everybody gets it. For the 2001/2 year it was £4,535, so we've written it in for you
Age-related allowance			If you or your spouse were aged over 65 at the end of the tax year, work it out on page 13 of the Inland Revenue Guide. The figure you want comes from box **w112**
Blind person's allowance			Enter this if you're entitled to it. For 2001/2 it was £1,450
Surplus blind person's allowance from spouse			Box 16.31 from the main body
Total of deductions and allowances		**w5**	**This figure gets taken to Table 11.6 on page 142**

TABLE 11.4 – DEDUCTIONS AND ALLOWANCES

Step 3 – Working out tax on all your taxable income

Here's where we bring together all your taxable income and work out the tax on it. There are three streams: non-savings income, savings income and dividend income. These need to be worked out separately and then added together. Not only that, but each of the strands is split into three sections – for starting rate tax, basic rate tax and then higher-rate tax. You have to add together the tax due at each rate of tax to get the total tax due on each source of income.

Before we start, you must work out your extended basic rate band of tax. That's basically how much income you have, beyond deductions, allowances and the starting rate, before you start paying tax at the higher rate. To work it out, we need to add certain pension and charitable contributions, which are non-taxable, to the basic rate band. You can do this in Table 11.5, below.

The only tricky one here is 'Gift Aid', which is taken out of your income after basic rate tax has been deducted from it. The charity concerned can then claim that basic rate tax back, so it ends up being as though you've made a gift that's that much larger, out of your pre-tax income. If you're a higher rate taxpayer, you also get relief for the higher rate tax on Gift Aid payments, but you get this yourself rather than the charity claiming it. The relief is given by increasing your basic rate tax band by the amount of the *gross* payment to charity (that is the money you hand over and the basic rate tax that they claim back). Are you still with me? Anyway, that's why you need to 'gross-up' any Gift Aid payments you've made by multiplying by 100 and dividing by 78. I'm afraid we're not out of the woods yet on Gift Aid, there's more to come in a little while but, for the time being, we can move on to non-savings income.

	Amount	Box Label	Comment
TABLE 11.5 – EXTENDED BAND OF BASIC RATE TAX			
Basic rate tax band	27,520		For the 2001/2 year this was £27,520, so we've written it in for you
Pension payments			Box 14.9 *plus* 14.11 from the main body
Gift Aid		**w15**	Box 15.5 multiplied by 100, then divided by 78. This figure also goes into Table 11.13 on page 149.
Total		**w16**	This figure gets taken to Table 11.6 on page 142

Non-savings income

You can work out the tax to be paid on your non-savings income by going through Table 11.6. Pay close attention to the comments – they tell you what to do!

If any box in the table is a minus amount, then put zero ('0') in the box.

	Amount	Box Label	Comment
Income		w6	From **w1** (the bottom line of Table 11.3 on page 138 of this book)
Allowances and deductions		w7	From **w5** (the bottom line of Table 11.4 on page 140 of this book)
Taxable income		w8	**w6** *minus* **w7**
Starting rate band	1,880	w9	For the 2001/2 tax year this was £1,880, so we've written it in for you
Income chargeable at starting rate		w10	The *lower* of boxes **w8** and **w9**
Tax due		w11	10% of box **w10** (take box **w10**, *divide* it by 100 and *multiply* by 10)
Taxable income over £1,880		w12	**w8** *minus* **w10**
Extended basic rate band		w16	From **w16** (from the bottom line of Table 11.5 on page 141 of this book)
Income within basic rate limit		w17	The *lower* of boxes **w12** and **w16**
Tax due		w18	22% of box **w17** (take box **w17**, *divide* it by 100 and *multiply* by 22)
Income chargeable at higher rate		w19	**w12** *minus* **w17**
Tax due		w20	40% of box **w19** (take box **w19**, *divide* it by 100 and *multiply* by 40)
Total tax due on non-savings income			**w11** *plus* **w18** *plus* **w20**

TABLE 11.6 – TAX ON NON-SAVINGS INCOME

So, the figure in the bottom line of Table 11.6 is the amount of tax that you have to pay on your non-savings income. Now we can work out the tax to pay on your savings income.

Savings income

For savings income, we have to start by adding together the different sources of income. You can do this in Table 11.7. The first box is only relevant to people who filled out the Partnership pages (and we won't go into why it's there), while the rest come from the main body of the tax return and are more relevant for most people. There's more about what goes in the various boxes where we covered them in Chapter 10. Remember that for the time being we're only dealing with non-dividend income.

'Interest where tax has been deducted' needs a mention because it has to be included to work out how much goes into the different tax bands. Don't worry, though, you're not being taxed twice, because you're taking the 'grossed-up' amount of income. In other words, the income that you would have got if tax had not been deducted. If it's relevant, then you'll have already worked out that figure and it will be in box 10.4 in the main body.

TABLE 11.7 - SOURCES OF SAVINGS INCOME

Sources of income	Amount	Box Label	Comment
Share of taxed partnership income			Box 4.70 on the Partnership pages
Interest where no tax has been deducted			Box 10.1 from the main body
Interest where tax has been deducted			Box 10.4 from the main body
Interest distributions from UK Authorized Unit Trusts & OEICs			Box 10.7 from the main body
National Savings			Box 10.8 from the main body
National Savings FIRST Option and Fixed-Rate Savings Bonds			Box 10.11 from the main body
Other income from UK savings and investments (except dividends)			Box 10.14 from the main body
Total		**w21**	This figure gets taken to Table 11.8 on page 144

You can now take the figure from the bottom line of Table 11.7, in box **w21**, into Table 11.8 and work out the tax on your savings income, just as you did for non-savings income. Things start to get a bit fiddly here because many of the figures will come back in from Table 11.6 on page 142. The reason for this is that you still get your allowances and deductions and the tax bands still apply, but *only* *to the extent that they haven't been used up with your non-savings income.* The numbers you bring forward might well be minus numbers, in which case you need to put in a zero ('0').

Notice also that the percentage used to work out your basic rate tax in box **w30** is 20 per cent, rather than the 22 per cent that we used for non-savings income (because the basic tax rate for savings income is only 20 per cent).

If any box in the table is a minus amount, then put zero ('0') in the box.

	Amount	Box Label	Comment
Income		w21	From **w21** (the bottom line of Table 11.7 on page 143 of this book)
Allowances and deductions		w22	**w7** *minus* **w6**
Taxable income		w23	**w21** *minus* **w22**
Starting rate band		w24	**w9** *minus* **w10**
Income chargeable at starting rate		w25	The *lower* of boxes **w23** and **w24**
Tax due		w26	10% of box **w25** (take box **w25**, *divide* it by 100 and *multiply* by 10)
Taxable income over £1,880		w27	**w23** *minus* **w25**
Extended basic rate band		w28	**w16** *minus* **w17**
Income within basic rate limit		w29	The *lower* of boxes **w27** and **w28**
Tax due		w30	20% of box **w29** (take box **w29**, *divide* it by 100 and *multiply* by 20)
Income chargeable at higher rate		w31	**w27** *minus* **w29**
Tax due		w32	40% of box **w31** (take box **w31**, *divide* it by 100 and *multiply* by 40)
Total tax due on savings income			**w26** *plus* **w30** *plus* **w32**

TABLE 11.8 - TAX ON SAVINGS INCOME

So the figure on the bottom line of Table 11.8 is the tax you owe on your savings income. Now we can move on to dividend income where, as you might have guessed, the process is remarkably similar.

Dividend income

There arc just two sources of dividend income that you might need to account for here – the ones that went in boxes **10.17** and **10.20** in the main body of your tax return. That is, 'dividends and other qualifying distributions from UK companies' and 'dividend distributions from UK authorized unit trusts and OEICs'. If you have entered anything in boxes **10.23** or **10.26**, 'scrip dividends from UK companies' or 'non-qualifying distributions and loans written off', then you should be using the Inland Revenue's *Comprehensive Tax Calculation Guide* (bad luck!). Anyway, assuming you've got nothing in **10.23** and **10.26**, then you can tot up your dividend income in the diminutive Table 11.9.

TABLE 11.9 – SOURCES OF DIVIDEND INCOME	Sources of income	Amount	Box Label	Comment
	Dividends and other qualifying distributions from UK companies			Box 10.17 from the main body
	Dividend distributions from UK authorized unit trusts and OEICs			Box 10.20 from the main body
	Total		**w33**	This figure gets taken to Table 11.10 on page 146

Now take the figure from the bottom of Table 11.9, in box **w33**, and transfer it to Table 11.10 on page 146, where we can finish working out the tax due on your dividend income.

Again, many of the figures come from the previous table (Table 11.8 on page 144), because we're interested in the amount of any deductions, allowances and tax bands that are left over after they've been used in that table. Remember to make sure that any minus numbers are entered as zero ('0'). Oh, and again, you'll see that the tax rates are different for dividends, so the percentages used to calculate boxes **w42** and **w44** are different again (10 per cent and 32.5 per cent, for the 2001/2 tax year, as it happens).

If any box in the table is a minus amount, then put zero ('0') in the box.

	Amount	Box Label	Comment
Income		w33	From **w33** (the bottom line of table 11.9 on page 145 of this book)
Deductions and Allowances		w34	**w22** *minus* **w21**
Taxable income		w35	**w33** *minus* **w34**
Starting rate band		w36	**w24** *minus* **w25**
Income chargeable at starting rate		w37	The *lower* of boxes **w35** and **w36**
Tax due		w38	10% of box **w37** (take box **w37**, *divide* it by 100 and *multiply* by 10)
Taxable income over £1,880		w39	**w35** *minus* **w37**
Extended basic rate band		w40	**w28** *minus* **w29**
Income within basic rate limit		w41	The *lower* of boxes **w39** and **w40**
Tax due		w42	10% of box **w41** (take box **w41**, *divide* it by 100 and *multiply* by 10)
Income chargeable at upper dividend rate		w43	**w39** *minus* **w41**
Tax due		w44	32.5% of box **w43** (take box **w43**, *divide* it by 100 and *multiply* by 32.5)
Total tax due on dividend income			**w38** *plus* **w42** *plus* **w44**

TABLE 11.10 – TAX ON DIVIDEND INCOME

If you add together the figures at the bottom of each of tables 11.6, 11.8 and 11.10, you'll get the total amount of tax you owe (so far at any rate). You can do that sum in Table 11.11.

TABLE 11.11 – TOTAL TAX ON TAXABLE INCOME	Type of Income	Amount	Box Label	Comment
	Non-savings income			From the bottom line of Table 11.6 on page 142
	Savings income			From the bottom line of Table 11.8 on page 144
	Dividend income			From the bottom line of Table 11.10 on page 146
	Total tax on Taxable income		**w48**	

We've now got a figure for the total amount of income tax that you're due to pay, but it would be too simple if that was what you actually owed. We now have to move to Step 4 where we deduct some more reliefs and allowances (and some Gift Aid).

Step 4 – Calculating tax due after reliefs, allowances and Gift Aid payments

Start by entering the total income tax figure from **w48** (in Table 11.11) at the top of Table 11.12 on page 148, then go down the table inserting the various reliefs and, at the end, take the reliefs away from the income tax bill. Most of the reliefs are at the starting rate of tax, that is 10 per cent, but for Venture Capital Trusts and Enterprise Investment Schemes, the relief is at 20 per cent (for the 2001/2 tax year).

The boxes labelled **w55** and **w56** are for the newly-introduced Children's Tax Credit. You may be able to claim this if you have a child living with you that was under the age of 16 at the start of the tax year, and the child is your own or living with you at your expense. There's more about this on pages 126 and 127 of Chapter 10. If it applies to you, you'll need to use page 16 of the *Tax Calculation Guide* to work out the figure to go in box **w55**.

	Amount	Box Label	Comment
Income tax before allowances and reliefs		w49	**w48** (from Table 11.11 on page 147)
Venture Capital Trust subscriptions			Box 15.3 from the main body
Enterprise Investment Scheme subscriptions			Box 15.4 from the main body
Total		w50	*Add* together the two boxes above (15.3 and 15.4)
Tax relief (at 20%)		w51	20% of **w50** (take **w50**, *divide* it by 100 and *multiply* by 20)
Married couple's allowance		w52	If you or your spouse were born before 6 April 1935, work it out on pages 14 and 15 of the *Tax Calculation Guide*.
Married couple's surplus allowance		w53	Box 16.32 from the main body
Maintenance and alimony		w54	Box 15.2 from the main body
Children's Tax Credit		w55	Were you entitled to the Children's Tax Credit (see pages 126 and 127 of Chapter 10), work out this figure from page 16 of the *Tax Calculation Guide*
Surplus Children's Tax Credit		w56	Box 16.33 from the main body
Total		w57	*Add* together boxes **w52**, **w53**, **w54**, **w55** and **w56**
Tax relief (at 10%)		w58	10% of **w57** (take **w57**, *divide* it by 100 and *multiply* by 10)
Total reliefs		w59	**w51** *plus* **w58**
Income tax due after allowances & reliefs		w60	**w49** *minus* **w59**

TABLE 11.12 – ADDITIONAL ALLOWANCES AND RELIEFS

The next section is a bit of a muddle. The idea behind the first few boxes is to make sure that, if you've made Gift Aid payments, then you're also paying enough tax to 'cover' the tax that the charity will recover from the Inland Revenue (we wouldn't want the taxman to be out of pocket, now would we?). If necessary, the Inland Revenue will restrict your allowances to make up the difference. The remaining boxes, **w64** to **w71**, take account of your dividend tax credits.

If you get a zero in box **w66**, you can ignore boxes **w67** to **w70**, enter the figure from **w65** into **w71** and carry on. Otherwise, you need to fill in all the boxes even if they do appear rather odd. Any minus numbers should be entered as a zero ('0'). Most of the boxes are just steps in the calculation and don't have names, so pay close attention to the labels!

If any box in the table is a minus amount, then put zero ('0') in the box.

	Amount	Box Label	Comment
Income tax due after allowances and reliefs		w60	From **w60** (in Table 11.12 on page 148)
Gift Aid payments		w61	From **w15** (in Table 11.5 on page 141)
		w62	22% of **w61** (take **w61**, *divide* it by 100 and *multiply* by 22)
		w63	The higher of boxes **w60** and **w62**
		w64	From **w33** (in Table 11.10 on page 146)
		w65	10% of **w64** (take **w64**, *divide* it by 100 and *multiply* by 10)
		w66	From **w34** (in Table 11.10 on page 146)
		w67	**w62** *minus* **w49** (**w49** is from Table 11.12 on page 148)
		w68	**w67** *multiplied* by 10 (that's the number 10, not a box label!)
		w69	**w66** *minus* **w68**
		w70	10% of **w69** (take **w69**, *divide* it by 100 and *multiply* by 10)
		w71	**w65** minus **w70**
Income Tax due after taking off tax credits		w72	**w63** *minus* **w71**

TABLE 11.13 – GIFT AID AND TAX CREDITS

Now we have to make adjustments to the figure in **w72** (income tax due after taking off tax credits) for Class 4 National Insurance Contributions, unpaid tax from earlier years and Student Loan repayments.

You will only have Class 4 National Insurance Contributions to pay if you were self-employed or in partnership during the year (and therefore filled out the Self-Employment or Partnership supplementary pages). In that case, assuming you want to calculate your own tax (which would be why you're knee-deep in this chapter), you'll need to fill out the worksheet at the back of the *Notes* to those pages to work out the income that you pay National Insurance on (it's slightly different from the income that you pay tax on). Now's your moment! You need to bring the figure from **box H** of that worksheet into box **w73** in Table 11.14 below.

If you have unpaid tax *from earlier years,* then it should be apparent from the 'Notice of Coding' (form P2) that you should have received from the Inland Revenue. Look at your latest 'Notice of Coding' for 2001/2 and, if there's a figure for unpaid tax from earlier years, then you need to copy it into box **w75** (in Table 11.14 below) **and** box **18.1** in the main body of your tax return. It may also be that your tax code changed during the year and that you have unpaid tax *from this year* (that is, the one you're covering in this tax return). In this case, there should be an estimated underpayment figure in your most recent Notice of Coding (form P2). That figure needs to be copied into box **w79** (in Table 11.15 on page 151 – we'll get there in a moment) and box **18.2** on your tax return.

Box **w76** is for Income Contingent Student Loan Repayments, which started to appear in August 1998. If you're making this type of Student Loan repayment and want to calculate your own tax, then you should have ticked 'yes' to ques-

	Amount	Box Label	Comment
Income tax due after taking off tax credits		w72	From **w72** in Table 11.13 on page 149.
Class 4 National Insurance Contributions		w73	From box H on the worksheet in the *Notes* to the Self-Employment or Partnership pages (if you filled them in, otherwise it's a zero)
Income Tax and Class 4 National Insurance contributions		w74	**w72** *plus* **w73**
Unpaid tax from earlier years		w75	From your Notice of Coding (form P2). Note that it's for *earlier* tax years, not this one. See comments above. This figure also needs to go in box 18.1 on the main body of the tax return
Income Contingent Student Loan Repayments		w76	If you ticked 'yes' to question 17 in the main body of your tax return, work it out on page 17 of the Inland Revenue *Tax Calculation Guide*. The figure is from box **w145** and it also needs to go in box 18.2A in the main body of the tax return
		w77	**w74** *plus* **w75** *plus* **w76**

TABLE 11.14 – CLASS 4 NI PAYMENTS, UNPAID TAX FROM EARLIER YEARS AND INCOME CONTINGENT STUDENT LOAN REPAYMENTS

If any box in the table is a minus amount, then put zero ('0') in the box.

tion 17 in the main body of your tax return, and now's your moment to work out the figure to go in box **18.2A** of the return, as well as box **w76**. To work the figure out, you need to go to page 17 of the Inland Revenue's *Tax Calculation Guide* and follow the boxes.

If any box in the table is a minus amount, then put zero ('0') in the box – except for box w80, which can be a minus amount (and, in fact, has to be if that's how it comes out).

	Amount	Box Label	Comment
Employment			From box 1.11 in the Employment pages
"			From box 1.30 in the Employment Pages
Ministers of Religion			From box 1M.50 in the Ministers of Religion pages
Self-Employment			From box 3.97 in the Self-Employment pages
"			From box 3.98 in the Self-Employment pages
Partnership (Short)			From box 4.77 in the Partnership pages
UK Land & Property			From box 5.21 in the Land & Property pages
UK Savings & Investments			From box 10.3 in the main body of the tax return
"			From box 10.6 in the main body of the tax return
"			From box 10.10 in the main body of the tax return
"			From box 10.13 in the main body of the tax return
UK Pensions etc.			From box 11.8 in the main body of the tax return
"			From box 11.11 in the main body of the tax return
Other income			From box 13.2 in the main body of the tax return
Total Tax Paid at Source		w78	*Add* together all the boxes above
2001/2 unpaid tax included in your PAYE Code for 2002/3		w79	See comments on page 150. This figure should also go into box 18.2 in the main body of the tax return
		w80	**w78** *plus* **w79**
Total Income Tax, Class 4 NI Contribs and Income Contingent Student Loan Repayment Due		w81	**w77** *minus* **w80** (**w77** comes from Table 11.14 on page 150). This figure should also go into box 18.3 in the main body of the tax return. **Note that this box is allowed to be a minus number (and has to be if that's how it turns out!)**

TABLE 11.15 – TAX PAID AT SOURCE AND UNPAID TAX FROM 2001/2 INCLUDED IN YOUR 2002/3 PAYE CODE

The final stage of Step 4 is to take away any tax that you've already paid 'at source' (that is, where you've received money after the tax has already been deducted) as well as any unpaid tax for the 2001/2 tax year that has been included in your PAYE Code for the 2002/3 tax year. To do this, complete Table 11.15 on page 151. Obviously you don't need to worry about filling in boxes that relate to supplementary pages you didn't fill in. The number that you end up with in **w81** should be transferred to box 18.3 in the main body of your tax return.

Step 5 – Work out what you have to pay the Inland Revenue by 31 January, or what they have to pay you

Are you still there? It's quite astonishing how complicated things have become, isn't it? It's all down to years and years of government tinkering. Much more of the same and it'll be pretty close to impossible. Where were we… There's a fair bit of awkwardness in Step 5, but many of the nastier bits are unlikely to apply. Avanti!

To start off, the figure we got in box **w81** at the bottom of Table 11.15 on page 151, needs to be transferred to box **w82** at the top of Table 11.16 on page 154.

You'll only have something to go in box **w83** if you ticked 'yes' to question 20 in the main body of your tax return: 'Have you already had any 2001/2 tax refunded or set off by your Inland Revenue office or the Benefits Agency (in Northern Ireland the Social Security Agency)?' Well, have you? If so, the figure needs to go in box **20.1** in the main body of the tax return and in box **w83** here.

Box **w84** is relevant to you if you have paid too little tax in earlier years because of the way your business profits are spread over different years. In particular, it'll be relevant to farmers, writers and artists. It may also affect you if you're claiming to carry back post-cessation receipts to the year your business ceased (you should know if that's you). What you need to do is 'work out the underpayment of tax or Class 4 National Insurance contributions by reference to the tax rates and circumstances of that earlier year. Recalculate the liability for that year… taking account of the adjustment' and enter the difference between the recalculated figure and the original figure in box **w84** (and **18.4** in the main body of your tax return). Ouch! Really what you need to do is consult a tax adviser or, at the very, very least, speak to your local Inland Revenue office.

Box **w86** is for people who have paid too much tax in an earlier year because they're claiming losses to be set against earlier years, or they're claiming to carry back retirement annuity or personal pension plan payments to an earlier year (see the comments on boxes **14.3** and **14.7** on pages 119–20 of this book and helpsheet *IR330: Pension Payments*), or they're a farmer, writer or artist claiming 'averaging' to reduce their income for last year. Again, a tax adviser or your local Inland Revenue office is your best bet here.

Box **w87** is for losses or pension payments for 2002/3 that you're claiming now to carry back to 2001/2. See the comments on boxes **14.4** and **14.8** on pages 119–20 of this book and helpsheet *IR330: Pension Payments*, but a tax adviser or your local Inland Revenue Office is probably the right answer.

Boxes **w88** and **w89** are for any tax that you've already paid on account. If you've made 'payments on account', then you should have received a Statement of Account from the Inland Revenue and this will give you the figures to go in the boxes.

If the amount of tax you owe for 2001/2 is less than £2,000 and your tax return is received by the Inland Revenue before 30 September 2002, then you can arrange for the tax to be collected through your 2003/4 PAYE code (assuming you have one, which you will do if you're an employee). This is what boxes **w90** and **w91** are trying to establish. So, if the figure in box **w90** is less than £2,000, you have a tax code and you want this to happen, then insert the figure from **w90** into box **w91**. Otherwise, leave **w91** blank.

Right, let's fill in Table 11.16.

	Amount	Box Label	Comment
Total tax, NI Contribs and Income Contingent Student Loan Repayments		**w82**	From **w81** (in Table 11.15 on page 151). Note that this can be a minus amount
Tax refunded in the year		**w83**	From box 20.1 (see the comments on page 152)
Tax due for earlier years		**w84**	See comments on page 152. If you do have a figure here it should also go in box **18.4** of the main body of your tax return
		w85	**w82** *plus* **w83** *plus* **w84**
Tax overpaid for earlier years		**w86**	See comments on page 153. If you do have a figure here it should also go in box 18.5 of the main body of your tax return.
Any 2002/3 repayment you are claiming now		**w87**	See comments on page 153. If you do have a figure here it should also go in box 18.8 of the main body of your tax return.
Any other payments or credits that have been made towards your 2001/2 payments on account		**w88**	See comments on page 153.
Any other payments or credits, not already included in **w86**, **w87** or **w88**, that have been made towards your 2001/2 tax bill		**w89**	See comments on page 153.
		w90	**w85** *minus* **w88**
Tax to be collected through 2003/4 tax code		**w91**	Enter the figure from **w90**, but only if it's less than £2,000, you have a tax code and you want to pay the tax through your 2003/4 tax code. Otherwise leave this blank. See comments on page 153.
		w92	**w86** *plus* **w87** *plus* **w88** *plus* **w89** *plus* **w91**
Tax owing (to be repaid)		**w93**	**w85** *minus* **w92**. **Note that this can be a minus number (if so, it means that you're owed tax rather than the other way around).**

TABLE 11.16 – WHAT YOU HAVE TO PAY BY 31 JANUARY (OR WHAT THEY HAVE TO PAY TO YOU)

So there it is. The figure in **w93** is, if greater than zero, what you owe the Inland Revenue and, if less than zero, what the Inland Revenue owes you. If you get exactly zero, then you're all square and it must feel as though it was hardly worth bothering. It's not over yet, though. Not quite yet. We still have to go through Step 6, the title of which, encouragingly, begins with the word 'finally'.

Step 6 – Finally, Consider whether you have to make payments on account for 2002/3

OK, we'll see if we can skip through this final bit relatively quickly. First of all, subtract both boxes **w76** and **w91** from **w82** to leave you with **w94**:

Amount	Box Label	Comment
	w94	w82 *minus* (w76 and w91)

If box **w94** is less than £500, you do not have to make payments on account for 2002/3. Wahey! Do nothing with boxes **w95** and **w96**. Enter zero in **w97** and complete box **w98**. This is your total payment due on 31 January 2003.

If box **w94** is £500 or more, then you'll need to make payments on account for 2002/3 if more than 20 per cent of your 2001/2 tax bill has not been 'Collected at Source'. This is what boxes w95 and w96 are about. So...

If box **w94** (tax not collected at source) is less than box **w96** (20 per cent of your 2001/2 tax bill), then you're in the clear. Enter zero in box **w97** and copy box **w93** (from Table 11.16 on page 154) to box **w98**. This is your total payment due on 31 January 2003.

If box **w94** is £500 or more and is equal to or greater than box **w96**, then you need to put half of the number in box **w94** into box **w97**. This then gets added to the figure from box **w93** (in Table 11.16 on page 154) to give your total payment due on 31 January 2003. The number in box **w97** also needs to be transferred to box 18.6 in the main body of your tax return (and for some reason you have to include the pence here).

If you do end up with a payment on account to make, you may be able to reduce this payments if you expect your income to be lower in 2002/3 than it was in 2001/2, if you expect your allowances or reliefs to be higher, or if you expect more of your income to be collected at source. If this is the case, then you

	Amount	Box Label	Comment
		w95	w63 *plus* w73
		w96	20% of w95 (take w95, *divide* it by 100 and *multiply* by 20)
Payment on account		w97	If w94 is less than £500 or less than w96, then enter zero. Otherwise, enter half the figure from w94. Box w97 must apparently include the pence and needs to go in box 18.6 of the main body of your tax return. See comments on page 155.
Total tax payment due on 31 January 2003		w98	w93 *plus* w97

must make a reasonable estimate of the difference between the income tax you expect to pay in 2002/3 and the income tax due on your 2001/2 tax return. You can reduce each of your payments on account by half this difference. If you want to do this, then you need to enter the amount of the reduced payment on account in box **18.6** (including the pence), tick box **18.7** and explain yourself in the additional information section, box **23.5** on page 9 of the return.

Part 2
The Health Check

Mr Micawber's Happiness/ Misery Test

Income is the life-blood of your personal finances. It's what provides the money you live on and the savings that you can put away for the day when it dries up (whether due to retirement or a period of unemployment). The curious thing is that some people earning a fortune can find themselves in financial difficulties, whereas those earning relatively little can find themselves very comfortable. It's all a question of cutting your cloth to suit your circumstances and it's summed up nicely by Mr Micawber, the debt-ridden landlord, to David Copperfield:

Annual income twenty pounds, annual expenditure nineteen nineteen six, result happiness. Annual income twenty pounds, annual expenditure twenty pounds ought and six, result misery.

The unfortunate fact is that for many people this advice is as hard to follow as it is simple, as Mr Micawber himself found when he was marched off to debtors' prison. The world is split into spenders and savers and it seems the spenders are doomed to misery. Well, not quite, but to avoid disaster, those who are naturally inclined to spend do need to apply more discipline. This is the first question to ask yourself in your financial health check.

How does my income match up with my expenditure?

This question is as relevant for the 'savers' as for the 'spenders' (or nearly anyway). There's no point putting yourself through financial penury to save money that you'll never actually need. In the language of Mr Micawber:

> *Annual income twenty pounds, annual expenditure ten pounds, result you only get one life and unless saving more than you need gives you a perverse sense of pleasure then you ought to get out and spend a bit more on yourself.*

Of course there's no point in spending money just for the sake of it, but the best way to maximize the happiness of yourself and those around you over your lifetime is to strike a sensible balance.

You also need to take a long-term perspective. At this point, we're not fussed about whether your net worth increased during the year because your bijou flat in Battersea jumped in value by 20 per cent or because your shares in Pink Pointsettas PLC doubled. These sorts of gain aren't sustainable and there's no point getting too excited when this happens, because it could so easily have gone the other way and sooner or later it almost certainly will.

What concerns us here is the level of any debts you have *or* the amount of money that leaves your current account destined for, you hope, greater things. The word 'or' here is of crucial importance because, other than your mortgage (which has a relatively low interest rate), savings and debts are not compatible. There's no point paying 14 per cent interest on your overdraft, while saving money in something (such as the stock market) that you hope might give you an annual return of only 10 per cent or maybe less. Put this another way: your excess sixpence should first be going to reduce your non-mortgage debts and then, when they've been dealt with, the excess money can go into savings. If you've currently got some of both, then you need to start by paying off the one with the other.

Right. Clear as mud? It's back to Mr. Micawber, with the help of the handy flow chart on page 160.

Mr Micawber's Happiness/Misery Flow Chart

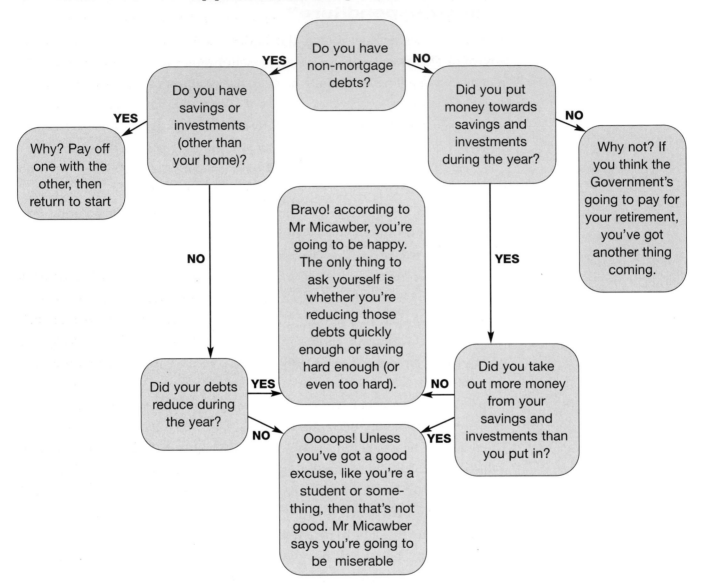

How did you do? Remember that you're trying to get an idea of the long-term picture. That means that if something unusual happened during the year, for instance if you had a windfall such as an inheritance, then you should exclude it from your sums. Similarly, if your income was lower than usual for any reason and it's likely to be higher in future, then you might decide to cut yourself some slack. Bear in mind, though, that it's best to be prudent: that big bonus you got last year may not reappear for some time, if ever, so you shouldn't count on it.

If you ended up in the misery box, then you'll need to think about how to increase your income or reduce your expenditure. For most people, the income side of the equation is pretty hard to budge, but that's not always the case. If you work on commission, or you're self-employed, then you might be able to achieve a bit by simply working harder. Alternatively, it might be a question of going to your boss to negotiate a pay rise, or even finding a new, better-paid, job. Perhaps you're in a job that you love, but which doesn't pay particularly well. In that case, look first at your expenditure as you try to balance your books, but if you can't, or don't want to make any headway on that, then a job you enjoy less is going to be better than a lifetime in debt.

Balancing the Books

On the expenditure side of things, first of all get a handle on where the money's going. If money flows through your fingers like water, then you probably need to spend a couple of months noting down everything that you spend. Pencil and paper works pretty well, but there are several different computer programs, such as Quicken, that not only help you categorize all your different expenses, but also produce nice charts showing you what's going on. Seeing where all the money goes really can be an eye opener. From personal experience, I was shocked to find that I was ploughing more than £50 per month into the golf machine in my local pub (didn't do much for my handicap, though). Most of that £50 per month is now making a big difference to my savings.

When you're producing your budgets, don't forget to include occasional expenses, like holidays or building repairs. If, for instance, you reckon on spending £1,000 every nine months or so on a holiday, then you'd want to include £111 (£1,000 divided by 9) per month in your budget for holidays. In the same way, if ad hoc repairs and maintenance to your house tend to cost you £500 per year, then you'd want to include £42 (£500 divided by 12) as your monthly repairs expenditure. Do you have a garden? If so, it probably absorbs a fair bit of cash each year, although most of it will be in the spring, so you'll need to spread that over the year as well. What about the phone bill? If you pay that quarterly, then you'll have to divide the average quarterly bill by three to get a monthly figure.

We've produced a basic table below, where you can list your monthly expenses, but if this is an issue for you it's probably worth making your own table and perhaps getting hold of one of the software packages.

	£
Mortgage/rent	
Insurance	
Utilities	
Telephone	
Other bills	
Groceries	
Clothing	
Travel	
Going out	
Other entertainment	
Other...	
Other...	
Other...	
Other...	
Total monthly expenses	

TABLE 12.1

To sum up on this income/expenditure lark, and at the risk of getting repetitive, the number in the total monthly expenditure box has to be smaller than your total monthly income. The difference between the two is what you're able to save (or use to reduce debts). How big that gap needs to be depends on how much you need to save, how long you've got and what you've got tucked away at the moment. We'll start, in Chapter 13, by looking at the last of these questions.

What Have You Got?

In the last chapter we covered income and expenditure, which you can think of as your personal profit and loss account. Here we're going to look at your personal balance sheet. That involves totting up all your worldly goods: firstly to see how much you've got, but also to check that everything's in the right place. The trick to doing this is to split your assets up according to the purpose that they serve.

My dictionary defines an asset as an 'item of value owned'. Of course, an asset wouldn't be much of an asset if it didn't have some value, but things can deliver their value in many different ways. The coat on your back keeps you warm in winter. The painting above the mantelpiece gives you a nice fuzzy feeling inside when you look at it. The cash that you have in your pocket has value because of the convenience of exchanging it immediately for something else in the shops. The money in your bank account can also be used to buy things, but it's much better if it also earns interest. You also might have some shares, which have a value because they entitle you to a share of a (hopefully) profitable business enterprise.

All your assets have a value and, to introduce another technical term, they deliver that value by giving you a 'return'. The return might be being kept warm, it might be that nice fuzzy feeling or… OK, you get the idea. It's vitally important to think of your assets like this. If something's *not* giving you a return, like the bread-making machine that's been doing nothing but take up space for the last ten years, then it's not giving you any value and it's not much of an asset. It goes further than this, though, because it's important that your total body of assets (your 'capital') is giving you the right blend of risk and return.

If you had all your money tied up in coats and paintings, you'd be faced with some tricky negotiations when you pop down to the shops for a pint of milk. In the same way, it's no good putting £1,000 into shares when you know you'll be needing it for a holiday in six months' time. By then the shares might still be worth £1,000, or more, but they might also be worth a lot less. If you know you're going to need the money soon, the bank's the place for it. It's horses for courses. You need enough clothing to keep you warm and covered up, enough paintings to keep you feeling fuzzy inside, enough cash (in your pocket and in the bank) for spending and to cover emergencies, and enough shares (or equivalent) to give you a fighting chance of keeping all this going when you retire.

You can really go to town on the categories for your personal balance sheet, but the purpose is to throw some light on your present circumstances, so it makes sense to keep things simple. To start with, in the table on page 165, we're going to stick with just four: chattels, savings, investments and debts.

Chattels

'Chattels' is just a legal word for your bits and bobs. We thought we'd use it because it has a beautifully Dickensian feel to it, and having started out with Mr Micawber we though we'd carry on with the theme. Estimating the value of all your chattels is a tricky task, but it's worth having a bash. Bear in mind that you don't need to know the value of everything to the nearest penny. All you're trying to do is get an idea of where your capital is tied up. So, at the very least, you can just go into each room of your house, tot up your guesstimates for the larger items and then add a bit for the smaller ones. Of course, you can go further with it if you fancy, but we don't really recommend it.

Savings

'Savings' is the cash, etcetera, that you have available for spending and emergencies in the near future (by which we mean less than about five years). Here we've given you subheadings for Bank Accounts, Savings Accounts and a couple of 'others'. So, you'll need to pull out your latest bank and savings state-

PERSONAL BALANCE SHEET	£
Assets	
Chattels	
Around the house	
Your home	
Car(s)	
Other ( )	
Total chattels	
Savings	
Bank accounts	
Savings accounts	
Other ( )	
Total short-term savings	
Investments	
Unit trusts and OEICs (including share-based ISAs)	
Investment trusts	
Individual shareholdings (including self-select ISAs)	
Pensions (defined contribution)	
Endowments	
Rental property	
Other ( )	
Total long-term investments	
Total assets	
Debts	
Relatively cheap debts	
Mortgage	
Other ( )	
Total relatively cheap debts	
Expensive debts	
Overdraft	
Credit cards	
Personal loans	
Other ( )	
Total expensive debts	
Total debts	
Total assets minus total debts	

ments for starters. 'Other' possibilities for savings are looked at in Chapter 16. They might, for instance, include premium bonds.

Investments

'Investments' covers what you have tucked away for the long term. We'll go into more detail in Chapter 17, but broadly speaking it includes anything that's connected with property or shares. That means shares themselves, but also any unit trusts, investment trusts and endowments that are invested in the stock market.

Debts

There is, of course, another section at the bottom of the balance sheet, for debts. We'll say more about debts in Chapter 14. For the moment, though, you need to split them into two categories. 'Relatively cheap debts' basically means mortgages and anything that charges interest at or below what a mortgage might charge. That includes, for instance, student loans and interest-free credit. 'Expensive debts' are any debts that charge a higher rate of interest than you'd get on a mortgage (for example, overdrafts, credit cards, store cards and personal loans).

With all this in mind, you can have a go at filling out your personal balance sheet. If it's all looking a bit tricky at the moment, then fill it in as we go through the next few chapters, which hopefully explain the different categories better. In any case, we suggest you do it in pencil, because you might well want to come back later and tinker with a few things.

Debts

The best way to understand debt is to think about where it comes from. Someone has lent you some money and that someone has had to get the money from somewhere. It doesn't just appear from thin air. A bank, for example, gets its money from people who deposit money with that bank; and they generally have to pay interest to the people who deposit money with them to make them do it. Even if they don't pay interest, the bank has to provide services (like cheque books and cash withdrawals) to make people part with their cash. So the money isn't free to the bank and, because the bank wants to make a profit, it certainly isn't free to you.

It might help explain things if we use a few numbers. Let's say that your sister puts £1,000 in a high interest account that pays her 5 per cent interest per year. Let's also say that the bank effectively releases that £1,000 to you by giving you an overdraft, on which it charges you 14 per cent interest per year. The bank is taking its 9 per cent in the middle (14 minus 5), and it calculates that this will leave it with a decent profit after taking account of its costs and the chances of you running off to the Bahamas and never paying them back.

So you'd much rather be the bank, or at least your sister. You absolutely don't want to be the one with the overdraft if you can help it. What really makes no sense at all is to be providing money to the bank yourself (and getting 5 per cent per year for it), while at the same time borrowing money back from the bank with an overdraft that costs you 14 per cent. Yet you'd be amazed at the number of people who have savings while at the same time being overdrawn or carrying debts on their credit cards. Is that you?

Expensive debts

Look back at your balance sheet on page 166. Do you have anything in the 'expensive debts' category? If you do, then your priority is to get rid of it – starting with the most expensive (that is, highest interest) first. If you have any savings and investments, use those to make a start. If you still have some debts left after that, then you'll want to think about how you can make them cheaper. You might, for instance, be able to get a 'consolidation loan' whereby a bank or finance company takes over all your debts at a lower average interest rate. Pay close attention, though, to any charges involved, stick to reputable companies and be very sure to look at the small print. There can be penalties for early payment and all sorts of other nasties. Remember – the priority is to clear the debts, and that's only going to be made easier by making them cheaper.

Now look at the chattels section of your balance sheet. We go into more detail about this in Chapter 15, but you may be able to sell some chattels to help remove your debt. You might, for instance, have a flashy car when a cheaper one might do. Not only might that give you some money to use to reduce the debts, but most likely it will also reduce your expenditure through cheaper insurance and maintenance. At the very least, you may be able to find some things that don't *really* need replacing as they wear out. That telly, for instance, could keep you going for another few years.

The next place to go is back to Chapter 12 and have another look at Mr Micawber's happiness/misery test. Your debts will get bigger if you spend more than you earn, so you need to find a way to cut your cloth accordingly. Perhaps you can cancel your Sky subscription or visit the hairdresser less than every month.

Almost everyone, myself included, has had trouble with debt at some stage during their lives (it's difficult not to, the way some loan companies try so hard to throw money at you) but, with some application, things can be turned around. The pain goes away very quickly once you've got on top of things, made a plan of action and are moving forward again. There's a discussion board on the Motley Fool website called 'Dealing with Debt' that is filled with people that are in debt or that have come through the difficulties and are trying to help others do the same. It's a very good place to go for tea and sympathy as well as practical tips. You might also consider contacting the Citizens Advice Bureau (local branches can be found via their website at **www.nacab.org.uk**), the Consumer Credit Counselling Service (**www.cccs.co.uk** or phone 0800 138 1111) or the Samaritans (**www.samaritans.org.uk** or phone 08457 909090).

Relatively cheap debts

The most obvious debt that falls into this category is a mortgage. We'll look at these more closely in the Homeowning chapter but, before tackling Chapters 16 and 17 on Saving and Investing, we need to say a few words about their compatibility with those things.

Mortgages are cheaper than other types of debt for a couple of reasons. First of all, there's less administration, per pound of debt, for the banks to do, so they can charge you less and still make a profit. Secondly, and most importantly, the bank takes a 'legal charge' over your house. Unlike people, houses have a very poor record of absconding to the Bahamas and this gives the bank extra confidence that they'll see their money again. For these reasons, lenders can still make a profit on providing mortgages, while charging only very slightly more than it costs them to get the money. So mortgages will tend to have an interest rate that sits just above the Bank of England's base rate (that's what they're talking about on the news when they say that interest rates have gone up, down or stayed the same), while good deposit accounts will have an interest rate that sits just below. (Occasionally you might find a mortgage charging even less than the bank interest rate, or you might find a deposit account charging more, but the only reason for this is that the bank concerned is trying to lure you in with an attractive rate. Make no mistake – they only do this because they fancy their chances at making it back off you eventually.)

So, it still costs you money to have savings at the same time as a mortgage (because you'll be paying more on the one than you're getting on the other), but this time it's only a little bit more. On the whole, the gap is sufficiently small for it to be worth getting on with your saving and, when you've got enough savings to cover your short-term needs, investing.

Where investing is concerned, mortgages are that bit more attractive. The reason again comes back to where the money comes from. The bank's depositors need their cash to be available to them at short notice (as we'll see when we look at your own savings in Chapter 16). That means that they can only expect the base rate of interest for it (or, in fact, slightly less). The bank, however, lends you the money for 25 years, on a typical mortgage. They can manage this feat of turning short-term deposits into long-term loans because they do a lot of it, and the cash flows from mortgages are very reliable. So, if more depositors than expected suddenly turned up wanting their money back on a given day, the bank would be able to borrow it from another bank (or even the Bank of England), using the cash flows from the mortgages as security.

The effect of this is that your bank can make its profit by lending you money at only a little above short-term interest rates, but it doesn't ask for the money back for 25 years. Over 25 years, you can *generally* do a lot better with the money than you could by simply sticking it in the bank. In other words, you can *generally* do better than the interest you're paying on the mortgage. This means that it *can* make sense to have stock market investments at the same time as having a mortgage (or other debt that charges the same or less in interest).

There are a lot of 'generallys' and 'cans' in the preceding paragraph and that's for good reason. While the stock market provided a better return than cash in the bank in every single 25-year period in the 20th century (that is, 1900-1925, 1901-1926, 1902-1927, you get the picture), we have no way of being sure that it will do so in future. Since the abolition of mortgage interest relief at source ('MIRAS'), there's also a confusion with tax. You pay your mortgage interest from your income after tax has been deducted from it, whereas, depending on how you're doing your investing (whether in an ISA or a pension or whatever), you will be suffering some tax on your investment returns. So your investments would have to make returns that much higher than your mortgage is costing, to make up for the tax you'll have to pay on those investment returns.

So, where does that take us? Well, it's far from cut and dried as to whether you should pay off your mortgage before you do any investing. You'll hear plenty of convincing arguments both ways. In fact, opinion is sufficiently split that deciding to do a bit of both is probably a pretty good way to go. That would be the effect of a repayment mortgage, where each month you pay off a bit of capital on your mortgage while, at the same time, putting more into long-term investments. We'll say more about all this in Chapter 17. For now, it's time to leave this contorted economic discussion and have a look at our chattels.

15

Chattels

We've already seen how chattels can do wonderful things like keep us warm and give us a fuzzy feeling inside. They can also drive us to work in the morning and a whole host of other things. In fact, it probably wouldn't be too much to say that our life would be impossible without them. They do, however, bring with them a couple of problems.

The first problem is that they tie up our capital. Even though we might take a lot of pleasure from a particular painting, the money we spent on it is money that hasn't gone into our investments. So we're effectively losing out on the return that we could be getting from the money if we had it stuck in the stock market. Before all you *Antiques Roadshow* buffs jump on me, though, things aren't so bad with a painting because paintings do tend to go up in value. Take a picture, for example, that was purchased for £100 in 1970 and is now worth £2,000. That amounts to an annual return of around 10 per cent. The stock market, by comparison, has returned 15 per cent per year, on average, over the same period, despite the recent falls. So the return that you've given up by having the picture instead of money in the stock market is around 5 per cent per year. That's what you've been paying for the pleasure of having the picture – and there's no harm in that.

Some things make even better investments than the stock market. Perhaps we should all have bought Steiff teddy bears or early Beatles memorabilia but we couldn't really have predicted that these would have done so well. All we can really say is that, on the whole, you'd expect an antique to provide slightly lower financial returns than shares *precisely because* they give us pleasure. After all, not much pleasure can be gleaned from a share certificate (especially since they no longer come with that elegant swirly writing). So, if people thought they could have their pleasure as well as the best financial returns, then they'd pay more for whatever it was until it cost the right amount. It's all about tying up your capital in something and what you get in return.

At the other end of the spectrum, there are chattels that go down in value over the years. The most obvious of these is a car. Say you bought a flashy car for £20,000 in 1995 and it's now worth £10,000. That adds up to a return of about minus 10 per cent per year. In the meantime, the stock market has returned a little over 8 per cent per year (if we include dividends). So the price you've been paying for the utility and the pleasure of your prize motor car is a whopping 18 per cent per year. So that's about £3,600 per year on the original £20,000 value, and that's before you even think about your insurance and the new brakes it needed a couple of years ago. Again, it's fair enough if that car is what you want and you can afford it, but what you need to think about is whether you can, *really*, afford it.

An accountant would deal with this by taking the reduction in value of the things on his balance sheet as a loss on his profit and loss account (and he'd call it depreciation). Ideally you'd do the same, but that really would be too much. What you should do, though, is think about the bigger items that decrease in value. Taking the example of a car again, if you think that every five years you're going to sell one car for £10,000 and buy another for £20,000, then you'd want to have an item in your budget of £2,000 per year (£167 per month) car expenses, in addition to the insurance and everything else.

As far as things that don't decrease in value are concerned, it's a matter of working out whether you've got so many of them that your pot of long-term investments is suffering. We'll look at how big that pot needs to be in Chapter 17. If you think it's not big enough, and you've got a big pile of underperforming assets in your living room, then it's at least worth considering whether the pile could be reduced to give your investments a kick start.

Your home, if you own it, is a peculiar sort of asset. Property has tended to make good returns over the years, so it's with good reason that people tend to think of it as an investment. In truth, though, your home is more like the painting above the mantelpiece. It should go up in value over the long term, along with the economy at least, but much of the return you get from it is in the form of having somewhere nice to live and not having to pay rent for it. In other words, you're getting a return from your home, but you're consuming that return yourself, by living there.

The best way to think of your relationship with your home is to imagine yourself wearing different hats. With one hat on, your investing hat, you are the owner of the property. With the other hat on, your consuming hat, you are the person who rents the property from yourself. So, the cost of your house to you is what you would be able to get if you rented it to someone else. At the moment that's around 7 per cent of the property value per year, but it goes up and down with interest rates like everything else.

Anyway, the fact of the matter is that while your house might feel like an investment, that's not really how things stand. The more accurate way to look at it is to think of it as a chattel. It's a pretty good chattel, like a quality antique, because its value should at least keep track with inflation and earnings growth over the years; but any returns over and above that are lost, because you're living in the house yourself. In any case, when we get onto Chapter 17 and try to work out how much you need to live on in retirement, we're going to assume that the mortgage is paid off and that you can therefore live in your home for free. On that basis, any money in your home isn't going to be available to you for generating a retirement income. We'll look more closely at your home and mortgage, though, in Chapter 18.

Savings

Savings are a reserve of the cash that comes in through your income, the idea being that the money is readily available to cover any planned or unplanned expenditure that crops up over the next few years. The first thing to note is that savings are there to complement our income. We don't need to have money saved in our bank account to pay for all the pints of milk that we might need over the next couple of years, because we can easily meet those costs out of our income (we hope). There are however, more lumpy expenditures that crop up.

Holidays are an obvious example. You probably take a holiday once a year, but unless you earn an awful lot, you're unlikely to be able to afford it out of one month's salary. What you need is to be saving a hundred pounds or so in each non-holiday month, so that by the time the holiday comes along, you have enough to pay for it.

How much do you need to save?

There are other examples of planned expenditures that you need to save for, such as the annual service charge (if you live in a flat), or that new kitchen, or even just Christmas (I'm writing this on 18 December and believe me…). So you need to divert enough of your income towards savings, so that you have enough to pay for the planned expenditures when they crop up. Try making a list of your planned 'lumpy' expenditures, along with their estimated cost and when the money's needed in the box on page 175.

It's all a bit vague (apart from anything else, it's a little tricky to add up the 'how soon' column), but putting it down on paper should give you an idea of

PLANNED EXPENDITURE	Expenditure	Cost	How Soon?
	Holiday		
	Christmas		
	Total		

how much money you're going to need tucked away in savings, and when. Then you can think about whether there's enough there already (lucky you) or whether you're tucking enough away each month to get you there in time.

Beyond planned expenditures, there are one or two things that you might call semi-planned expenditures. Repairs to your car are one example. Another would be calling out a plumber/electrician/pest-control person to sort out your home. You know it's going to hit you sooner or later, but you're really not quite sure when. Again, think about your life, and your various bits and pieces, and try to imagine what might crop up in this category. Again, we've given you a table so you can put pen to paper. This time, though, it's a lot harder to work out what to put in it. Coming up with the eventualities is hard enough, but it's even harder to put a value on them. How much will it cost to repair your car if you have some, as yet unspecified, mechanical failure? Well, how much did it cost last time? Even better, how much did it cost the last three times, divided by three?

SEMI-PLANNED EXPENDITURE	Expenditure	Estimated Cost
	Car repairs	£500
	Total	

This time, you have a choice, depending on how close you like to sail to the wind. If you're very much a downwind sort of person, you might want to have enough tucked away to cover all the semi-planned expenditures on your list if they happened all at the same time. On the other hand, if you're more the 'close-hauled', boat-tipping, mast-creaking kind of soul, then you might reckon that you'll only get stung for one of these events in each year. In that case, you might be happy to keep just enough to pay for one at a time and then restock the reserve when something happens (keep your fingers crossed, though). Most people will be somewhere in the middle of all this, but you can't really work out where you are unless you think about what might crop up.

Finally, you need to think about totally unplanned types of expenditure that might hit you. Here we're talking about redundancy, unplanned pregnancy, a sudden flit across the world because Betty in California is tying the knot – you know the sort of thing. What you need to keep back to account for this type of thing really is hard to quantify. Even so, it's easier for you than it is for me. I'm writing this book for people in all sorts of different situations whereas you, at least, have some idea of your own. Do you work as a civil servant or for a flighty start-up company? Are you having regular (or even irregular) sex without contraception? Are Betty's emails indicating a very cosy state of affairs with Pete, the plumber from Pasadena?

After thinking about how likely any of these things are, you need to think about how they might affect you financially. You might be entitled to attractive maternity rights through your job, but then again you might not. If you lose your job, how much money would you leave with (in other words, how long is your notice period and what rights do you have to any redundancy)? How long do you guess it would take to find alternative employment?

If you're a couple with two incomes, or even an individual with two incomes, this will also make a difference. How likely is it that both incomes dry up at the same time? If both incomes are in the same sector of the economy, or even the same company, then the chances are greater than if one of you works in advertising and the other as an insolvency practitioner.

You can actually drive yourself mad thinking about all the possibilities and that'll just make losing your job (and perhaps the pregnancy) more likely. Ultimately, deciding how much you need to cover unplanned expenditure is so hard that it becomes easy. You'd be very brave to live your life without enough to cover at least three months' expenditure whereas, assuming you're vaguely employable, you'd probably be overly cautious to have more than 12 months' worth. Most people will find themselves somewhere in the middle of this. Say six months?

On to that six months (or whatever it is), you can add whatever you feel you should have reserved for semi-planned expenditure and what you need, from time to time, to meet the planned expenses (over and above those that you cover out of income). One way or another, that probably leaves you with the equivalent of nine months' normal living expenses and for most people, assuming they're doing some saving (which would go on hold in an emergency), that adds up to, say, six months' income. Of course, depending on your circumstances and attitude to risk, it might be more or less than this, but it's a basic sort of benchmark. In particular, if you've got two incomes, you might go a little lower than this on the basis that it's that much less likely for both incomes to disappear at once (and that much more likely that one would be replaced relatively soon if they did).

So, after all that, how much have you got tucked away in savings? Is it enough? If not, then your first priority should be to make it so that it is. That might mean putting your long-term investments on hold for the time being and it might even mean revisiting your budget in Chapter 12, to find a few pounds extra to save each month.

What should you do with your savings?

Having worked out (or, rather, guessed) how much you need in the way of savings, the next thing to worry about is what to do with them. The bottom line with this is to remember what they're there for. They need to be secure and relatively accessible. Right away, then, we can forget about things like shares, which have a very uncertain value over the short term. What good are savings if, when the holiday or that bill for car repairs or even that redundancy arrives, you haven't got the money any more because there's a nasty stock market slump? Shares also aren't very accessible since they cost a fair bit of money to buy and sell.

Cash is king
Nope, you've guessed it, the basis for your savings is good, honest, cash. What you can do, though, is make sure that the cash is earning a decent rate of interest, while it's waiting for its call-up. If you're aiming to have, for example, £15,000 in

savings, then that could be earning interest of perhaps 5 per cent per year (depending on current interest rates). That amounts to £750 per year, which is a lot of money to give up by just leaving it to rot in a zero interest current account.

There are, in fact, a number of Internet-based banks springing up these days that, because of their ability to keep costs low, offer current accounts with what look like deposit account rates of interest. There's a guide to picking them on the Motley Fool website at **www.fool.co.uk/banking/banking.htm**, and it's certainly something to consider. Perhaps, though, you like the service, or whatever else it is, that you get from your current bank. If that's the case, there's nothing much wrong with having a few thousand pounds in a low-interest current account. But it's worth being aware of what it costs you. Interest of 5 per cent on, say, £3,000 pounds amounts to £150 per year, or around 40p per day. So if you were thinking of economizing by not buying a newspaper each day, then your bank account might be costing you as much. On any basis, though, it's worth having enough in any bank account to avoid it going into overdraft. When that happens, you can forget the 5 per cent you might be earning elsewhere, because it'll be costing you more like 14 per cent. I won't bore you with another rant about debt – if you want a refresher, go back to the beginning of Chapter 14.

Another point that ties in with this is how many current accounts to have: a particularly relevant question for couples. The thing to bear in mind is that to prevent overdrafts, you need to have a thousand pounds or so, depending on how much you spend, in each account that you have. More accounts therefore means more money that could, perhaps, be working harder. Even if you get a decent rate of interest on your current accounts, you'll generally get a higher rate of interest by having more money in one account. So, on the whole, a proliferation of bank accounts is a bad thing, since it means your money isn't pulling its weight. Another way to look at it is to think about the bank. More accounts equals more admin for them. That means more cost and, one way or another, they'll probably want you to pay for it. Having said all that, I'm not suggesting that couples embark on a headlong rush into joint accounts. There are so many more personal considerations, such as independence and convenience, to take into account. From a purely financial point of view, though, the fewer accounts the better (though it's a relatively small thing).

Beyond the float in your current account (which, of course, will go up and down as holidays etcetera get bought and paid for), you really need to be thinking in terms of deposit accounts, and this is a matter of shopping around for the best interest rates. To get the very best rates of interest, you may need to look at 'notice accounts' where you have to give, for example, three months' notice to get at your money. If you stand to get three months' notice from your employer if you lose your job, then that would fit quite nicely, but it wouldn't do as a store of money for your holiday or those car repairs.

It's worth keeping everything in perspective, though. You can wear yourself out looking for the best interest rates and ultimately, although it's worth making sure you get a *good* interest rate, it only makes so much difference if you get the best. A difference of 0.5 per cent, for instance, on £15,000 amounts to only £75 per year. Sure, it's worth having, but it's probably not worth poring over Deposit Account Weekly and filling in an application form every few months. The ideal is probably simply to check once every year or so that your account is still paying a competitive rate of interest. So do that now! Most broadsheet Sunday newspapers have a table of the best interest rates available in their Money section. If you're a long way off, then you'd want to change, but if it's marginal then what the heck. You never know, you might be top of the list next year.

Individual Savings Accounts

Each year, you can tuck away up to £3,000 in a cash ISA (which is short for Individual Savings Account) and, if you do so, then you get the interest on that £3,000 tax free. If, say, you're getting interest on that £3,000 at 5 per cent, then you'd be getting £150 in interest. A basic-rate taxpayer would pay £30 on that interest, deducted at source, while a higher-rate taxpayer would pay £60. On the whole, you'd say that that's worth having. After all, if it's worth having the interest, then it's worth having it tax free, especially if you're a higher-rate taxpayer. The trouble is that you have only one ISA allowance of £7,000 per year, and all of this can go into a stocks and shares ISA if you like. We'll talk more about investments and ISAs in the next chapter but, while we're here, it's worth pointing out that cash ISAs are all very well, but you probably get more bang for your buck, on the tax front, with a stocks and shares ISA. So you'll probably want to start by using ISAs for your investments and shelter any of your remaining allowance in a cash ISA.

Current account mortgages

It may seem a little odd to flip suddenly into mortgages when we've been talking about savings, but current account mortgages can provide you with both. They basically work by including your mortgage as a huge overdraft in your bank account. So, say you buy a house for £80,000 and have a deposit of £10,000. You will start off with an account that has a balance of *minus £70,000* and you'll be paying interest on it, just as with a normal mortgage. Imagine that the £70,000 is also your borrowing limit on the account. Each month your salary goes in and every penny that you manage not to spend will gradually go to reducing the mortgage.

If you save hard and manage to get the balance on your account up to only *minus* £60,000, then that £10,000 you've got between the balance of minus £60,000 and the limit of £70,000 is still available to you. So, what you've effectively done is save £10,000 but, and here's the really clever bit, you don't actually have the cash. Instead you have a smaller mortgage. So you get to have your savings cake and eat it. You can have your stash of savings without actually having to have the cash sitting around idly. You'll be saving interest on your mortgage at a higher rate than you could be getting on a deposit account. You also save tax, because you're not actually receiving any interest (the taxman doesn't tax you for mortgage interest you're not paying). We'll say more about these little beauties in Chapter 18, Your Home and Your Mortgage.

Other possible homes for savings

You will hear people talk about 'medium-term' savings, but it's never very clear what this means. After all, you can't predict whether that unplanned emergency will crop up this year, next year, in five years' time or never, but you need the money to be available when it does. So putting this type of reserve in something designed for five years or so doesn't make much sense.

One example of this would be 'guaranteed' stock market products. These, for example, might promise you your money back whatever happens to the stock market, plus a bit extra if you leave the money there for the full seven years and the stock market does the right thing. The reality is that the guarantees on your money cost a lot and the returns are rarely that much better than you'd expect from a good deposit account. You might also stand to get no interest at all if you need the money before the seven years are up.

Another possibility as a medium-term investment are bonds whereby you effectively lend money, for a number of years, to companies ('corporate bonds') or to the government ('gilts'). Over the years, the safest of these (particularly the gilts) give you the same sort of interest that you'd get from a bank account – it's just that it is generally fixed for several years in advance. The trouble with this is that their value goes up or down depending on how interest rates move, after their rate has been fixed. So, in the shorter term, they have an uncertain value (although generally much more certain than shares) and that means cash is still better for those emergencies.

Gilts and corporate bonds might make sense for planned expenditure that's still some way off. School fees are an example of this; but over periods of more than five or ten years, shares tend to do quite a lot better (as we'll see in the next chapter), so there's still a pretty narrow window where they make the best sense.

Corporate bonds will pay a little more interest than you can get on a gilt or on cash in the bank, because there's the risk of the company going bust. The trouble is that to reduce that risk you really need to buy a lot of them, and that means investing in 'corporate bond funds', which are a form of pooled investment that invests in many different bonds. And there's a cost to this. The funds will charge 1 per cent a year, or sometimes more, to manage the money; and this puts a pretty big hole in the extra interest you were hoping for.

At the end of the day, it's hard to make an argument against cash as a store for your short-term savings (save for what we said above, about current account mortgages). It's readily accessible, has a predictable value in the shorter term and, if you do a little shopping around, you should get a fair enough rate of interest. If you really, desperately, want some more excitement, then you might think about premium bonds. You can have up to £20,000 invested in these and they can be cashed in at any stage. The prizes are worked out so that they can be expected to pay an acceptable (just about) rate of interest, which varies along with the base rate. Of course, some years you might not get very much interest (or even none), but then you might hit the jackpot and that's where the fun comes in.

Investments

So, you've got rid of any non-mortgage debts, as we talked about in Chapter 14, and you've managed to pull together enough savings to let you sleep soundly at night, as described in Chapter 16. Now you've finally arrived at the chapter on investments. This is where you put the extra money after everything else is taken care of. It's more important than that, though, because your investments are there to finance your retirement. So rather than think of them as a repository of anything that's left over, you really need to start from the other end: work out what you need and then make sure there's enough left over each month to get you there. So how much do you need?

How much you should be tucking away for the future is one of the hardest questions in finance: right up there with how to value shares and how the Bank of England sets interest rates. It involves making guesses about a whole range of things, most of which don't lend themselves very well to guessing. Just because something's difficult, though, doesn't mean you shouldn't have a go. After all, where would we be if the Bank of England simply said 'Well, it's tough. So tough, in fact, that we haven't got a clue. We should probably just stick interest rates at 10 per cent and leave them there forever'?

So, it's a tough business but, Fools that we are, we'll have a bash at it. What we can do is take a tip from the Bank of England and get an understanding of our limitations. They know that their assumptions (guesses) about the future will turn out to be wrong, so they account for it by reviewing them regularly in the light of how things turn out. Once a month, they sit down and look at all the data again and tweak interest rates if necessary. As far as your investments are concerned, you don't need to do it every month, but once a year you should sit down, do some sums, and tweak the amount that you're putting by. And, as you'll no doubt have guessed, that moment is now!

Estimating your retirement income needs

The first guess to make is how much you're going to need to live on in retirement. You wouldn't want to reach retirement and find that you can no longer live in the manner to which you've become accustomed. But there's little point spending your working life investing so hard that you have a miserable time (if you do this, you probably wouldn't know what to do with the money when you finally got to use it, anyway). So the aim should be to maintain your standard of living in retirement, and you need to guess at what that might cost.

To make it easier, you can do it all in today's money. We can use this trick because, when we eventually look at what you might get as a return on our investments over the years, we'll deduct what's needed for the pot of money to keep pace with inflation. In fact, we'll do more than that, and take off enough for the pot of money to keep pace with the average earnings of people all over the country. After all, we don't want our retirement income simply to keep pace with inflation if we suddenly find that, due to economic growth, everyone is now earning that much more and we can't afford the latest gizmos. To put it another way, it wouldn't have been enough, thirty years ago, to think of having enough to buy a telly in retirement, even if we adjusted the cost of it for inflation. These days, to maintain the 'equivalent' standard of living that you enjoyed back then, you'd be wanting a telly, a video recorder, a computer and all the rest of it.

You also need to bear in mind that your life will be a little different when you reach retirement. You'll hopefully have paid off the mortgage (we're going to assume you have, which is why we didn't include your home as an investment in Chapter 13). Also, any kids will most likely have left home, there won't be the cost of commuting to work and a whole host of other things. On the other side of the coin, you probably have an idea of the hobbies that you'd like to fill your time in retirement, and these might cost a bit. Fishing rods aren't free and neither, for that matter, are fishing trips. And of course there are other, less pleasant, side-effects of getting older, like needing extra medical care. Anyway, you need an idea in your mind's eye of how much income, in today's terms, you'll be needing when you retire. It's best to think about this figure *after* tax has been deducted from it – in other words, the actual number of pounds you'll need for spending.

So, umm and ahh a bit, wave your finger in the air if you like and come up with an annual after-tax income that you'll need in retirement. It might seem a little arbitrary, but it's the only way to do it and it does need doing. Remember, too, that you'll be tweaking your numbers each year, so you can home in on a more accurate figure as you get closer to it. Anyhow, think of a number and enter it here:

> Best guess of annual income needed in retirement

Estimating income from other sources

From this figure, you need to deduct any income that you expect to receive from sources other than your own personal saving. To start with there's the State Pension, which is worth around £5,000 per year (before tax). The trouble with this is that its value relative to everything else has been falling for many years now, and we'd suggest you exclude it from your plans. Instead it can operate as a sort of safety valve (though probably not much of one).

There are also 'final salary' pensions. These, also known as 'defined benefit' pensions, generally work by giving you a retirement income of, say, one sixtieth of your final salary for each year that you've worked for the company. That way, 40 years' employment will lead to a pension that adds up to 40/60, or two-thirds, of your final salary. The beauty of this design is that it automatically maintains your standard of living into retirement (on the basis that you only need two-thirds of your former income when retired).

There are, however, one or two problems. To start with, they don't necessarily keep pace with inflation very well. On top of this, most people don't stay with the same employer for very long these days (at least not for a lifetime). These two problems can, in fact, combine to leave you with lots of not very valuable pensions by the time you retire. In any case, final salary schemes are mostly confined to the public sector nowadays, as well as a handful of very large companies. If you do have one, then you need to work out how much, in today's money, it's likely to give you in retirement, *after tax* of course. You can then deduct that from the income you'll need to leave you with what you have to generate from elsewhere. Be conservative, though. You could easily find yourself with a new employer in five years' time, and that juicy final salary pension might not look so juicy then.

With other types of pension, called 'defined contribution', what you get depends on how much has gone into them over the years and how the investments within the pension fund have performed. You can pay into them yourself, but quite often an employer will add something as well. The way to treat these is to ignore them for the time being. It's all investing and we're trying to work out how much you ought to be doing. When we get there, we can deduct any contributions that your employer makes to your pension from what you need to put by yourself.

So, you can now enter the amount of income you need to generate from your investments, after deducting anything you expect to get, after tax, from final salary pensions.

Best guess of after-tax income to be generated from investments

How big a pot do you need?

OK, so now you should have some idea of the after-tax income that you'll be needing to generate from your investments in retirement. Now we need to work out how big a pot of investments you'll need to produce that income. For the sake of this example, we're going to go for a target income of £15,000 and we're going to try to get there in 20 years' time. We're going to use 5 per cent as the return you can get from your investments, while at the same time allowing the investments (and therefore the return you get from them) to grow along with inflation and economic growth (we'll explain where the 5 per cent comes from later on).

So, if you're getting 5 per cent per year from your pot of investments and you need £15,000, then £15,000 is going to be 5 per cent of your pot of investments. That works out like this:

£15,000 = pot multiplied by 0.05
which, by dividing both sides by 0.05, can be rewritten as
£15,000 divided by 0.05 = pot = £300,000

So, roughly speaking, if you're looking at having today's equivalent of £15,000 per year, after tax, in retirement, then you will need a pot of money worth today's equivalent of £300,000 to produce it for you. You can now do the same sum for yourself and put the answer in here:

Best guess as to the size of pot needed to produce retirement income

When will you retire?

You've now got an idea of the size of the pot that you need to scrape together. The next thing to think about is how long you've got to do it. When do you expect to retire? The answer to this isn't 'when I'm forty', because you'll find, when we get there, that to do this you'd need to be investing all of your salary and more. Believe me, the sums turn out pretty nasty as it is. Be realistic. Unless you're a trader in the City earning a fortune, aim for some time in your late fifties or early sixties. How far away is that? Enter the number in the following table (which, you'll notice, is beginning to expand).

Best guess as to the size of pot needed to produce retirement income	
Years to build pot	

How much have you already got?

Of course the other major factor that affects how much you need to save is how much you've got already. Hopefully you answered that question when you put together your personal balance sheet in Chapter 13. So, how much, if anything, do you have in the investments category?

Unfortunately, to make our guess as good as we can, we need to adjust the value of the different investments, to account for the tax we have to pay on the income they will eventually produce. The way to do this is to imagine your tax return when you retire and think about how much tax you'd be paying on each source of income (if the same tax rules apply).

So, if you guess that your income will be half basic-rate and half higher-rate tax in retirement (because that's what it would be today), then that would put your overall tax rate at around 30 per cent (that is, around halfway in between). On that basis, you'd need to knock 30 per cent off the value of any pensions you have, to account for the 30 per cent tax that you expect to end up paying on the annuity that the pension provides you with. You'd have to do the same with other investments that will be subject to income tax. For instance, if you have shares held directly, outside of an ISA, then as a higher-rate taxpayer, you'd have to pay an extra 25 per cent tax on the dividends you get from them. So, you'd need to knock 25 per cent off their value. The idea is to adjust the value of your different investments downwards, to account for how much of their value will end up being taken away from you by the taxman. Bearing this in mind, copy the figures from Your Personal Balance Sheet on pages 165–66 into the table below and adjust them to account for tax.

Remember that we're only playing with best guesses. Even if you're 10 per cent out, it shouldn't matter too much. If none of this is making much sense, just take off 25 per cent of the value of any investments that aren't tucked up in an ISA. You shouldn't go too far wrong.

TAX ADJUSTMENTS FOR EXISTING INVESTMENTS	Investments	Value now (£)	Percentage adjustment to account for future tax	Adjusted value (£)
	Unit trusts and OEICs (including share-based ISAs)			
	Investment trusts			
	Individual shareholdings (including self-select ISAs)			
	Pensions (defined contribution)			
	Endowments			
	Rental property			
	Other ( )			
	Other ( )			
	Total			

The next thing to do is to work out how much this will be worth when we retire. In other words, how much of our pot will be accounted for by investments that we've already put aside. To get this, we need to 'compound' whatever we've already got (adjusted of course) at the rate of 5 per cent per year until we get to retirement. Compounding just means multiplying the adjusted value of our investments by '1.05 to the power of the number of years until retirement'. So, if you've already got, say, £30,000 tucked away and there are 20 years until retirement, then you have the following sum:

$$£30,000 \times 1.05^{20}$$

The 1.05^{20} is just shorthand for multiplying by 1.05 twenty times. The easiest way to do this is to start by multiplying the 1.05 by 1.05, twenty times. 'Scientific' calculators will have a special button on them for doing this. Otherwise, I'm afraid, it'll be a matter of using the multiplication button (and you'll need to do it two or three times to make sure you've not lost count). Anyway…

$$£30,000 \times 1.05^{20} = £79,599 \text{ (to the nearest pound)}$$

So, if you have £30,000 already and you have 20 years to retirement, then you could knock £79,599 off the total pot you've got to reach. So, do the following sum for yourself:

$$[\text{value of pot already}] \times 1.05^{[\text{years until retirement}]}$$

Bear in mind that the investments we're talking about here are just the investments you have stored away, and which have the opportunity of making a proper investment return. I'm afraid it doesn't do to deduct the value of any equity you have in your home because, as we saw in Chapter 15, you're consuming a large part of the return you get from your property by living in it. Besides, we're not factoring the cost of a mortgage into the income you need in retirement, and you will need somewhere to live. Of course, if you have a rental property that is making a proper return by being rented out, then you could include that, but only if you reinvest the rental income in shares or something rather than spending it.

Anyway, having worked the numbers out for yourself, insert them into the table below:

		HOW MUCH DO YOU NEED TO COBBLE TOGETHER FROM NOW ON
Best guess as to the size of pot needed to produce retirement income ('A')		
Years to build pot		
Value of current investments (with a bit knocked off, where appropriate, to take account of tax)		
Contribution that current investments should make to retirement pot ('B')		
Best guess as to total pot you need to reach out of what you tuck away from now on		

First of all, multiply your required pot by 0.05. Then, divide this number by 1.05. Then put the resulting number to one side in a box marked 'leave until later'.

Now put 1.05 to the power of the number of years that you've got until retirement. (Remember how we said earlier that this 'power of' stuff was just shorthand for multiply by this number that many times? It'll be easier if you have a 'scientific' calculator – if you have a computer, there'll be one on there). Take the answer from this and subtract 1. Put the answer to this in a box labelled 'keep handy'.

Finally, take what's in the box marked 'leave until later' and divide it by the contents of the box marked 'keep handy'.

How much we need to add to our investments from now on

Now we've got a figure for what we need to produce from additional savings from now on. Next, we can work out how much that means we need to add to our investments, on a monthly basis. Unfortunately, this is where the sums get a little hairy. Not only do we have to do more of that fiddly compounding, but we have to compound something that we're adding to each month. What you really need here is a compound interest calculator (there are plenty on the Internet, including one on the Motley Fool website at **www.fool.co.uk/school/compound.htm**), but without that, you'll have to settle for an ugly formula. How about this one…

$$P = \frac{a(1+r)((1+r)^n -1)}{r}$$

Don't panic! I just thought I'd start by showing you what we're up against. It also means that the people out there who are good at maths can play around a bit (they like that).

'P' stands for 'pot' and 'a' stands for the amount you're saving per month. 'r' stands for the investment return and, since we're using 5 per cent as our investment return, the '1+r's become '1.05's. 'n' is the number of periods that you're investing for. To keep things relatively simple, we'll stick to using 'n' as a number of years. That should give us an amount to invest per year. We can then divide that by 12 to give us the amount to save per month. (Compound interest officionados among you will probably be aware that this is an approximation, and we'd be more precise doing everything in months, but hey, we've already made plenty of approximations and this one's a very small one. It does make the sums a lot simpler.)

We've turned things around and spelt them out in the box alongside called Go Figure, for those of you that prefer English to mathematics. So, take the numbers that apply to you and work them through.

And the answer is… a rabbit. No. Sorry. That's not it. The answer is the number of pounds you need to invest per year until retirement to live happily ever after. More useful, in almost all senses, than a rabbit. You can divide that number by 12 to give you a number to be saving monthly. How did you go? You've not done it yet? OK, to make you even more comfortable, we've followed our example through to its conclusion in the box on page 190.

So £6,349, I'm afraid, is the number of pounds you'd need to save per year, over 20 years, to put together an after-tax retirement income of £15,000 per year, assuming you've already got £30,000 tucked away. You can divide it by 12 to get a number for what you need to save each month, and that comes to £529. It's a big number, isn't it? Thankfully we can throw some good news in to make things a bit easier. The first is that because of the way we've worked things out, as we said at the beginning, inflation and earnings growth ought to take care of themselves.

You can take away from the amount *you* need to save each month any money that your employer puts into defined contribution pensions for you. Unfortunately, you can't take off the money that the government effectively puts into your pension fund, because the contributions are made tax free. The reason is the same reason that we adjusted the value of your accumulated pension fund downwards to account for what you'll have to pay on the income from it. Since we've come up with a figure for the retirement income we need *after* tax, then the pot that we must put together doesn't take account of it. So the tax that gets added to your pension contributions should be thought of as a provision for the tax you'll have to pay on your pension income, and *ignored* as far as how much you need to save is concerned.

Repeating the process each year

Because everything is being worked out in terms of today's money, when we do the sums again next year, money will be worth a slightly different amount (generally a bit less), so you'll need a slightly different amount to keep you happy in retirement (generally a bit more). You'll also have a different amount of savings already tucked away (hopefully a bit more, depending on how well your investments have actually done) and 12 fewer months to get the money together.

So you'll need to go through the process again, from start to finish. The result will be a slightly different amount that you need to save each month for the next year to keep on track. It may be more and it may be less, though most likely it will have gone up a touch due to inflation and growth in earnings. But that's OK, since we hope our earnings will have gone up by this amount as well. You really need to go through this process once a year and, guess what, your annual financial health check is the ideal time to do it!

Of course, just like any sums, all this does is produce a number. You will then have to decide what to do about it, according to your circumstances. If you're young, with no family but a tidy income, then you might decide to save

AND THE ANSWER IS...

Remember we needed to get £220,401 together (our pot is reduced by £79,599 to account for the £30,000 we already have) over 20 years, and we're expecting 5 per cent as our annual investment return.

We multiply 220,401 by 0.05 (and get, roughly, 11,020). Then we divide 11,020 by 1.05 (and get 10,495). So we put 10,495 to one side in our box marked 'leave until later'.

Now we put 1.05 to the power of 20 (and get 2.653). We then subtract 1 from 2.653 (giving us 1.653). We put the 1.653 in a box labelled 'keep handy'. Finally, we take the 10,495 (from our box marked 'leave until later') and divide it by 1.653 (from our box marked 'keep handy') and we end up with £6,349.

a bit more than the sums tell you to. That way, when you've got a couple of kids and a whole host of other expenses, you'll have enough tucked away already to make the monthly savings figure that much smaller. You may expect to earn significantly more in a few years' time; in which case you could choose to save a bit less, in the expectation that you'll be able to afford the bigger monthly number that will appear from the sums at that stage.

Going through the process each year at least lets you know what should be par for the course. If you can shoot a few birdies early on, then you'll be in a better position to cope with some tricky holes later on. On the other hand, if you've got some tough holes at the beginning, then it's better to make a bogie than just give up! Repeating the process also means that how much you save over the years gets adjusted to take account of investment returns as they actually materialize. In other words, although we're only dealing with approximations, even mere guesses, things should work out because we'll keep adjusting our guesses in the light of what's actually happening. The one thing, however, that is very unlikely to change is our best guess about future investment returns. As we'll see in a moment, the 5 per cent figure comes from looking at what's happened in the stock market over a hundred years or so. Just because the stock market might have jumped by 20 per cent last year, or slumped by 20 per cent (which, as it happens, is closer to the mark), doesn't affect our guesses about the long-term future. Nor, for that matter, do any of the guesses about the next few years in the stock market that you'll read in the Sunday newspapers.

Investment returns

Now we can have a look at where the 5 per cent figure comes from. At the same time we can see why the stock market is the best place for your long-term investments. Shares, what you get in the stock market, are 'real' assets. They represent part of a business enterprise and, as such, they naturally take account of inflation and growth in average earnings. After all, it's those business enterprises that pay people's wages out of their profits. By attaching your long-term investments to the profits of those businesses, you also effectively attach them to the earnings that everyone is taking home.

By keeping money in the bank, in the form of cash, you don't achieve this. That pound represents a pound, pure and simple. If the economy suddenly puts on a spurt, whether because of inflation or because we're just becoming more productive, that pound could be worth relatively less. The profits of businesses in the economy, on the other hand, will still be worth an amount, relative to average wages, similar to before.

So shares are going to be the most appropriate store of value over the long-term. It's a happy coincidence that they've also tended to produce the best long-term returns. In fact, it's not that much of a coincidence. The reason that it's not surprising is that the economy wouldn't be doing very well if that wasn't the case. If shares do badly for a long period of time, this means that companies' profits, in real terms, must be drying up. If that happens, where's the money going to come from to pay all the interest on the cash? Perhaps more importantly, where's the money going to come from to produce taxes for the government? Companies are what drive the economy forward. They produce the profits that they can then use to pay people's wages, pay interest on their borrowings and pay tax. One way or another, economic policy needs to be set so that they can carry on doing so. Otherwise we'd all go broke! And the effect of going broke wouldn't be good for the value of those pound notes.

Over a period as short as five years, shares can look pretty scary. Enough to make cash look relatively appealing (which is why we wanted to use cash for five-year savings in the last chapter). For every five-year period from 1918 to 2000 (that is, 1918-1923, 1919-1924, 1920-1925… you get the picture), the returns from cash and shares are given below (the figures come from the CSFB Equity-Gilt study and all the figures are after inflation).

Returns on shares and cash over five-year 'rolling' periods since 1918			
	Average Annual Return (%)	Highest Annual Return (%)	Lowest Annual Return (%)
Shares	8.2	32.1	-18.8
Cash	1.6	12.5	-4.9
Shares beat cash in 79.5% of five-year periods			

5-YEAR PERFORMANCE

Shares do best, on average, but the range of returns varies much more. In other words, they're riskier. As our time periods get longer, though, this effect gets smaller. It stands to reason. After all, a ten-year period is two five-year periods put together, so you get an averaging effect. The returns for ten-year periods are shown on page 193. Much better, but still slightly scary if you have a very sensitive disposition.

10-YEAR PERFORMANCE

Returns on shares and cash over ten-year 'rolling' periods since 1918

	Average Annual Return (%)	Highest Annual Return (%)	Lowest Annual Return (%)
Shares	8.2	18.5	-6.0
Cash	1.6	9.8	-3.3

Shares beat cash in 97.2% of five-year periods

Once we get to 20-year periods, though, there's very little contest. Cash has beaten shares in only one out of 62 periods and even then, it only won by a slither (a mere 0.3 per cent per year). Just to make the point more forcefully, we'll cast a quick eye over the 30-year periods. By the time we get here, things have become a paradise for the long-term investor in shares. In fact, the London Stock Market has never lost out to cash. In their *worst* period (1944-1974) shares managed an average annual gain of 2 per cent, while cash could only manage a 2.4 per cent average gain per year in its *best* period. For the period 1920-1950, when cash was producing its best return, shares were busy generating 9.4 per cent per year. So, it's pretty clear what works best over the truly long term. And, if you start investing for retirement as early as you ought to, then it is a truly long term undertaking.

So, now we can address where that 5 per cent figure comes from. As you'll see from the tables, the average annual return for shares since 1918, after inflation, was 8.2 per cent. From this we take off a further 2 per cent to account for average earnings growth over and above this (this has been a relatively stable figure since our data begins in the 1960s). Then we need to take off 1 per cent or so to account for charges (it would be nice to assume that investing costs you nothing, but unfortunately it's not true). So that leaves us pretty close to 5 per cent, which we see as a nice round number (and remember we're dealing with estimates – even over 30-year periods, the real return from shares has varied from 2.0 per cent to 9.4 per cent).

Spreading it about

The other point to make about these average returns is that they are exactly that: averages. Averages of the whole stock market. Or, rather, averages of large representative parts of it. So, if you're just going to put all your investments into moneyfromether.com, then things will look very different. Quite likely you'll end up with nothing, but there's a chance you could hit the jackpot. Very few shares end up producing anything like the average on their own.

Just as doing it for a lot of years smoothes out your likely returns, so does going for a decent spread of shares. Simply on the basis of eggs and baskets. Once you've got up to about 12 to 15 shares from different industry sectors (in sensible proportions), it's beginning to get very likely that you'll get reasonably close to the market average. If you made it 30 shares (again from different areas of the market and in sensible proportions), then it becomes very difficult not to be very close to the market average. The trouble is that, all other things being equal, as the number of different shares goes up, so does the cost of getting them. That would be reason to reduce the 5 per cent figure we're using as our expected investment return, and that could put a large hole in our sums.

What you need to decide is whether you want to try to do better than average or just settle for getting the average. There's a big WARNING to make here. Trying to beat the market average tends to incur extra costs. That reason alone means that most people that try to do it fail. So, for once, there is an awful lot to be said for being average.

Being average

In investment terms, being properly average comes down to doing one of three things. First of all, you can invest via an index tracker. These are funds that are designed to give the performance of the overall stock market. Hold on, isn't that just what we wanted? Yes, it is. Fantastic! They tend to cost from 0.5 per cent to 1 per cent of your invested money per year. Not surprisingly, being at the 0.5 per cent end of things is best.

The second way to be average is just to buy a load of different shares (like about 15 or 20 from different industry sectors in sensible proportions) and leave them alone (perhaps adjusting things from time to time to make sure the proportions remain sensible). Over many years, you're unlikely to miss the market's performance by much and you might save yourself that 0.5 per cent per year. The trouble with this is that if you want the money to be invested in some form of wrapper to protect it from tax (like an ISA or a pension), then you'll quite likely have to pay around 0.5 per cent per year anyway.

On top of this, if you're adding £x to your investments each month, then that's going to cost extra as well, if you're going down the individual shares route. An index tracker, on the other hand, will let you add your £x per month, straight out of your bank account, with the cost of doing so all included within the 0.5 per cent fee.

Given how we're so keen on these index tracker thingies, it's not surprising that a whole section of our website is devoted to them. You can find it at **www.fool.co.uk/isas/trackers/trackers.htm.**

Not being average

As I've already said, trying not to be average tends to result in being below average. That's what professional fund managers find – the vast majority of them fail to beat the average over the long term – and that's what most private individuals find as well. The problem is that everyone is fighting against each other in what, for these purposes, can be thought of as a zero-sum game. Everyone has the same shares to invest in and one person's gain is another person's loss. Of course, you can try to make sure that you get the gains and someone else gets the losses but how, exactly, is that achieved?

What people tend to find (and tend isn't really a strong enough word) is that all the shifting around that's required to try to beat the average results in extra costs, and that just results in a greater chance of being below average. The typical managed unit trust might charge around 1.5 per cent or more of your money per year, or about 1 per cent more than an index tracker. Not surprisingly, on average, they tend to perform about 1 per cent per year less well. The private investor who trades in and out of shares in the hope of doing better than average will most likely have higher costs than this. So, it's all very self-defeating.

What you're really looking for when comparing investment funds are factors that show *persistence*. It sounds a bit like some sort of rash and that's not a bad way of looking at it. You want to find things affecting a fund's performance that will stick to it like a rash. You can see all sorts of patterns in the historic performance of a fund, but unless it's something that's likely to *persist* into the future, then it's no good to you at all.

One of the most obvious things that people look for in a managed investment fund is its recent performance record, say up to the last five years or so. Is that likely to *persist* into the future? The answer, (according to research undertaken by the WM Company, amongst others) is a pretty resounding 'no'. So, even though it's tempting to pay a lot of attention to recent past performance, it's unlikely to tell you very much.

As a record of consistently good performance gets longer and longer, though, you might begin to conclude that it is telling you something. Not because of itself, but because it might suggest that there's something else that's *persisting* in the performance. A good example of this is the legendary American investor, Warren Buffett. After thirty or forty years of consistently good performance, few people would put it all down to luck. More likely there's something else that's persisting. He keeps costs very low at his investment vehicle, **Berkshire Hathaway** but he's probably just very good at picking shares. The trouble is that it takes a very long time to become confident about this ability – and now that he's at last everyone's favourite fund manager, he must be close to retirement. There aren't going to be many, if any, funds around with this type of performance record, and the likelihood of it continuing into the future.

The National Lottery is a good example of what we're talking about. In its first year of operation, the number 5 was drawn an impressive ten times, compared to a shocking performance by the number 39, which appeared only once. Would you conclude from this that the number 5 was more likely to appear than the number 39 in future? You certainly shouldn't! Some numbers *have* to be drawn more than the others. It would be more unbelievable if all the numbers were drawn exactly as expected (especially since they should each come out 6.3673469 times). But if, after twenty years, the number 5 was still coming out ten times as often as the number 39, then you'd be thinking it might be heavier or something. No doubt the authorities would spot that, though, and shave a little off it.

One type of investment fund, other than the trackers that we've talked about already, has shown persistently good performance over many years. These funds are called 'investment trusts' and are actually companies that invest in other companies. The ones that we're interested in are the very big ones. The likes of Foreign and Colonial and Alliance Trust are worth well over a billion pounds. The beauty of them is that as they get bigger, they become relatively cheaper per pound invested in them, and, being companies, they're legally obliged to pass these benefits on to their shareholders (that is, the people who've invested in them). This means that they tend to have lower costs and, over the long term, they therefore tend to do that much better. You won't often hear about them from so-called 'independent' financial advisers, because they won't get much (or any) commission from selling them to you. But that, of course, is precisely the reason they get a head start. Perhaps the less said about that the better (who ever said the Motley Fool didn't pull its punches). If you want to find out more about investment trusts, you can do so at the Association of Investment Trust Companies, or AITC for short. The web address is **www.aitc.co.uk**. While we're at it, a good resource for all investment funds, including unit trusts and OEICs, is **www.trustnet.com**.

If an investment is consistently performing badly over many years, then it can also become a warning sign that there is something beneath the bonnet that's causing the bad performance. Much has been made of the lousy performance of 'endowments' over the last ten years (and more), and rightly so. They consistently perform well below the stock market averages and, sooner or later, you have to begin to wonder why. Endowments can often carry more cash than other investment funds, and, as we've seen, cash tends not to do too well over the long term. More importantly, though, endowments carry some very hefty charges and that acts a brake on their performance.

All we're really saying here is that you can't tell much about the performance of your investments on a one-year basis. Instead, you need to think about factors that might persist, but focus on long-term performance to judge whether they're showing their face or not (and that means at least five years, and preferably many more). Instead of asking yourself whether your particular investment fund has performed well over the last year, ask yourself whether similar types of investment, with a similar approach to investing and a similar level of charges, have performed well over the last twenty years or more. That's likely to tell you a great deal more about it.

Before we move off the subject, we should mention that the other way to try to beat the averages is to pick the shares yourself. As I've said, the odds are against you and they get heavier as your costs increase, but that's not necessarily a reason not to have a bash at it. In fact, much of the discussion on the Motley Fool's website is devoted to trying to pick shares that will beat the averages. If you fancy having a go, first of all remember that there's no rush. The market will still be there tomorrow, so there's no reason to charge in just because your mate seems to have made a killing. What you want to do is develop a strategy that has at least a chance, in your opinion, of showing persistently good performance. That's very definitely no easy task, so it's well worth spending some time getting to grips with things. No doubt you've guessed, but a good place to do that is the Motley Fool website.

Protecting your investments from the taxman

So we've established that your long-term investments should be in shares, and we've worked out that you can most likely give yourself the best returns from shares, with minimum risk, by being cheap and average. Isn't life wonderful? For most people, who are saving monthly, a cheap index-tracking unit trust is going to be the best way forward. One thing remains, and that is the question of how to keep the taxman out of your trough. This essentially means putting a nice, cosy, tax-protective wrapper around it – and that brings us to pensions and individual savings accounts (ISAs). There are also certain insurance products that can save you some tax but, as will become clear, we don't much like them as investments in the first place, so that rather counts them out. Let's start with pensions.

Pensions

Pensions are best thought of as deferred income. You effectively say to your employer, 'Don't pay me that bit of income now. Instead, let's put it somewhere where it can wait until I'm retired and need it.' So, since you're not taking the income now, the government doesn't charge you income tax on it. Instead, it waits until you are paid the money in retirement, when it most certainly *will* tax you on it. In the meantime, while the money's waiting for you to need it, it gets invested in some form of fund, generally linked to the stock market, where it can increase its value relative to the rest of the economy.

It's important to think of pensions like this, because it puts their tax position in focus. All that's happening is that you're deferring your income and, quite reasonably, the government agrees to forgo the tax on that income until you actually receive it. That's not quite the free money that it's sometimes made out to be.

The reason that pensions are attractive, from a tax point of view, is that the alternatives are not too rosy (except for ISAs, which we'll come to in a moment). After all, if you simply took the income now and invested it, you'd get taxed twice on it: once when you earn the money, and once when your returns from the invested money get taxed. Getting taxed twice is not so great.

Pensions come in all sorts of shapes and sizes. First of all, there are the 'defined benefit' or 'final salary' pensions that you might get from an employer (if you're lucky). If you're offered one of these, then you should generally take it. The way to account for it in your investing plans is to think about the benefits that it's designed to give you and, for the period that the benefits are accruing to you, consider that that much of your retirement income is being covered.

Other pensions are 'defined contribution'. These involve putting money into a fund, which is then invested in the stock market until you need it. That's the basis of them, but they come in all shapes and sizes. There are schemes organized by your employer as well as personal pensions. There are also things called SIPPs (self-invested personal pension) whereby you yourself choose what they're invested in.

As with other types of long-term investment, the trick to maximizing performance is to minimize costs. With a SIPP, that means exercising restraint and not trying to be too clever (it also means using one of the very cheap SIPPs that are springing up on the Internet these days). With a personal pension, it basically means going for a 'stakeholder' pension, since these have to have costs below a certain level. With an employer's pension scheme, it's a question of going to your employer and saying, 'Hey, why is our pension invested in xyz fund where the charges are a whopping 2 per cent per year, when we could invest in an index tracker and pay so much less, thereby enhancing the investment performance?' It may or may not give you some brownie points.

Especially since the advent of relatively cheap and transparent pensions (by which we mostly mean stakeholder pensions), they're not a bad thing. However, there are still one or two problems. First of all, there are limits on how much you can put into them. These are based on your age and how much you earn – see the box on page 119 for the exact figures – and on the whole are pretty high. But if you're a high earner, you might want to save more.

A bigger problem is that they're not very flexible. Once the money goes in, you can't get it out again until you retire, and that has to be after the age of 50. Whether or not you reach the limits for the amount you can save in a pension, most people will prefer to have at least a portion of their long-term savings in an accessible form, in case of a change in circumstances.

A further problem with flexibility is that you're forced to use most (75 per cent for personal pensions) of your pension pot to buy an annuity when you do retire. Annuities do have the benefit of lasting until you finally visit the great tax office in the sky, but in the meantime, they don't make particularly good investments. That's especially so if you have a long retirement, since their returns can get left behind by inflation and growth in average wages.

There's a whole lot more about pensions in the pensions centre of the Motley Fool website at **www.fool.co.uk/pensions/pensions.htm**.

Individual Savings Accounts

Whether or not you go for a pension, you're likely to want to keep at least some of your long-term savings in more accessible form. For this, an Individual Savings Account (ISA) should be your first port of call. The principal difference between pensions and ISAs, apart from the flexibility issues discussed above, is that you put money into a pension out of your *pre-tax* earnings, but you'll eventually get taxed on the income you take from it; whereas with an ISA, you pay into it out of your *post-tax* earnings, but the eventual income will be tax-free. All things being equal, this amounts to the same thing. This is all because of a peculiar mathematical principle called, rather grandly, 'multiplicative commutativity'. All it really means, though, is that with multiplication, it doesn't make any difference what order you do it in.

Consider the position of Henrietta, the higher-rate taxpayer. She earns £1,000, invests it, and gets 9 per cent growth for three years before drawing income at a rate of 5 per cent. She can either put £1,000 into a pension (but then lose 40 per cent of her income at the end) or she can put £600 into an ISA (but get the eventual income free of tax). Each year's income will end up being the same for both the ISA and the pension, since you're multiplying by the same numbers – just in a different order. It looks something like this:

Earnings   Tax — — —-Growth— — —-   Income   Tax

ISA: £1,000 x 0.6 x 1.09 x 1.09 x 1.09 x 0.05   = £38.85

Pension: £1,000   x 1.09 x 1.09 x 1.09 x 0.05 x 0.6 = £38.85

All we've done is shift the 'x 0.6' in our calculation from the beginning to the end. So, not surprisingly, the answer comes out the same. This position is, however, complicated by several factors. To start with, it assumes that the income you're aiming for in retirement is the same as in your working life, and that therefore so is your tax rate. In practice, most people will aim for a slightly lower income and therefore lower tax rate in retirement (after all, they should have paid off the mortgage, and any kids will probably have left home). That will make the pension route a bit more attractive because there's a greater tax saving on the money going into the pension than there is on the money that eventually comes out of the ISA.

Another point is that the income tax benefits of an ISA are not quite as simple as they seem at first. The income from cash, government bonds (aka gilts) and corporate bonds in an ISA attracts full tax relief. That's all well and good, since a lower-risk approach is likely to mean more of these in retirement. The problem is that you don't actually get full tax relief on the income you get from shares. Shares suffer tax at source on their profits, in that the company pays corporation tax; but, even if your shares are wrapped up in an ISA, you don't get that tax back. At least, though, if you're a higher-rate taxpayer, you don't have to pay any additional tax. So, if you plan to carry on owning shares in your ISA after retirement (and that's part of the attraction of going down this route), you'll only get a tax benefit to the extent that you're a higher-rate taxpayer at that point.

There are two basic types of ISA: the Maxi-ISA and the Mini-ISA. It's pretty important to be clear about the differences because, in each tax year, you are only allowed (assuming you're a UK resident aged eighteen or over) to invest in one of the two types. Each type has three separate components: cash, stocks and shares, and insurance. The difference between the two is that in the Maxi, they're all mushed together into the same account; whereas with the Mini, each of the bits are in different accounts. It's perhaps easiest to think of the Maxi as being like one big teapot, into which you can put up to three different types of teabag (that is, one teabag for cash, one teabag for stocks and shares and one teabag for insurance). Since it's all in one teapot, only one person can be mother – in other words, you have to pick one financial organization to run the whole Maxi-ISA for you.

Similarly, you can think of the Mini-ISA as being like three small teapots, each of which can contain a different teabag (except you can't have the same type of teabag in two different pots). So, if you like the interest rates on some-one's cash Mini-ISA, but you don't like the charges on their stocks and shares Mini-ISA, then you can open the cash Mini with them, but go to someone else for the stocks and shares Mini. Before we leave the teabags analogy, it's worth just saying that we don't much like the taste of insurance teabags. It's a mistake to get insurance and investment mixed up at the best of times, and we really can't work out who'd want to put insurance policies into an ISA. It looks as though we're not the only ones. Few financial organizations offer them and very few people have taken them out.

For the 2002/3 tax year, you'll be able to put £7,000 into a Maxi-ISA. As much of this as you like can go into the stocks and shares component, but you can only put up to £3,000 into the cash component. For Mini-ISAs, the limits are

£3,000 for a stocks and shares Mini and £3,000 for a cash Mini. Each new tax year brings the opportunity to make fresh subscriptions to an existing ISA, or to open a whole new ISA. Of course, if you keep opening a new ISA each year, things are going to get pretty complicated; so to simplify matters, transfers from one ISA into another are allowed. However, the components must remain the same. So, once you've gone for the stocks and shares component of a Maxi-ISA or a stocks and shares Mini, you can move it around all over the place, but it must always remain in stocks and shares. Similarly, when you've gone for a cash component, it must always stay in cash. Any transfers like this don't count for the purposes of each year's allowances.

As you can imagine, you can only really put cash (and one or two things that are very like cash) into a cash ISA. The fun starts when you get to the stocks and shares bit. Here you can put in most of the things that you might want to. You can put shares in it, so long as they're quoted on a major stock exchange, you can put most unit trusts and investment trusts into it and you can put gilts and corporate bonds (IOUs issued by companies) into it. You can even hold a bit of cash in it, but this must be for the purpose of buying the other investments that we've just mentioned. You can't hold cash in a stocks and shares component 'for the sole purpose of sheltering interest on cash deposits from tax'.

The biggest problem with ISAs, like most things in the financial world, is that they cost you: generally not very much, but it's worth keeping a close eye on. If you decide to invest via some form of fund anyway, then the provider will almost invariably throw in an ISA wrapper for free. On that basis, there can be no harm in it. You should make sure, though, that the unit trust itself is nice and cheap. Ideally it should have a CAT mark, which means it meets certain government-prescribed standards on Charges, Access and Terms. To get a CAT mark, charges have to be below 1 per cent per year, and that will most likely mean that the fund's an index tracker. If you want to put your own hand-picked shares into an ISA, it will probably cost you more, although some stockbrokers are offering ISA wrappers for very low (and in some cases no) fixed annual fees these days.

It won't surprise you to hear that there's an ISA centre on the Motley Fool website at **www.fool.co.uk/isas/isas.htm**, where you can explore these charming things some more.

Insurance products
The final form of tax-protective wrapping that you should know about is life assurance. Some life assurance, the good kind, does exactly what it says on the

tin, in that it pays out a sum of money if you die. However, there are also life assurance policies that pay out even if you don't die. In other words, they're life assurance products with a savings and investment element added on. Generically, they tend to be known as endowments, and we really don't like them at all.

Why? Well, you tend to get the worst of all worlds. To get the tax protection, you have to hold on to them for a long time (at least ten years, or 75 per cent of the length of the policy, whichever is longer), so they're not very flexible. They're also far less transparent than, say, an ISA, and the financial companies that provide them tend to take advantage of this fact to build in some hefty charges.

A large number of endowments are also of the 'with-profits' nature and we suggest you're especially wary of these. Essentially, there's one big pot of money over which all the endowment holders of one particular product provider will have an interest. The interest is provided by what you put in, plus 'bonuses' awarded annually, plus a big bonus at the end. The trouble is that it's not entirely clear who owns what. The recent Equitable Life debacle, where any number of judges, lawyers, accountants and actuaries have been arguing for years now about who gets what, demonstrates the problems. We'd suggest that you keep your name tag firmly attached to your savings, and that means avoiding with-profits investments. If you're not going for with-profits (the alternative being called 'unit-linked'), then you can invest more cheaply and more effectively via a cheap ISA.

Avoid!

Wrapping up on investment wrappers

Investments outside of an ISA or a pension suffer because they don't have an income tax benefit either on the way in (like pensions) or on the way out (like ISAs). So, with your long-term investments, you should start by using up your annual pension and ISA allowances. How much pension and how much ISA you might want is going to come down to how flexible you want to be. The more you want to be flexible, the more you'll want to go for ISAs, but bear in mind that there will most likely be a small cost attached to doing this compared to a cheap pension.

Of course, another thing that flexibility brings is responsibility. One very good reason for going the pension route is to keep your grubby mits off the money until retirement.

One final point to throw into the pot is that governments of all persuasions are pretty fickle about tax benefits, with old ones going and new ones appearing on a regular basis. That means that you have to be careful about letting tax issues dominate your investment thinking. After all, they could change at any moment. Having said that, the best you can do is to take advantage of the system as it stands at any one time. So wrapping your savings up in a pension, an ISA or both is likely to be much better than using no wrappers at all.

If you're in the fortunate position of being able to invest so much that you use up your pension and ISA allowances, then you'll need to invest unprotected. The biggest problem with this is the potential for capital gains tax. Dealing with this headache (for it can be) is covered in Chapter 8, starting on page 84.

Your Home and Your Mortgage

In Chapters 13 to 17, we've looked at the different assets and debts that you have, whether they suit your circumstances and whether you've got enough of them. At various points along the way, we've stumbled across your house and your mortgage, made one or two comments about how they're a bit different from other assets and debts and moved swiftly along. It's high time, you might think, that we got properly to grips with the subject since, for most of us, a house and a mortgage is the single biggest investment we make and the biggest debt that we take on. Important stuff.

Property as an investment

The first thing we need to work out with property is whether it makes sense to own it at all. One way to look at this is to say that, like shares, property is a real asset. It has an economic value that's determined by what people are prepared to pay to live in it. Over the years, as average earnings in the country go up, so will the amount that people are prepared to pay to live in a given home. If people were prepared to pay around a quarter of their income on housing in 1900, then there's no reason why they shouldn't be prepared to pay a similar, *relative*, amount now. So, property has a value in that you can live in it, and that value tends to keep up with the economy that it's in. Excellent. Already, that sounds like a solid long-term proposition, but there's a simpler way of looking at things.

You see, just because *you* decide not to own your home, that doesn't mean that nobody owns it. Someone has to own every house and, if you don't own it yourself, you'll have a landlord that you rent it from (if it's council property, then the council will be the landlord). Landlords clearly think it's worthwhile owning property, or they wouldn't do it. They either tie up their own money, or they borrow money on a mortgage, just as you would have done if you'd bought it yourself. They then go and charge you just enough rent to pay for the upkeep of the property and still provide a good enough return to justify them tying up their money, or a good enough return to pay the mortgage *and leave them with a profit*.

So, if it's profitable for your landlord to own your house, you have to ask yourself why you shouldn't just *be your own landlord*. That way, you can make the profit that your landlord would have been making from you. In fact, it makes even better sense, since you, yourself, are the most efficient person to be owning your home anyway. You don't need to charge yourself a deposit, you don't need to worry that you might run off without paying rent, and you don't need to worry that you might start squatting in your own home (or let anybody else do so). A landlord needs to charge a tenant just a little more than otherwise to take account of the chances of these things happening but, if you do the job yourself, you know that they're not going to happen. You therefore effectively save yourself money. It's really not much different from cooking your own food instead of going to a restaurant.

So, on the whole, you'd expect it to be worthwhile to own your own home, but there are some big 'buts'. First of all, you have to take on some risk. The landlord we discussed above might have ten or more properties, and might have the financial wherewithal to play the game for decade after decade. Individuals who decide to be their own landlord (the mega-rich aside) will most likely have to settle for one property. But you do have the advantage of doing it for decade after decade after decade. Mortgages typically last for 25 years, but even after that you expect to carry on owning property (it's just that you'll have paid off the debt you took on to buy it). So most people are able to look at investing in their home as an undertaking of up to fifty years, so long as they don't overstretch themselves.

Another point about property is that it's an awkward thing to invest in. You can't just set up a standing order for £100 per month to buy a share in the 'property market average', as you can the 'stock market average' when you purchase an index tracker, since there is no such thing as a 'property exchange'. When you buy a property, it's like buying an entire private company (that is, one that isn't listed on any stock exchange). This means that the process of buying and selling property is expensive – involving, amongst other things, surveys, legal fees, and extra stamp duty.

You also have to buy property in very big chunks. Since most of us can't afford to buy these big chunks outright, we tend to have to borrow big sums of money to do it. When we borrow money to buy a house, we are borrowing a fixed (that is, 'nominal') sum to invest in a real asset. This is called 'gearing'. If we buy a house for £100,000 with a £90,000 mortgage, then we have invested £10,000 ourselves. If the house then increases in value by 10 per cent to £110,000, the value of the £10,000 that we put in has actually increased by 100 per cent to £20,000. However, the flip side to this is that, if the value of the house falls by 10 per cent to £90,000, then the value of the £10,000 that we put in has fallen by 100 per cent, to zero. Our short-term risk is dramatically increased but, since we expect the value of our house to increase over the long term (if only because of inflation and increases in average earnings), our long-term returns should also be increased. This gearing effect is, for many, one of the attractive aspects to property as an investment.

Collecting the benefits while minimizing the risks

All this tells us a few key things about buying our own home. First of all, it's generally a good thing to do, if you can afford to. Secondly, it is a risky thing to do in the short term and, if you do take the plunge, you have to make sure that you really can stick it out for the very long term. You need to think of it as a life-time investment. You can change properties in the meantime (although you wouldn't want to make a habit of it, since the costs are pretty hefty), but you need to think of yourself as being invested in property, as a class of asset, for pretty much the rest of your life. The key to collecting the benefits while mini-mizing the risks is to be very sure of lasting the course.

Mortgages, as we'll see, tend to last for 25 years. If interest rates rocket skywards in ten years' time, you should feel very confident that you will be able to keep paying the interest on your mortgage. Rocketing interest rates generally mean high inflation, and you'll feel the pain of that in your wallet each month. High inflation, though, also means that the amount of money you had to borrow for the mortgage in the first place will start to look more and more insignificant, which means that high interest rates are not necessarily a bad thing for the *long term* value of your property. In fact, much of the increase in house prices over the last thirty years can be put down to high inflation, despite the high interest rates that have often accompanied it.

In the *short term*, though, high interest rates can be a very bad thing for the current value of your property and, if increases in interest rates mean that you can't keep paying the interest on your mortgage, then you'll generally find that it is absolutely the worst possible time for your bank to repossess and sell your home. Apart from the possibility of some nasty 'negative equity' (where the value of your house is less than the value of your mortgage), economic conditions are likely to be bad, and it may be hard to find employment.

This is beginning to sound very scary, but it isn't really meant to. It's just a warning that if you're playing a long-term game, as you do with shares and property, then you need to make sure you can keep playing through to the end. Buying your home is a good thing to do, but be careful, keep well within yourself and don't get caught short. We talk about this sort of thing at length in another of our books, the *Motley Fool UK Investment Guide*, and it's well worth repeating some of it here.

Which property, when and for how much?

The questions of which property to buy, when to buy it and how much to pay are often the questions that cause people most headaches, but if you think about things in simple terms, this needn't be the case. The answer to the first question is easy. You are buying your own house, as we've said, to be your own landlord. So, the house that you buy is the one that you want (and can afford) to live in. It really is as simple as that. Find the house with the wonderful view, the rambling garden, the short journey to work or the gentle stroll along the lane to your local pub, and buy it.

To buy a house and live in it just because you think it will make a good investment is putting the cart before the horse. You only have one life, and to spend it living in a house that doesn't work for you is a *big* waste of time. Besides, why are you so much surer that it will be a good investment than the person you're buying it from? The better the prospects for an area, the more the property should be costing you in the first place. In any event, you should have sufficient confidence in your own taste: if you buy something that you like and you look after it, the chances are that there'll be someone who wants to buy it from you when the time comes for you to move on.

So you buy the house that you want to live in, but when do you buy it? Well, you'll be pleased to hear that the answer to this is just as easy. You buy it when you want to and when you're able to. Just as you shouldn't try to time the short-term fluctuations of the stock market, you shouldn't try to time the short-term fluctuations of the property market. The state of the market should take account of people's expectations about interest rates and prices in the future and there's no point in holding off because Leo, your estate agent friend, thinks that 'the market looks a bit toppy at the moment'.

In our experience, people who hold off from the property market because they are expecting a big crash suffer a similar fate to those who hold off from the stock market for the same reason. There are always reasons for thinking that the market might fall in the short term, just as there are always reasons for thinking that it might rise. All that we can say with any degree of confidence is that, over the long term, investing in property is a good thing to do. So, when you can afford to buy a home, find the one that you want (and can afford) to live in and go for it.

How much should you pay for your dream home? Well, given the answers to the previous questions, you can probably work out what's coming. You pay what it costs. Here, though, there are some very important riders. First of all, you should only be buying a house that is genuinely up for sale. It's not going to make sense for you to pay twice as much than a house is worth because the current owners love it so much that they don't really want to sell. The only way that you can get a proper guide to the value of a house is if it is on the market.

Next, you look around your dream home and you're told that the asking price is £100,000. What do you do then? Well, you 'um' and you 'ah' and, making sure you don't sound too keen, you say that you want to go away and think about it. You are now in a negotiating situation and there is a large amount of money at stake. Have a look around some similar properties in the area and find out their asking price. Preferably, you should find out how much similar properties have actually sold for. Is your dream home in the same ball park? Be very careful about anything that the seller's estate agents tell you – remember whose side they're on. Another thing to do is to think about how much it would cost to rent the home. The rent that you'd have to pay should always be a good bit more than the cost of a 100 per cent mortgage (to pay for upkeep and to give the landlord his profit).

When you've thought carefully about all this, you put in a tentative offer to the seller's estate agent. Don't be afraid of pitching it quite a bit below the asking price: if nothing else, you can learn a lot about the property's value from the response you get. The last thing you want is an immediate acceptance of your first offer. If you get this, you'll know you've pitched it too high. The seller will always tend to pitch the asking price higher than the price they expect to get, so you should always be very reluctant to go above this price. If someone else is interested and the bidding gets above this level, then it's probably a good idea to walk away and start looking for another dream home. There will be others, you just have to keep dreaming.

The final point to make about how much you pay is a repetition of a point that we've already made. Too many people fall into the trap of buying as expensive a house as they can afford. **Don't do this**. It can be very tempting – we all want somewhere nice to live and it's a very good way to impress our friends, but it's a really appalling idea. If you can't keep up the mortgage payments, for the long term, then you might end up with nowhere to live, and your friends won't be very impressed at all. Work out how much the mortgage interest is going to cost you and double it. If things got this bad, could you keep up the repayments? It's bound to be painful, but if you think they'd be too high then you perhaps need to be looking at something a bit cheaper. The bottom line is that to play the mortgage game profitably, you need to be able to play it for a long time, through good times and bad.

From a health check point of view, then, you need to ask yourself, periodically, whether you're living in the right house and whether you can really afford it. If you decide that you're currently a bit overstretched, then you need to consider what to do. Selling up and moving somewhere smaller might be the answer if things are very tight, but it's a last resort: after all, as we've said, buying and selling property is an expensive business. There may be other options. For instance, you might have a room that you could let if things got really bad. Not ideal by any means, but better than going belly up on your mortgage. If you have some savings and investments already, you might be able to make a one-off payment to reduce the size of the mortgage and reduce your risks in one fell swoop. It all comes down to being as comfortable as possible with your mortgage.

Mortgages

Mortgages are what enable most people to buy homes. Not only that, they enable us to go in for a bit of this 'gearing' lark which, as we've seen, can be a nice little earner over the long term. So, it's a little unfair that mortgages get such a bad press, generally appearing after the word 'bloody', as in 'it pays the bloody mortgage, I suppose', when referring to one's line of work. A mortgage is a tool and 'just like any other tool, Marion, it's as good or as bad as the man using it' (with thanks to George Stevens' 1953 blockbuster, *Shane*). Also, just like any other tool, understanding how they work is the trick to getting the most out of them.

A mortgage is the cheapest form of long-term loan there is. It's cheap because the lender takes your home as security for the loan, and houses are unable to change their name and leave the country. If you don't keep up your repayments, then the lender steps in, sells the house for what it can get and keeps enough to repay the loan. Simple as that. When the lender sells the house, they'll only get what the house can fetch at that time. There's no obligation for them to wait 'until the market recovers'; they just go in and do it. If that means that the money *you* had put into the house goes up in a puff of smoke, then that's hard cheese. In fact, if the lender can't get enough for the house to cover the loan, you'll still owe them the difference and they can come after you to get it.

The up side, as far as we're concerned, is that the rate of interest is very low – only a percentage point or so above what the government pays to borrow money and, since the government prints the stuff and effectively carries no risk at all, that's a pretty good deal. It is this fact that makes mortgages compatible with savings and investments, whereas just about all other forms of debt should be paid off before you get into any saving. It is, however, only Foolish if you keep well within yourself. Sorry, did we make that point before? It must be beginning to grate now. It's just that we think it is the single most important thing in this whole chapter.

Anyway, we've made our point now and we promise to drop the matter, except maybe for a quick mention at the end for those readers who lost patience with all this rambling and skipped ahead. Now, where were we?

Oh yes, mortgages are a good cheap way of borrowing money (can you hear the sound of tongues being bitten?). As with any loan, there are essentially two things that you have to do with them. You have to repay the capital on the loan, and you have to pay the interest on it. It is how you do these things that makes one mortgage different from another.

Repaying the capital on your mortgage

There are basically two ways of doing this. Either you pay it back bit by bit over the course of the mortgage (which we'll assume to be 25 years, but this can vary) or you can pay none of it back at all over the 25 years, and pay it all off in one go at the end. The first of these approaches is called a repayment mortgage and the second is called an interest-only mortgage. On top of these basic approaches, there is another, called a current account mortgage, which is essentially a hybrid of the two.

If you've got a mortgage, then your first health check task is to work out which of these types it fits into. One way to do this is to look at your annual mortgage statement (you did keep it somewhere safe, didn't you?) and see what's happening to the amount you owe. If it's going steaily downwards, then you'll be on a repayment mortgage. If it's staying exactly the same, then you'll be on an interest-only mortgage, and if it's jumping about all over the shop, then you'll be on a 'current account mortgage'. If your mortgage statement just looks like a jumble of large numbers, then you'll want to phone up your mortgage company and ask them about it. They make a profit by lending you money, so don't be afraid to ask them how it all works.

Repayment mortgages

With a repayment mortgage, you start with a large pile of debt on which you have to pay a large amount of interest. On top of this interest, you pay back a tiny bit of the capital each month. As each month goes by, the amount that you owe is reduced and the amount of interest therefore falls as well, allowing you to pay back a bit more capital. The mortgage is structured so that the payments remain broadly level (subject to fluctuating interest rates) but, as time goes by, an increasing amount goes on repaying capital and a correspondingly decreasing amount goes on paying the interest. By the time you get to the last few years of the mortgage, most of the monthly payments are going into paying off the capital and the amount you owe starts falling more and more quickly until, at the end of the mortgage, it is all paid back.

The beauty of this approach is that if you keep making the payments, you know that, come what may, at the end of the mortgage you'll have paid everything back. For this reason, repayment mortgages are the least risky way of repaying a mortgage. A lot of people prefer to do it like this. It makes good sense, since you've already taken on a fair bit of risk by having a mortgage at all.

On the health check side of things, repayment mortgages are very low maintenance, at least as far as repaying the capital is concerned, precisely because the repayments are designed to leave you with no mortgage at the end of 25 years. All you have to do is decide that you're still well able to afford the repayments and, well, keep making them. There's more to do on the interest rate side of things, but we'll come to that in a moment.

If you still want to feel as though you're doing something useful, you can check your mortgage statement to see how much less you owe now than you did last year. The trouble is that you'll need at least an 'A' level in Maths to work out whether it has fallen by the right amount, because it's designed to fall more and more quickly as time goes on. It really doesn't matter, because the mortgage company works it all out so that your mortgage is gone by the time you're finished.

Interest-only mortgages

The riskier option, but the one that is potentially more profitable, is to go for an interest-only mortgage. With this approach, you owe the same amount of capital and therefore have to pay the same amount of interest (subject to fluctuating interest rates) throughout the term of the mortgage. All you do each month is repay the interest. How, then, do you repay the capital? Well, in addition to repaying the interest, you put a bit aside each month into investments of one sort or another and then, at the end of the mortgage term, you use the accumulated pot of investments to repay the mortgage. In this case, you are taking a risk as to whether you can repay the capital. If your investments don't do their job, then you might have a shortfall when the time comes. The up side is that, if your investments more than do their job, then you might have a tidy sum left over.

The way to think about interest-only mortgages is that the money you are investing each month is money that you're not using to repay the mortgage. If you're investing £100 per month then, after ten years, you will have added a total of £12,000 to your investments. This is £12,000 that you could have used to repay the capital on your mortgage. For it to make sense to invest the money rather than use it to repay the capital on your mortgage, the investments need to be making a greater return than the rate of interest you're being charged on your mortgage (that is, on the capital that you haven't repaid).

To have a chance of doing this, you really need to be investing the money in the stock market and, if you do so, then there is a good chance that an interest-only mortgage will work in your favour. After all, the rate of interest that you pay on your mortgage is linked to the rate of interest on cash deposits and, as we saw in Chapter 17, the returns from shares tend to leave cash deposits miles behind over the long term.

With an interest-only mortgage, therefore, *you are effectively borrowing money at mortgage rates in order to invest in the stock market.* In the past this has proved to be a profitable thing to do and there are good reasons to think that this will remain the case, BUT there is no doubt that there is risk involved. In fact, having borrowed money to buy your house, you are now borrowing money to invest in the stock market. For many people this is too much borrowing and too much risk and they prefer to go the repayment route. One thing is for sure: if you do decide to go for an interest-only mortgage, make sure that you think long and hard about the risks involved and your tolerance for them before you do it.

As well as introducing risks, interest-only mortgages bring in a whole load of complications to your health check, because you need to work out whether you're investing enough to pay off the capital when the mortgage comes to an end. At the beginning, your lender will have a pretty firm idea about this and they're likely to point you in the right direction. However, as interest rates change, so do the returns that you're likely to get on your investments, so you need to change the amount you invest to account for it.

One rough and ready way of doing this is to make sure that any money you save from interest rates going down should be added to your investments. So let's say you start off with a mortgage that costs you £400 per month in interest and that your mortgage company says you ought to invest £100 per month to repay the capital. If interest rates fall, so that you're only paying £300 per month, then you'd want to increase the rate of your investing to £200 per month. That works out nicely, since you're still earmarking the same amount per month to your mortgage and it should also get you to the amount you need to pay off the mortgage when the time comes.

Unfortunately, it doesn't work the other way around. If interest rates increase, so you have to pay £500 per month in interest on your mortgage, then you should still invest the £100 per month that you started with. However, the plus side is that higher long-term interest rates most likely also mean higher long-term rates of return on your investments. So, by keeping with the £100 per month, you're most likely being conservative and could well end up with a little extra in the end.

So, for your health check, you need to look at your monthly interest payments compared with when you started your mortgage and, if they're lower, then you should add the difference to what you're investing each month.

If you want to be cleverer than this, you can try to work out how much you need to invest more precisely. The method is the same as the one in Chapter 17, which we used to work out how much you needed to invest to produce your retirement pot. You need to replace your retirement 'pot' with the total size of your mortgage, 'what you've already got' with what you've already invested for repaying your mortgage, and the number of years until retirement with the number of years left on your mortgage.

The difficulty is that although your income requirements in retirement are linked to inflation and increases in average earnings, what you need to repay your mortgage is not. We can't do the same neat trick and ignore inflation and growth in average earnings, so coming up with an expected rate of return on our investments is that much harder. The place to start is the 5 per cent return that we reached in Chapter 17, as our expected return from shares over the year, but then we need to add something to it to account for inflation and growth in average earnings. You could argue about this until the cows come home, but it's likely to be between 0 per cent and 5 per cent, depending on how conservative you're being. We'd suggest you stick to being fairly conservative and we're going to use a figure of 7 per cent.

Anyway, you can see in the box below where all this might take us (if it doesn't make any sense, you'll want to go back to page 189, where it's explained a bit more clearly).

Let's say we have an interest-only mortgage of £100,000, with 15 years left to run and we've already got investments worth £20,000 earmarked to pay it off. We'll also use the middling conservative figure of 7 per cent as what we expect to get as an investment return.

The £20,000 that we've already got should become £55,181 in 15 years' time. We get this by compounding it up at 7 per cent per year for 15 years – in other words, multiplying it by 1.07 a total of 15 times. That's the same as doing '1.07 to the power of 15', and then taking that number and multiplying the £20,000 by it. You can write it out like this:

$$£20,000 \times 1.07^{15} = £55,181$$

So, from what we invest from now on, we need to get to £44,819. Using the same process as for our retirement in the box on page 189, we...

...take the 44,819 and multiply by 0.07 (giving us 3,137). Then, we divide the 3,137 by 1.07 and put the resulting number, 2,932, to one side in a box marked 'leave until later'.

Now we put 1.07 to the power of 15, giving us 2.759, from which we subtract 1, to leave 1.759, which we put in our box labelled 'keep handy'.

Finally, we take the 2,932 from our box marked 'leave until later' and divide it by the 1.759 from our box marked 'keep handy'. That leaves us with £1,667, which is our guess as to what we'd need to invest per year to pay off our mortgage.

So, for our theoretical mortgage situation, we'd need to invest £1,667 per year, or roughly £139 per month. Since we're being conservative, why don't we call it £150 and we might have a little left over at the end if things work out well.

It pays to be conservative, because you're also investing for your retirement at the same time. If you invest more than you need to pay off your mortgage, that's all well and good and will help fund your retirement. If you don't invest enough, then your retirement pot is going to have to make up the difference.

That brings us neatly to another point about interest-only mortgages. You need to keep the investment pot for them mentally separate from your retirement pot, at least when working out how much you need to put into them. The reason is that when guessing what we needed to live on in retirement, we assumed that we'd paid off the mortgage. So, what we got as our required retirement pot was over and above anything that we needed to pay off our mortgage.

Just like your investing for retirement, though, all we get out of these sums is a number, and we need to work out what to do with it. If you're currently single and earning pretty well, then you might decide to invest more heavily, so that you can ease off a bit later on. Similarly, if you're currently out of work, then your priority is not paying off your mortgage in however many years' time, but making it through to your next employment without having to raid what you've already got invested. So you might give yourself an 'investment holiday' on the basis that you'll make it up with knobs on when you're back in work.

There's also a pleasant side effect to doing the sums again each year, because it takes account of what has actually happened, as opposed to what you guessed might happen. If the investments haven't been doing too well and you've therefore not actually been investing enough, then as time goes on, the sums will tell you that you need to be investing more. If your investments have done well, and you've therefore got a tidy sum already tucked away, then the sums will tell you that you can perhaps ease off a little, thus leaving you more to put towards your retirement pot.

The final decision to make about interest-only mortgages is which vehicle you should use to do the saving. Traditionally, this type of mortgage has been backed up by an endowment policy. We looked at these briefly in Chapter 17, and it's very safe indeed to say that we don't like them one little bit. They're expensive, inefficient and inflexible and the major pay-off they provide is to the person who sells you the policy – not you. Back in the Dark Days of the late 80s, well over two-thirds of British mortgages were backed by endowment policies.

Following the justifiably horrendous press that they've received recently, we're pleased to say that this figure is now down to below 10 per cent. Still, in our opinion, it's about 10 per cent too many.

You've still got to do something to avoid capital gains tax on your mortgage investments though, so that leaves us with pensions and ISAs. Pensions are a possibility, so long as the 25 per cent lump sum that they'll deliver to you at retirement is going to be enough and is going to arrive at the right time; but really, you'd want to think about that as a little cash for a rainy day.

The clear winner, for most people, is going to be a stocks and shares ISA. Again, we talked about these in Chapter 17 and you may have one anyway for retirement purposes; in which case, you can pay in a bit extra each month to deal with your mortgage. Remember, though, to have a rough idea about how much is for retirement purposes and how much is for the mortgage. If you're paying in a total of £400 per month and £100 is for your mortgage, then you'd reckon that a quarter of what's there is mortgage money, and the other three-quarters is retirement pot.

Of course, if you're investing so hard for retirement that you haven't got any room left in your ISA, then you'll have to think again. Interest-only mortgages really only make sense if you use a tax-protected investment vehicle, so you might need to think about switching to a repayment mortgage.

What you should put into your ISA comes down to the same sort of factors that we looked at for long-term investments in Chapter 17. You want something that's based on shares, you want a good spread of them and you want it to have low charges. An index tracker will tend to have the best mix of these things. In fact, it'll probably be top of the tree on both spread of investments and charges.

Current account mortgages

The Aussies, bless them, are famous for only a few inventions, but they've hit on some real 'beauts' – for, alongside Don Bradman's pull shot and Lance Hill's rotary hoist washing line, you can add the current account mortgage. This effectively allows you to carry your mortgage debt in a bank account. Your lender sets a limit on how much you can borrow and then, so long as you keep below this, you can let the total amount of your mortgage debt fluctuate, upwards or downwards.

This means you can treat it like an interest-only mortgage if you want, where you just pay the interest each month, or like a repayment mortgage where you pay back a bit of the actual loan each month. You can repay the loan more quickly than the traditional 25 years or, if you like, you can pay it back more slowly.

If all this is sounding as though current account mortgages are supremely flexible, then that's because they are. Be careful, though, because with flexibility comes responsibility. If you don't make the effort to reduce the mortgage, then it won't reduce. In fact, if you're allowed to skip a few interest payments and do so, then the mortgage will actually increase. If you're the interest-only mortgage sort of person and you're using the money saved to invest, then you might not see this as a problem. But you need to make sure that what you are doing is a conscious and well-considered decision and not just a bit of financial slackness.

Another benefit of current account mortgages is that you can effectively use them to save cash tax free and in a very high interest account. The reason for this is that any 'savings' you put into (or rather leave) in your current account are, instead of actually being cash savings, effectively knocked off the outstanding amount to repay on your mortgage. Imagine that you have £10,000 that you want to save in cash. With a normal mortgage, the interest payments that you make will not be affected, as your mortgage and your bank accounts are completely separate. This means that, ISAs aside, you'll pay tax on the interest that you're getting on the £10,000 in a deposit account.

With the current account mortgage, on the other hand, the cash that you save goes directly towards paying off your mortgage. You can get the cash back out at any stage but, in the meantime, you're not paying tax on any interest that you've earned, because you haven't earned any. Sounds bad, hey? £10,000 saved and not earning any interest. What's the point in that? Well, by reducing the amount of your mortgage by £10,000, you've reduced the amount of interest that you have to pay on it, which more than corresponds to the interest you would have earned on the money in a deposit account.

The current account mortgage lets you have your cake and eat it. Because your overall borrowing can go up and down, you can effectively have a cash reserve without actually having any cash. Neat, hey?! Before we get carried away, we should say that, at the moment, the market for this type of mortgage is relatively young and there are only a few of them around. This means that the competition among the providers is fairly limited, and you might have to pay a slightly higher rate of interest than you would for a more conventional mortgage. Still, you might well feel that it's worth it for the advantages and, as these things become more popular, as they certainly should, so the interest rates will become more competitive.

Paying the interest on your mortgage

The first thing to get a handle on here is where interest rates actually come from. Knowing the answer certainly won't make you sparkle at parties, but it is one of those things worth knowing anyway. The answer is that they are set by the Monetary Policy Committee (MPC) of the Bank of England. If the MPC thinks that the economy is doing rather too well, potentially setting off a nasty bout of inflation, then it will put up interest rates to slow things down. On the other hand, if the MPC thinks that the economy is going too slowly, and that inflation is not a real threat, then it will bring interest rates down to try to get things going again. The MPC tries to make small adjustments well ahead of events (about 18 months ahead), so as to avoid the need to make big adjustments later. If it fails to put up interest rates when it should, then the chances are that inflation will increase and, ultimately, rates will have to go much higher than they otherwise would in order to bring it back under control. It's a case of a stitch in time saving nine.

The base rate is effectively the rate of interest at which the government borrows money in the very short term. The government has the best credit rating there is, so if it is prepared to pay 6 per cent to borrow money, then everyone else will have to pay a bit more. After all, why would a bank take only 5 per cent from you and me if it can get 6 per cent from the government? How much more everyone else has to pay depends on how good a risk they are. If you put your house up as security, then you're a very good risk and you should only have to pay slightly more than base rates, perhaps 0.5 per cent to 1 per cent more.

Tracking and variable rate mortgages
When you get a 'tracking' mortgage, your interest rate 'tracks' the base rate. Say you get a tracking mortgage on which you pay the base rate plus 0.75 per cent. This means that if base rates are 5.75 per cent, then you will be paying 6.5 per cent. If base rates go up by 0.5 per cent then you'll be paying 7.0 per cent. Fair enough.

Variable rate mortgages are similar to this, but perhaps not quite so good since they are slightly less predictable. In this case, your mortgage provider sets rates pretty much how it likes. It has savers to whom it must pay interest and it wants to make a profit, so it would like to charge you as much as possible. However, it can't charge too much or all its borrowers will simply move to someone else who's charging less, and then where will it be? Taking all this into account, each lender's variable rate is likely to float around a bit above the base rate. In fact, it is likely to float around at about the same sort of premium to base rates as a tracking mortgage. The difference, and the reason for preferring the tracker, is that with the tracker you know exactly what the deal is and it's not subject to the fickleness of your mortgage provider. (By the way, don't get confused with index trackers here – we're talking about something different. A tracking mortgage simply refers to the way the interest rate is calculated. An index tracker is a type of investment you may or may not be using to pay off the mortgage in the end.)

With variable rate and tracking mortgages, the major health check issue (not surprisingly) is to make sure that you're not paying over the odds. Start by finding out the current base rate (it'll be in the broadsheet newspapers, or just ask someone who knows about these things). Then compare this with the interest rate you're being charged. That should be clear from your latest mortgage statement, but if it's not, phone up your mortgage providers and ask them. If you're paying more than 1 per cent over the base rate, then you should seriously think about moving your mortgage to a building society or bank that charges less.

Whatever you're paying, though, it's worth having a shop around to see if you could be paying less. Probably the easiest way to do this is to use the Internet. The various banks and building societies will have their different mortgage offerings set out online, but there are also online mortgage brokers that help you search through the offerings from a wide range of providers. A good place to start is the Motley Fool's online homeowning centre at **www.fool.co.uk/homeowning/homeowning.htm** (but then we would say that, wouldn't we).

Fixed rate mortgages
With a fixed rate mortgage, as the name suggests, your interest payments are fixed for a certain period. This period is typically anything from a year to ten years or sometimes even more. So, if you have a mortgage with the interest rate fixed at 7 per cent for five years, your monthly interest payments on the outstanding capital will be set at that rate for five years.

To understand properly how fixed rate mortgages work, you need to think about the gilt market. In just the same way that the base rate determines what interest rate the government pays on its short-term debt, the 'redemption yield' on gilts determines the interest rate that the government pays on its medium- and long-term borrowings. The 'redemption yield' on gilts therefore also dictates the interest rate of fixed rate mortgages. Most broadsheet newspapers will have a list of gilts, together with their yields, somewhere in the business section. If you are looking at a five-year fixed rate mortgage, then you want to compare it to the redemption yield on gilts with a maturity date five years from now. In other words, if it's now 2002, then you want to look at a gilt called something like Treas 5 per cent 2007. Make sure you're looking at the column for redemption yields, rather than the column for the interest yield or flat yield (which are different).

As with variable rates and trackers, you will generally pay a small premium (of perhaps 0.5 to 1 per cent) to the rate that the government pays (that is, the redemption yield on the relevant gilt). So, if you are offered a five-year fixed rate mortgage at 6 per cent and you see that the redemption yield on a five-year dated gilt is 5.5 per cent, then you know that it's a pretty fair deal. Sometimes you might see a deal where the interest rate is less than the gilt yield. If this is the case, then there is often a catch in the form of a lengthy tie-in period or something similar. If not, then the provider is probably relying on enough borrowers being too lazy to move when the rate eventually goes up. If you go for something like this, then make sure you're not the lazy type because it could end up costing a lot more in the long run.

The effect of a fixed rate deal is, of course, that your repayments will stay the same for the period of the fix. This provides a bit of certainty for your budgeting. However, once you have fixed the deal you are, to a greater or a lesser extent, committed to it for that period. If interest rates go up, then you'll sit back smugly, thanking your lucky stars that you decided to fix your interest rate and congratulating yourself on your vision and perspicacity. On the other hand, if interest rates fall, then you will have to watch enviously as variable rate and tracking mortgages get cheaper and cheaper, while blaming your spouse for talking you into a fixed rate mortgage in the first place.

In this situation, it will cost you to get out of the deal. This is entirely reasonable, since you wouldn't let the bank back out of the fixed rate deal if the rates went up, and you can't have it both ways. Different mortgage deals have different penalties for copping out early. There is no such thing as a free lunch and, where the penalties for early redemption are slack, the borrower will have to pay for this with a higher interest rate. So, if you hunt around for the cheapest five-year fixed rate deal on the market, don't be surprised if it also contains the toughest redemption penalties. If you want the cheapest interest rate, then you'll have to accept the least flexibility. If you don't like the idea of being tied in, then rather than looking around for slack redemption penalties, you should probably be looking at a tracking or variable rate deal instead.

Because the point of a fixed rate mortgage is to set things in stone for a few years, there's less to do on the health check side of things. That said, you should check to see that what you're paying isn't way above current base rates or what you can get on other mortgages. If you're way out of line, then it might be worth checking the terms of your mortgage to see if you can change to something that's cheaper.

The other thing is to check to see when your fixed period ends. Interest rates can change a fair bit over five years or so, and it can come as quite a shock if you come off an advantageous fixed rate and the interest you're paying suddenly shoots up. You want to be aware of what's coming at you well ahead of events so that you can plan accordingly.

Bells and whistles

What we've done here is try to simplify the important elements of a mortgage. However, there are literally thousands of different types of mortgage on the market. They are littered with extra frills like 'cash-back' deals and 'discounted rates'. We don't much like this sort of thing. It all sounds terrific, but they're generally just a way of muddying the waters so that the providers can end up charging more. They know we love a discount and they know that dangling some cash before our eyes (to buy that washing machine) is going to get us right where they want us. Remember that there is no such thing as a free lunch and the more unnecessary bells and whistles that attach to a mortgage, the less likely it is to be the best value. *Keep things simple.*

The way the interest is calculated on your mortgage is an entirely separate issue from whether the mortgage is a repayment type or an interest-only type. This means you can have a repayment fixed rate, variable or tracking mortgage or an interest-only fixed rate, variable or tracking mortgage. Sorry if by now this seems ridiculously obvious to you, but it is a point of confusion for quite a few people – so we just wanted to make sure it was all completely clear.

Summing up on mortgages

First of all, decide how you want to repay the capital. If you want the least risky option, then this will mean a repayment mortgage. If you can stomach a bit of risk, then there's a very good chance that an interest-only mortgage, backed up by good Foolish investments, will work out better in the end. If you want the maximum flexibility over your repayments, then one of the new current account type mortgages might suit.

As far as paying the interest is concerned, bear in mind that no one, despite what they might want you to believe, knows where interest rates are headed. If anyone really knew what was going to happen, they'd be busy making a fortune on the gilt market. They certainly wouldn't be trying to sell you a mortgage. The gilt market takes into account the market's best guesses, and is therefore the best guide as to where interest rates are heading. Fixed rate mortgages are dictated by yields in the gilt market. The yields in the gilt market, in turn, are dictated by the market's best guess as to where the base rate is headed, and the base rate dictates the interest rates on variable rates and tracker mortgages.

Phew! Anyway, the effect of all this is that, all things being equal, a fixed rate mortgage should reflect what the market expects a variable rate or tracking mortgage to cost you over the same period. In other words, it should make no real difference which type of mortgage you go for (so long as you get the cheapest available of the type you're looking at) and you shouldn't get too het up about it. However, for peace of mind, there's a lot to be said for a straightforward five-year fixed rate deal. At least that way you know where you are for five years and can budget accordingly.

Finally, we just want to return to that point that we made several times at the beginning of this chapter. The best mortgage is one that you can easily afford – even if interest rates rocket. For the whole homeowning thing to work well, you must make sure that you can stick it out for the long term, through good times and bad.

Insurance

Seventeenth-century London merchants were faced with a perplexing problem. On the one hand, there was huge wealth to be gained by ferrying various riches back from newly-discovered exotic locations around the world. On the other, they could land up penniless if their one and only boat, with its expensive treasure all bought and paid for, went down in a storm or was set upon by pirates on its way home. It was essentially a very profitable business, but how could they justify the risks?

No doubt some merchants were sitting around in Edward Lloyds' coffee house on Tower Street discussing this very problem, when an enterprising spark hit upon the solution. They could get together and *share* the risks of their various voyages. It was brilliant. A merchant could go into Lloyds' coffee house, explain to his colleagues the details of a particular venture and they could agree to stump up a share of any losses in return for a small fee. This fee they called an *insurance premium* and an entire industry was born. Well, perhaps not. People have been sharing risks with each other since the Stone Age and before, but this is the earliest known example of it being so organized. Lloyd, an enterprising soul himself, even laid on a special news service so that people knew when a ship had gone down.

Anyway, this isn't a history book, so it doesn't matter much. What does matter is that it explains the origins, and therefore the purpose, of insurance. Our merchants only went looking for insurance out of necessity. After all, the premiums they had to pay cut into their profits. But when the necessity was there, when there was a risk that they just couldn't live with, they jumped on it. Out of this come our two basic Foolish principles of insurance:

Only insure against risks you can't afford to bear

and

Always insure against risks you can't afford to bear

These days, Lloyds of London is a relatively small part of the insurance market. Most of the insurance we might need in our daily lives is instead provided by large (and rich) insurance companies. They take on a particular risk for thousands of people and can accurately predict how many times, among these thousands of policies, things are going to go wrong. And, very importantly, they work it out so that they charge us enough of an insurance premium to make a profit (mostly). That means that the insurance is generally a good deal for them and will generally cost us money over the long term.

Imagine, for example, that you are insuring yourself against losing your nice watch. The watch is worth £100 and the insurance company works out that there's a one in 20, or 5 per cent chance, of it having to fork out the £100 in any given year. It therefore expects the insurance policy to cost it, on average, £5 per year and it therefore charges you £6, so it can make £1 per year in profit from you.

So, one option is to smooth out the cost of losing your watch by insuring it, but this will cost you, on average, £6 per year. The other option is to meet the cost of replacing the watch yourself as and when you lose it. This makes your budgeting more complicated, because you might suddenly need to find £100; and conceivably you have to find the £100 for several years in a row if you have bad luck, but it should only cost you £5 per year, *on average*.

So insurance is a means of paying to reduce life's uncertainties. It makes sense to use it when those uncertainties are too much to cope with, but it makes no sense when the uncertainties are relatively trivial – you'd be just paying extra for no real reason.

You can therefore think of insurance as forming a balance with your savings and investments. If you insure your household contents against theft or damage, then you don't need to have so much in your cash reserves to meet these exceptional costs when they occur. By reducing your need for cash savings, you can potentially make better use of your capital by having more of it tucked away in long-term investments.

Similarly, if you have a family that's dependent on your income then you will need some life insurance, unless you have so much tucked away in investments that your dependents could manage on the proceeds of your will. Although in that case, you'd perhaps say that your family wasn't dependent on your income.

The key to getting insurance right is to understand the risks that you face and to strike the right balance between the insurance, your savings and your investments –the idea being that you're covered against what life might throw at you, while at the same time making the most of your capital and not contributing, unnecessarily, to insurance company profits.

Having decided what you want to cover with insurance, it's then necessary to find the right policy. Read the small print! An insurance policy is no good to you if it doesn't cover what you need it to, and it will be more expensive than it needs to be if it covers things that you don't need it to. With this in mind, we can have a look at the more normal types of insurance.

Car insurance

If you've got a car, then you need some car insurance, because that's the law. The legal minimum is third party insurance, so called because it's what's necessary to cover any damage that you cause to others, or 'third parties'. Whether you want to take your insurance further than this depends on the principles we've just been discussing.

For example, if your car is a veritable banger, worth a few hundred quid, then you might choose just to go for the minimum and cover the cost of any damage to it out of your own money as and when it crops up. On the other hand, if you've got one of the new Ferrari 550 Maranellos then, unless your name is Gates, Rothschild or Al Maktoum, you'd probably reckon that the cost of replacing a total write-off is more than you can live with. On that basis, a 'comprehensive' policy, which pays out for damage to your own car as well, will probably suit.

Most people will be somewhere in between these two extremes and the insurance you'll need will depend on the value of the car, how much money you've got and your need for general peace of mind. Bear in mind, though, that if you don't have a comprehensive policy, then you'll need to have a bit extra in your cash reserves to cope with any accidents that take place.

Pay attention to the small print on fully comprehensive policies. Often you'll find that there will be some form of penalty for making a claim, or some sort of bonus for not making claims – the 'no-claims bonus'. Alternatively, you might have to pay the first £x of any claim that you make, called an 'excess'. These conditions can be a good thing, in that they should reduce the cost of your policy – but you must make sure that the policy covers what you need it to and no more, and then make sure that your finances elsewhere make provision for it. So, if you have an 'excess' of £500 on your car insurance, then you'll need to have a cash reserve that can cope with the occasional £500 hit; but you can be safe in the knowledge that, so far as your car is concerned at least, it's not going to be more.

Home contents insurance

A basic home contents insurance policy covers the contents of your home (you probably guessed that) and, for most people, it's well worth having. If you are burgled tomorrow, or have a fire, could you afford to replace the TV, the video, the sofa, the clothing, the jewellery, etc, etc? When you start to tot up the cost of the bits and bobs around your home, as you might have done back in Chapter 15, it can come to a staggering total.

It's important not to confuse insurance on the things in your home (that is, the contents) with any insurance you might have over the actual home itself. The latter is commonly called 'buildings insurance' and it's there to pay for your home to be rebuilt if it, er, falls down or something. If you have a mortgage, then your mortgage company will insist on you having some of this, to protect their security, but it's something that you need anyway. Few of us, after all, can really afford to stump up to rebuild our houses or flats. It can get even worse than this, especially if you live in a flat, because things that you do in your property can affect the properties of others. If you live on the top floor of a block of flats and have a leak of some sort, you could end up damaging everybody else's flat underneath.

Returning to your contents insurance, assuming you have some, it's worth reminding yourself of its precise details from time to time, and checking it against a rough inventory of what it's expected to cover. Generally, the policies will have a limit on them and this can fall behind reality if you've been upgrading some of your bits and pieces.

You can get all sorts of add-ons to a basic home contents policy. Many will provide cover for your personal belongings when they're outside the home itself, which might be very handy if you tend to go everywhere with your camcorder. But every extra will need to be paid for, so make sure you're covering the risks you need to, but no more. Also, like car insurance, you might find a policy that incorporates an excess or a no-claims bonus. That's fine, and might make the policy cheaper, but you must make sure that you're aware of what you're getting and organize yourself to take account of it.

One final point on the subject of home contents is that you might find it advisable to keep a list of your high value items. In some cases, it might even be worth having a photo. After all, if burglars swiped all your jewellery tomorrow, would you know exactly what had gone, be able to describe it and put a value on it? Impeccably trustworthy you may be, but an insurance company will need these details to process a claim.

Medical insurance

There's a line of thought here that says you don't really need medical insurance until it's too expensive. As a young person, the type of emergency situation that you might encounter is generally dealt with admirably by the National Health Service. As an old fogey, those new hips can be done far more quickly privately, but then the insurance companies are fully aware of how much they cost and you'll have premiums to suit.

Really, though, medical insurance simply comes down to personal whim. Some people wouldn't be without it, while others regard it as an unnecessary luxury and a few more won't touch it on political grounds. You're likely to have a pretty good idea as to whether you want it or not, and nothing I can say will change that; so I'm not going to try. As ever, though, you need to make sure it covers what you want it to. Some policies will offer you a choice of hospital, while some won't… that type of thing. Just be sure you know what you're getting.

Travel insurance

It's all very well having car, contents and medical insurance, but it won't do you much good if you then take a driving holiday to Spain, lose your camera and get injured in a car accident. Depending on the type of policy you have, it may well stop working when you leave these shores. You need to know what you're no longer covered for and organize some specific travel insurance to suit.

Things you might want to consider covering include the cost of the holiday itself, medical expenses and personal belongings. Then there's cars again. Be very careful with insurance on hire cars. In a foreign language, you can easily find yourself signing up for third party cover, but if you're driving on the wrong side of the road in, let's say, Rome, then comprehensive cover is probably more prudent.

Things get even more complicated with your own car. Your UK car insurance policy will automatically give you at least third party or the legal minimum cover in European Union countries as well as a few others. You can extend this to the same level of cover that you get in the UK, though there may be a small charge for doing so. The thing to do is phone up your insurer and ask. It's also worth getting hold of a 'green card' which demonstrates you have the legal minimum cover for the country you're in or, at the very least, packing your Certificate of Insurance.

Life, income protection and critical illness

The most important thing to understand about 'protection' insurance is that it is there to deal with risks you can't afford to bear, just like any other insurance. Life insurance, for example, deals with the risk of you dying and not leaving your dependents with enough to get by. What this type of insurance definitely isn't is some sort of consolation for you or your family in the event of disaster striking.

Bear in mind that every penny you spend on insurance is a penny you haven't invested. By keeping insurance to the minimum, you can ultimately aim to have enough invested so that you or your partner can toodle off to the great stock market in the sky without having to worry. Of course, until you reach that level of wealth, you need to be making sure that your dependents could manage if you were no longer around. You're not trying to provide them with a windfall: if you want to do that, the best way is to invest more.

With this in mind, we can take a look at the three most common types of 'protection insurance': life insurance, critical illness insurance and income protection insurance.

Life insurance

Life insurance is designed to provide financial protection for your dependants in the event of your untimely death. There are a couple of points to note about this straight away. First of all, you only really need it if you have dependants (although more on that in a moment). Secondly, it only pays out if you die. The flip side to this is that it is the *only* type of insurance that pays out if you die. We will see below that critical illness insurance and income protection insurance only pay out if you survive for a bit.

To determine how much life insurance you need, consider the position of your dependants after your death. What would be their sources of income and what income would they need? Then think about how much money they would need to generate that income. Index-linked gilts and shares yield around 2 or 3 per cent, so you will only be able to provide an inflation-proofed income of perhaps £3,000 per £100,000 of insurance cover. It is therefore highly unlikely that you will be able to replace all the lost income. The answer to this is that you probably shouldn't try. Your partner, if they don't already, will probably need to work in the event of your death.

If there isn't anybody that you need to provide for in the event of your death, then you don't need to bother with life insurance. Except that there are circumstances in which it may be required. The most obvious example is with a mortgage. Frequently, a mortgage company will require you to take out life insurance. This is so they won't have to go to the trouble of selling your house if you die during the loan period. It doesn't provide any benefit to you unless it makes your loan cheaper. The best thing to do here is to try to get away with as little as possible.

Critical illness insurance

This is designed to pay out a (tax-free) lump sum in the event of your suffering from a number of specified serious illnesses, or if you have to undergo certain types of surgery. The intention is to provide a sum of money to alleviate the additional cost of living with the particular condition. So, in contrast to life insurance, the policy only pays out if you survive. It also only pays out if you contract one of a defined list of illnesses. In other words, if your illness isn't on the list, you won't get a penny. Illnesses that are frequently not covered include Alzheimer's, Parkinson's, motor neurone disease and AIDS. Injuries resulting from accidents may also not be covered, so it's very important that you know what's on the list.

The trouble with critical illness insurance is that you don't know what illness you might contract, so you have no idea what needs to be on the list. Sod's law dictates that you'll probably go and get the wrong illness. The real problem is that it deals with *causes* rather than *effects*. The risk you need to insure against is not having a stroke itself, but the financial effects of your having a stroke.

You can liken critical illness insurance to an insurance policy that pays out a specified amount if thieves break into your house, through the front or back door or through a ground floor window, regardless of whether they actually take anything. What's the good of that? The policy would be a waste of time if they got in through the skylight and made off with everything. What you really need in this situation is something that pays out according to the effects – in other words, a policy that pays out for the cost of replacing things that are burgled, burnt or otherwise damaged. In terms of protecting your livelihood, this is something that pays out if you can no longer earn your income – for whatever health reason. This is called income protection insurance or permanent health insurance.

Income protection insurance

This is designed to pay a regular income if you become unable to work due to long-term sickness, accident or injury. There are two very obvious and important differences between this and critical illness insurance. First of all, in the event of a successful claim, you receive an income as opposed to a lump sum. Secondly, whether a policy pays out or not depends on whether you are 'unable to work', rather than whether or not you contract a specific illness. The definition of 'unable to work' varies from policy to policy, but might mean 'an inability to do your own job', 'an inability to do your own or similar job' or 'an inability to do any kind of work'. The cost of a policy will vary according to what definition it includes. It is also worth noting that there are likely to be a number of exclusions in a policy. For instance, most policies will not pay out for injuries caused by alcohol or drug abuse.

Assuming that you, or your dependents, rely on your income from work, then income protection insurance is likely to be of benefit to you. Of course, if you are already retired, then it won't make sense. Think about what income you would need if, for some reason, you became unable to work. Then think about any other sources of income you might have in these circumstances. You may be entitled to statutory sick pay from your employer and/or a variety of welfare benefits. If you have a pension, you might also qualify for early retirement due to ill health. The job of income protection insurance is to try to bridge the gap.

Summing up on insurance

Everyone has their own ideas about the risks they're prepared to live with, and those they're not. As we said before, you need to insure against those risks you can't afford to bear, but it's wasteful to insure against risks you can live with. The important thing is to understand the gaps that you want it to bridge. Decide on the type of policy you need, then go out and find the cheapest one on the market (making sure that it does the right job); then organize the rest of your affairs appropriately. One slight rider to this is that you'll find that the most common types of insurance are the cheapest, because these are the ones that are exposed to more competition. So, as far as possible, it'll pay to stick to the more common types and build up an appropriate balance from there.

Finally, for more information try the Motley Fool's insurance centre at **www.fool.co.uk/insurance/insurance.htm** and the Association of British Insurers at **www.abi.org.uk**.

And Finally...
Top 10 Tax Saving Tips

Welcome to the end of the book! How does it feel? Is your tax return currently winging its way to the Inland Revenue, and have you reached that serene plateau of financial consciousness that we talked about back in the introduction? Clear of debts, a tidy pile of cash and steadily growing investments? No? Of course not. That's just not how it works. You can't wave a magic wand over your finances and make things OK. All you can do is work out what needs to be done. You then have to set about doing it. Some things, such as using cash savings to pay off credit card debts, can be done relatively quickly; but most things will take a lot longer. If you're like the vast majority of the population, you won't have enough put by to finance your retirement, and that's something that could take years to rectify. But, by running through the health check, you are now on the right path, at least. You understand what needs to be done and you can therefore set about doing it.

When you come to do your tax return and run through your health check next year, you'll notice a couple of things. First of all, the process will be that much easier. You'll have your tax return from this year to copy from and you'll have a better idea of where you're going with your health check. As an added bonus for getting through the book, you'll have our top ten saving tips (see page 233). Secondly, whether you're paying down debts, saving up an emergency reserve of cash, or piling money into long-term investments, you should find yourself a step closer to where you need to be. As the years pass, you'll get closer still and eventually, one day, you'll find that everything is how it should be.

There is no great secret to planning your finances. It really doesn't take much time, and no great intellectual prowess is required – although we'll admit there were a couple of nasty sums. What you have to do is take action according to what you find, and that requires discipline and patience. If you find that you're spending too much and don't have enough savings, then there's only one way to solve the problem: spend less, save more – and wait.

Top Ten Tax Saving Tips

Most people are very keen to pay less tax but, strange as it might sound, that's the wrong position to take. Tax headaches are a good thing, because they indicate that you're making money. In fact, the bigger the headache, the better you're doing. So, the first thing to do is get the right investments for your situation and, after that, you can think about maybe saving yourself some tax. If you let tax considerations dictate the investments that you go for, you're putting the cart before the horse and you might end up covered in manure. Or something like that anyway.

In any case, saving tax is more difficult than it sounds. People have been trying to exploit loopholes for years and years and the government has been systematically closing them up; to such an extent that there aren't too many left. Instead, what we have is a series of benefits and allowances and reliefs and goodness knows what, that are generally designed to encourage us to do certain things. But just because the government thinks something is a good idea doesn't mean that it is, especially not in your own particular circumstances.

For example, the Government reckons it's a good idea for businesses to spend lots of money on computers and other information technology equipment, so it offers extra capital allowances to encourage businesses to invest in it (effectively, you can set the costs of the investment against your profits). But no amount of capital allowances will make it a good idea to spend money on a fancy new computer system if your business just doesn't need it.

So it's really not worth letting tax incentives lead your thinking. Is that clear? OK, well on that basis, we can get on with some tax saving tips. In fact, 'tips' is probably the wrong word, but every tax book ever written includes some, so we thought we probably should. Instead of tax saving tips, just think of them as suggestions for ways you can take advantage of the tax system if you happen to find yourself in certain situations.

1. Reducing your income
It might not sound like much of a tax saving tip, especially in the light of what's

just been said about making money first and then worrying about tax; but there are a few ways to reduce your income without affecting your wealth.

The best way is to reduce your income, while at the same time reducing your expenses, or converting expenses into expenses that can be set against your tax bill. A couple of examples might make this clear.

Using investments to reduce your mortgage would be an example of the first case. Imagine, for example, that you've got £10,000 of straight cash savings paying interest at 5 per cent per year, and a mortgage charging interest at 5 per cent per year. In this case, you'd be paying £500 on the mortgage interest and getting £500 interest on your savings. Unfortunately, the latter will suffer tax (of £200 if you're a higher-rate taxpayer), and you'll be out of pocket by that amount. If, on the other hand, you used the cash to pay off your mortgage, then you'd have no tax bill and you'd be that much better off.

In practice, the interest on your savings will be less than you pay on the mortgage, so you do even better by paying off the mortgage. A slick way of doing this so that you retain access to the 'cash' for emergencies, is to use a current account mortgage. These are explained on page 217 of Chapter 18. You could also look at the comments about paying off your mortgage in Chapter 18.

A variation on this theme arises if you rent out property. Say you've got a £100,000 home that you live in, a £100,000 investment property and a mortgage of £50,000. It's better to have the mortgage on the investment property rather than your home, because it can be set against the rental income that you pay tax on.

Another way to reduce your income while not hurting your finances is to use investments that tend to give you more capital growth at the expense of income. Capital gains are treated differently from income, in that tax only gets charged when you make a disposal of an asset; and, even then, you can make gains up to the limit of your capital gains tax exemption (£7,500 for the 2001/2 tax year) each year without paying capital gains tax. Watch out though. This is one of those classic situations where focusing too much on the tax considerations could leave you in the horse manure we've already mentioned.

2. Using your annual capital gains tax exemption

Every year, you get the benefit of your personal exemption from capital gains tax. That means that you can make a certain amount of capital gains before you start to have to pay tax on them. For 2001/2, the exemption was £7,500. The thing is that you can't carry the exemption forward. So, if you let your investments build and build for decades and then decide to sell them, you'll have only that year's exemption to reduce them, and all the exemptions in all the intervening years will have been wasted.

The alternative is to sell some of the investments intermittently and reinvest the money. If you make sure you only create gains of less than the personal exemption, then you won't have to pay any tax. You will, however, increase the 'cost' of your investments, so that when, and if, you come to sell up in years to come, you'll have less capital gains tax to pay.

Deciding what to sell and when is the tricky part, and it's guesswork really. After all, you can't know how your different investments will do in the future. There is a discussion of some of the issues in Chapter 8, starting at page 93.

3. Tax-protected investment wrappers

Of course, you can avoid the issue of capital gains tax completely and, to a lesser degree, income tax, if you tuck your investments away in a nice tax-protective wrapper. The obvious ones are Individual Savings Accounts (ISAs) and Pensions, and these are discussed in detail in Chapter 17, starting on page 198.

A recent development with pensions is that you can pay into them even if you don't have an income. In fact, even a child can have one. For the 2001/2 tax year, a non-earner can contribute up to £2,808 to a pension, which increases to £3,600 when you include the 'tax rebate' that gets added (even though you're not earning). So it might be worth providing funds to a non-earning spouse or child for them to use to contribute to a pension.

As ever, though, you should first decide whether a pension makes sense for you as an investment. Be especially careful of using a pension simply for the much-touted tax benefit. The tax that gets added to the money you contribute can be thought of as a provision for the tax you'll have to pay when you draw your annuity income in retirement. With ISAs, you don't need that tax provision because the income from them doesn't get taxed. This is explained, hopefully a little more simply, on page 200.

4. Tax-favoured investments

As well as investment wrappers, there are some types of actual investment that have the benefit of tax incentives. For example, with things called Venture Capital Trusts and Enterprise Investment Schemes, you get a string of income tax and capital gains tax benefits – the theory being that the government likes you to invest in young companies (it's important for the economy that someone does). These are, however, very risky.

At the other end of the risk scale, there are various tax-free National Savings products. These include premium bonds, index-linked savings certificates, children's bonus bonds and fixed-interest savings certificates.

This is definitely an area where you shouldn't let tax considerations lead your thinking. The important thing is to get the right balance of risk and reward on your investment for the relevant time period. National Savings often don't pay the greatest interest rates, so much of the supposed tax benefits are lost. You may be better off with a high interest deposit account, a cash ISA or a current account mortgage for your low-risk savings. Some of the options are considered in Chapter 16.

5. Marriage

There are many better reasons, and few worse, for getting married than to save you paying as much tax. But, if you do decide to enter that honourable estate, then there are quite a few ways it can help reduce your tax bill.

To start with, one of you might have a lower marginal tax rate than the other. For example, if one of you doesn't work, then it's worth putting investments in that person's name, so that they come within the personal allowance and don't get taxed at all. Even if you both work, there'll be a benefit if one of you is a higher-rate taxpayer and the other only pays tax at the basic rate. At this point, I'm supposed to warn you that x per cent of marriages break up, and that you should think about this when you transfer assets between yourselves, but I shan't. If you break up, the lower earner is probably the one who needs the assets anyway; and, besides, the Divorce Court will have the final say on who gets what.

The capital gains exemption is also a personal thing, so each spouse will get one and it might be worth making use of both, subject to costs and a few other things (have a look at page 93). There are, in fact, an extra couple of tricks that you can play as a married couple. First of all, you can move investments between you *without* triggering capital gains tax. That means you can always shuffle an investment over to the best person to sell it. If you both have share portfolios, you could also try swaps. If I sell Tesco and you sell Barclays, I can buy back Barclays and you can buy back Tesco. That way, your combined portfolio hasn't changed, but you've managed to use both your capital gains exemptions and you haven't had to wait 30 days to buy the shares back as you would have done if you'd been single. For archaic reasons, it's called a 'bed and spouse', which seems fair enough. As ever, you should weigh up the costs of selling the assets against the potential tax savings. There's more about it all on page 93.

For elderly couples, which means those where one person was born before 6 April 1935, there's also the married couple's allowance to consider. This goes to the husband in the first instance, but it may be worth transferring it to the wife, if the husband can't make full use of it. Where one party of the marriage is blind, you also have the blind person's allowance to consider. There's more detail on these allowances on page 116.

A final point for married couples to think about – if one of you is self-employed, then the other spouse, assuming they're on a lower tax rate, should be paid a fair salary for any assistance they provide to the business.

6. Children

If getting married for tax reasons is a bad idea, having children for tax reasons is worse. Apart from the overwhelming moral issues, children are extremely expensive. So, even if children enable you to shave a fraction off your tax bill, they'll add many times that to your bill for just about everything else. Still, as with marriage, if you find yourself with children, then there are some tax issues to be aware of.

For starters, there's the Children's Tax Credit. You qualify for this if you have a child under the age of 16 at the beginning of the tax year, living with you for at least part of the tax year. The relief is given at a rate of 10 per cent for up to £5,200 of income in the 2001/2 tax year. If you're a higher-rate tax payer, though, the credit is reduced by £2 of allowance for every £3 of income that gets charged at the higher rate, meaning that you get nothing if you earn much over £41,000. You won't be surprised to hear that if either or both halves of a couple are higher-rate tax payers, then the highest earner has to claim it. You can only receive one credit per household and you only get one however many children you have. To claim the credit, you must fill in a claim form, which is available from the Inland Revenue's document orderline on 0845 9000 404.

Children, like adults, have a personal allowance that prevents them from paying tax on their income below £4,535 (for the 2001/2 year). They can't normally get near that, though, because if they make income of more than £100 per year, it's treated as the parents'. Even so, that should enable you to hold a thousand or so pounds' worth of savings and investments on behalf of your child, without it getting taxed (with things like shares, you have to hold them on behalf of the child because they can't own them themselves until they're 18).

Having children means you ought to have a will, apart from anything else, to appoint guardians in case of your death. You or your spouse might have to pay inheritance tax if you're worth over £242,000, so you should also think about ways to reduce that. There's no inheritance tax on leaving your assets to your spouse, but there is on giving assets to children. A common trick is for the first spouse to leave up to £242,000 to the children. That way it doesn't get taxed and the value of the estate of the second to die is reduced, meaning less tax. These are things to discuss with the person who draws up your will.

7. Make charitable donations via Gift Aid

Giving money to charity has a long and proud history. Amongst millions of unsung heroes, the likes of King Hammurabi of Babylon, Moses, Buddha and Benjamin Franklin have all done their bit for charity. It was the great Chinese philosopher, Confucius, who said around 500 BC that 'he who wishes to secure the good of others has already secured his own'.

So we can agree that it's good to put a bit back. The Government thinks so, too, and gives tax relief on charitable donations. The trouble is that they need to know about it. If you put a pound in a tin from time to time, then that's a fine thing, but the charities would do better out of it if you made a donation through Gift Aid or a payroll giving scheme.

With Gift Aid, you can make any donation, large or small, regular or one-off, and the charity gets to claim some tax back. In fact, in the 2001/2 tax year, a £10 payment to charity through Gift Aid would enable the charity to claim another £2.82 from the Inland Revenue. That payment represents the basic rate tax you had paid on the money donated. If you're a higher-rate taxpayer, you can then reclaim the additional higher-rate tax you've paid through your tax return (see page 124). That means you can afford to make a larger donation for the same money!

For the donation to be eligible for Gift Aid, you need to make a written or oral declaration to the charity to that effect. Normally there'll be a form to fill in. The declaration can be in respect of one gift or more (whether made previously or later).

Payroll giving is a simpler way of sorting it all out if you want to give money to the same charity (or charities) regularly. Your employer doesn't have to offer it, but many do. Because it's all sorted through Pay As You Earn (PAYE), you get immediate tax relief at your highest rate of tax on the payments that you make. As an added bonus, the government is adding 10 per cent to all charitable gifts made this way up to 5 April 2003.

8. Claiming for expenses

Roughly speaking, the taxman aims to tax you on your income and gains, less the expenses of getting those income and gains. So, it stands to reason that one of the best ways to save tax is to make sure you claim for all your expenses. Few people do.

As an employed person, the ideal solution, is that your employer refunds you for the expenses that you've incurred. These will then net off against each other in the tax return. As far as the employer is concerned, these expenses are then a cost of the company, reducing its profit and the tax that it pays. Where expenses are not refunded by your employer, you can still claim them on your tax return, so that they reduce your taxable income and therefore the tax you pay. The trouble is that if your employer wasn't prepared to foot the bill, the Inland Revenue will take some explaining that it was 'wholly, exclusively and necessary for your employment', and that's the test.

The best people to tell you the sort of expenses you can claim for the work you do are the payroll people at work. Obvious things to check on are where you use your own things, like a car or a computer or a room in a house for work. You should also claim for any tools or specialist clothing that you only use for work, for work-related travel (but this excludes the daily commute) and any fees you have to pay to a professional or trade body. There's more about all this on pages 26–28 and in the Inland Revenue leaflet *480: Expenses and benefits – a tax guide.*

For self-employed people, it's a question of reducing your taxable profits so that the tax you pay is less. For that, you need to make sure that every expense you can legitimately claim as a business expense is deducted. Broadly speaking, this includes all the costs you incur 'for the sole purpose of earning business profits'. There is a list of examples on page 7 of the Inland Revenue's *Notes on Self-Employment.*

You need to make sure you claim for your expenses with capital gains tax as well. If you spend money renovating an antique then you can add the cost of the repairs to what you paid for it for the purpose of working out the capital gains. So you should keep good records of this type of expense and be ready to claim it when the time comes.

9. Making use of allowances and reliefs

Depending on your circumstances, you may be entitled to various tax allowances and reliefs. To start with, there's the personal allowance, which everyone gets and you don't need to claim. It increases, depending on income when you hit 65, so you'll need to let the Inland Revenue know your age through a tax return or claim form if you're to get the increased amount. There's a leaflet, *IR121 – Income Tax and Pensioners*, that can tell you more about this.

There is also the children's tax credit and the married couples allowance, which were discussed above. Some maintenance payments may also attract tax relief, depending on how they were set up. Finally, there's the blind person's allowance, which we looked at on page 124.

The Inland Revenue produces a handy leaflet called *IR90 – Tax Allowances and Reliefs*, which starts off with the line 'We do not want you to pay any more tax than you have to'. You can't say fairer than that!

10. File your return and pay your tax on time!

To finish off, we get to the easiest way to reduce your tax bill, and that is to file your tax return and pay the tax on time! To make life easiest on yourself, you're best to get the return in by 30 September following the end of the tax year. The deadline, though, is 31 January. If you miss that date, then there's an automatic £100 penalty. It's also the date for paying your tax, and you'll start to suffer interest and various surcharges if you're a late payer.